IMAGES
of America

ST. BERNARD

I0806194

ON THE COVER: The entrance to Procter & Gamble Company's Ivorydale Plant in St. Bernard, Ohio, is pictured here. Founded by William Procter and James Gamble, the early soap and candle company relocated here in 1885. As one of the largest employers locally and worldwide, it continues as a major presence today, providing ingenuity and imagination in marketing and development of a wide line of products. (Courtesy of Procter & Gamble Archives, Ed Rider.)

IMAGES
of America

ST. BERNARD

Marjorie N. Niesen

ARCADIA
PUBLISHING

Copyright © 2011 by Marjorie N. Niesen
ISBN 978-0-7385-8284-9

Published by Arcadia Publishing
Charleston, South Carolina

Printed in the United States of America

Library of Congress Control Number: 2011924851

For all general information, please contact Arcadia Publishing:
Telephone 843-853-2070
Fax 843-853-0044
E-mail sales@arcadiapublishing.com
For customer service and orders:
Toll-Free 1-888-313-2665

Visit us on the Internet at www.arcadiapublishing.com

To the people who live, work, and raise families in St. Bernard, and to the local businesses who employ them now and in the future—they embody our history.

Contents

ACKNOWLEDGMENTS

Melissa Basilone provided answers, advice, suggestions, and patience with issues that inhibited timeliness, as did John Pearson, for which I'm grateful. My team, Michael and JoAnne Niesen, Jan Boylan, and Barb Jennings were invaluable, especially with computer issues, interviews, and availability. Thanks to Mayor Bill Burkhardt, Elaine Sipe, Heidi Culbertson, Phil Stegman, the St. Bernard Police and Fire Departments, Greg Lipp, Mike Haarman, Paul Myers, and Gerry Wiedmann. St. Bernard City Council support is appreciated as well. Pat Ballard, Carolyn Ungruhe, Don Wess, Tom Boehm, Bruce Broxterman, Robert Niehaus, Eileen (Speed) Fiebig, Kay Heller Phillips, Nancy Broerman, Daniel A. Nurre, Gail (Bittner) Nurre, Patrick Condon, Steven Schildmeyer, Dodie Strittholt, Mary Jo and James Royston, Marilyn VonderMeulen, Sharon Beringhaus, Fr. Joseph Folzenlogen, SJ, Jim Sicking, Jerry Doerger, Richard Doerger, and Cathy Wilson shared family information and/or photographs.

Special interviews were conducted with Ed Rider and Lisa Mulvaney (Procter & Gamble); Alan Wedgeworth (St. Bernard Soap Company/Trillium); John Kilgour and Tina Neer (J.M. Smucker Company); vice president Mark Miller (PMC Chemicals); Stephen Bittner (Cincinnati Catholic Cemetery Society); Ken Kistner (Kistner Monuments); Douglas Baxter (Wilbert Baxter Company); Greg Morschak (Hummel Industries); Albert Reilly and Mike Ward (Rough Brothers); Louis Rauh (Antique Boat Connections); Ann Kling and Anne Shepherd (CMC Cincinnati Historical Library); Sue Kathman (Kiddie Korral); Dr. Mimi Webb and Pam Carroll (St. Bernard-Elmwood Place School District); Principal Jeff Eiser and Paula Blessing (St. Clement School); Brother Chris Meyer, OFM, Fr. Bill Farris, OFM, and Bill Carey (alumni office of Our Lady of the Angels High School and Roger Bacon High School); former mayor Barbara Siegel; Delores Rutemueller; Annabelle Walden; and Carla Tobergte (*Valley Courier*). Also interviewed were Chris Vidas (Chili Time Restaurant); Scot, Carrie, and Chris Inderhees (LaRosa Restaurant); and Dorothea Jones (DJs Image Salon). Identification of some historic photographs was made by Romilda Berling, Mary Boehm, Brenda Hunda, PhD, Tim and Linda Bollmer, Michael Schildmeyer, Ruth Wallenhorst, Ed Junker, and Fr. Howard Hudepohl. To those who expressed interest and encouragement, without all this help the book would not have been published. Unless otherwise noted, photographs are from the St. Bernard archives. Thank you.

INTRODUCTION

This pictorial presentation is only a glimpse of the community many have called home. Thousands have been employed here. In this limited space, we hope to remind readers of events, experiences, and mostly good times. Today's travelers along the Interstate 75 Mill Creek corridor give only a passing glance to today's industrial complex where Ivory soap was the springboard for the Procter & Gamble Company, still manufactured today. John Ludlow and his family were property holders along the route on Mill Creek in 1793 adjacent to today's expressway location. The militia from Ft. Washington in 1778 was based near here, between Ludlow and White's Station, and marched through this area while traveling north to expand the Northwest Territory along that creek, which is now banked in concrete. Today, one can trace some of the former Miami and Erie Canal that began Ohio's growth here. Ross and Chester Lakes no longer host wooden sailing canoe races, and no one would guess today's industrial railroad yards were formerly Buckeye Trotting Park. This is the spot of the eighth United States Fair in 1860, as well as Camp Harrison, where Union soldiers prepared for the Civil War in 1861. The railroads were a major catalyst for new business and industry, and the honeymoon recreation era was over.

Surrounded by Cincinnati, Norwood, and Elmwood Place, St. Bernard is the old-fashioned small town that made good. Residents have been energetic, industrious, imaginative, and forward-looking enough that Cincinnati has tried annexation on more than one occasion. Why did people come to St. Bernard? They came to settle, work, and raise families. Many came to visit or be buried in the local cemeteries: St. John in 1849 and St. Mary in 1876. Small shopkeepers found ideal business with the mostly German populace. Saloons were especially popular. A local, solid, blue-collar workforce was available close to businesses that paid decent wages. Churches and schools gave opportunities for prayer and learning.

Local government developed favorably and started with the village incorporation in 1878. City incorporation included Ludlow Grove by 1912, when St. Bernard was the first city in the Mill Creek Valley. New subdivisions developed gradually as farms diminished and demand increased, primarily after World War I and World War II veterans searched for places to live. By the 1960s, urban renewal for the North Vine Street sector created a major change in the look of St. Bernard, as the mix of homes and businesses around Ross Avenue and Vine Street were purchased. Here was a new post office and two new shopping malls. Improvements to maintain and update St. Bernard continue for growth and prosperity, with city services second to none.

City of St. Bernard

Bill C. Burkhardt, Mayor E-mail: bburkhardt@cityofstbernard.org

An invitation from the Mayor of the City of St. Bernard, Ohio

Dear Reader:

As we enter the 100th Anniversary of the incorporation of the City of St. Bernard, Ohio, I would like to extend to you my personal invitation to join us in the celebration of our heritage.

This brief review in pictures of our evolution from the United States' early western frontier of the Symmes Purchase to the present, demonstrates what we believe makes St. Bernard great.

St. Bernard is a city with the true small town spirit that reaches out to touch all corners of the globe. Nestled in the heart of the Ohio valley, the ease of transportation to and from potential markets has given us an economic advantage. Sound investment by entrepreneurs with foresight coupled with a dedicated home grown work force has built our strong base. Quality products have had their start in St. Bernard. For example, Procter & Gamble Company's Ivory soap was a springboard to numerous product lines used throughout the world.

A key to the success of the earliest settlers, farmers and businessmen was the opportunity that St. Bernard presented; this is still true today, 100 years later. St. Bernard is a family city built by generations with a long tradition of services second to none. We are proud that this small community with humble beginnings can still guarantee opportunity for independence, growth and prosperity.

I sincerely hope that you enjoy this glimpse into our past. We hope you will visit us in the future.

Best Wishes,

Bill Burkhardt

Bill Burkhardt, Mayor

110 Washington Avenue, St. Bernard, Ohio 45217 (513) 242-7770 Fax: (513) 641-1840
www.cityofstbernard.org

One

MILLCREEK TOWNSHIP

The "Cincinnati Sea" is a local term representing the time when the ocean covered most of the United States and parts of Canada 450 million years ago. Glaciers in the depositional processes in the ocean covering this region created the local bedrock, and glacial outwash carved the landscape to generate hills that gave the sand, gravel, and fertile ground underlying much of the Ohio Mill Creek area. Interim generations have scraped the land and reshaped it, which provided a livelihood and a home for many. Water helped form the boundaries of the community, including Mill Creek to the west, Bloody Run Creek to the north, and Ross Run to the east. Bloody Run Creek was named for a place where two government packhorse men were reportedly killed. Native burial mounds can be found in nearby Norwood, and remains of an Indian were discovered buried along Mill Creek—evidence of early Native American life. Other boundaries include former Kemper land to the east and Mitchell Avenue to the south.

John Ludlow was the first settler of record along the part of Mill Creek that eventually became St. Bernard. Ludlow came west, where his half brother Israel Ludlow had been a surveyor of the Northwest Territory for George Washington. In 1788, Fort Washington along the Ohio River housed the militia in what became Cincinnati, where John Ludlow was the first sheriff. In 1793, he obtained property he named Ludlow Grove and established mills along Mill Creek. This was part of land purchased by John Cleves Symmes between the Little and Great Miami Rivers. He settled between Israel Ludlow's Station in Cumminsville to the south and White's Station to the north, seeking refuge there during frequent Indian raids. Troops from Fort Washington included Harmar's expedition, Gen. St. Clair's troops, and Mad Anthony Wayne's campaign, who came through with plans to defeat the Native Americans. This opened up Ohio territory for new settlement with relative peace by 1813. Between Israel Ludlow's Station and White's Station was a base for militia. For recreation, the soldiers raced their horses on what became the Buckeye Trotting Park. With primitive beginnings, adventurers and those who were crowded out of eastern cities came to the area, and many put down roots that lasted for generations. Before long, new families such as Kemper, Kaylor, Attemeyer, Schulhof, and Schroeder would arrive, working industriously and construct from scratch what was to become a city one day. Just 10 miles north of present-day Cincinnati and the Ohio River, this small community became a world influence for change and economic growth.

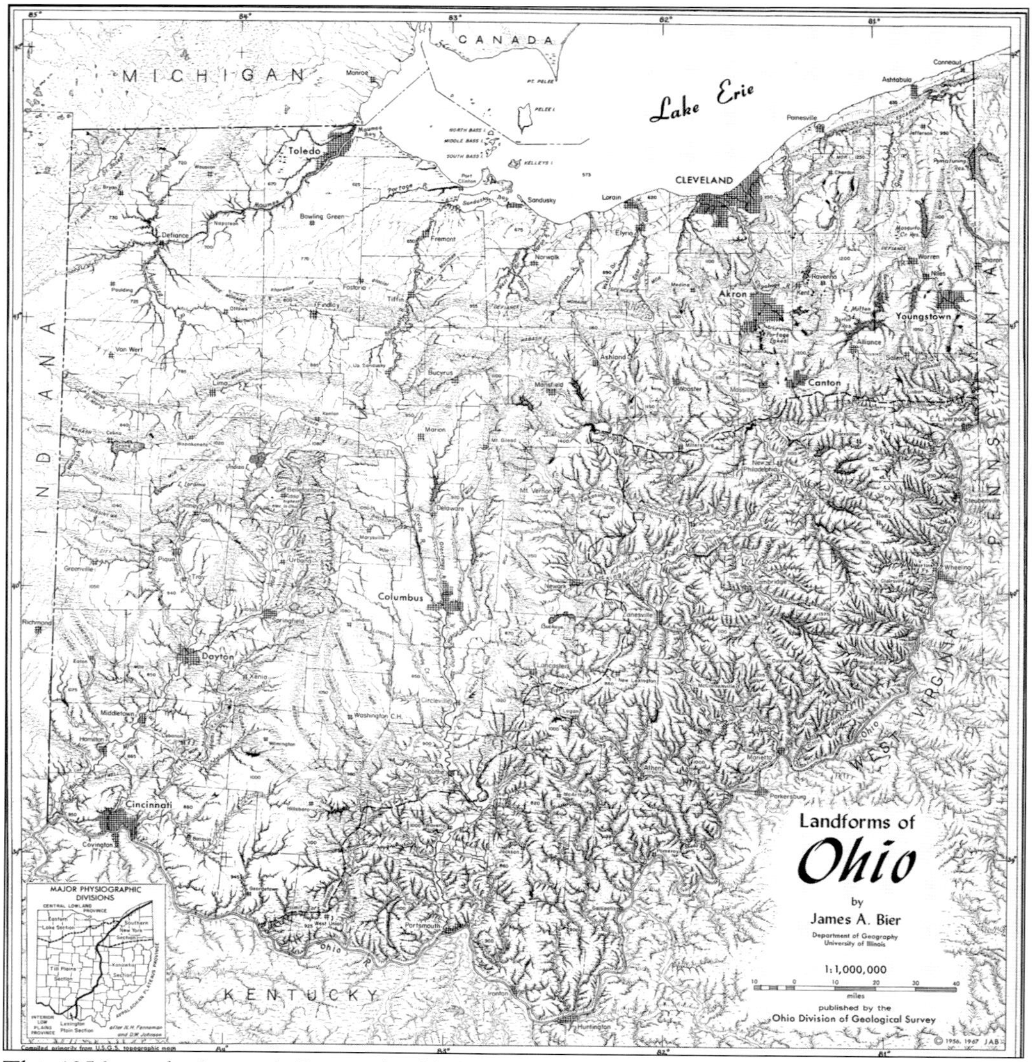

This 1956 map by James A. Bier and published by the Ohio Division of Geological Survey shows the geology of the area, which supported early settlements and industries. The hilly topography, which consisted of sand, clay, and varieties of stone, provided the natural resources needed to construct Ohio's buildings, roads, and even fine pottery. (Courtesy of the Ohio Department of Natural Resources.)

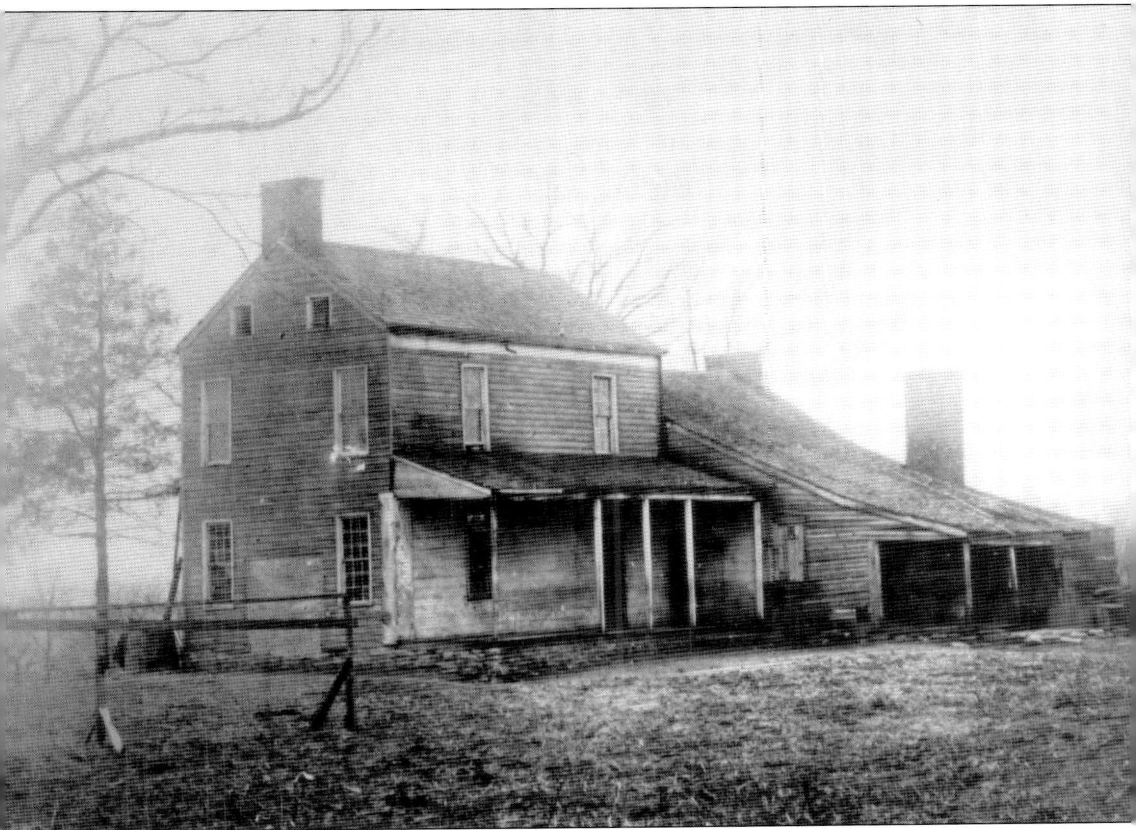

This was the home of John Ludlow and his family, who was the first settler of record in 1793. His half brother was Israel Ludlow, a surveyor of the new Northwest Territory. He established mills on the Mill Creek and battled with Native Americans who came along Mill Creek en route to the Ohio River and Kentucky hunting grounds. Militia also came here to eliminate opposition to settlement for immigrants and adventurers coming west. John Ludlow served on the Mill Creek Township, and his son William later served in the legislature. Following purchase from the Ludlow family of 76 acres of property, William Procter and James Gamble used this home for their first office in St. Bernard until completion of the new factory that was being constructed on-site. Present-day June Street was a private drive until the new company was established. (Courtesy of Procter & Gamble, Ed Rider.)

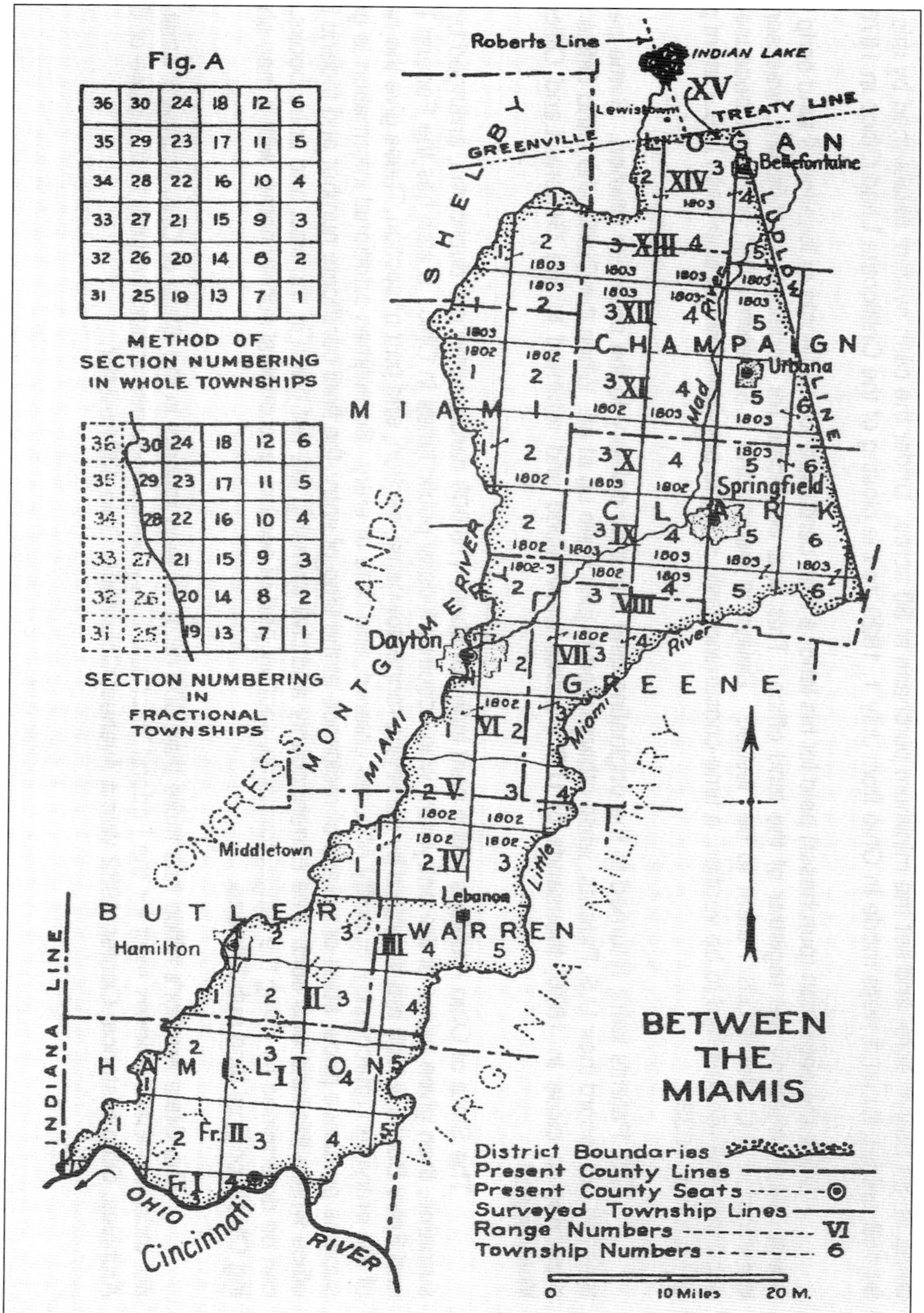

John Cleves Symmes purchased land that included the area that became St. Bernard. This 1925 map by civil engineer C.E. Sherman, published by *Ohio State Reformatory Press*, shows the total area of the Northwest Territory, of which this community is a small part. (Published with permission by the Ohio State Historical Society.)

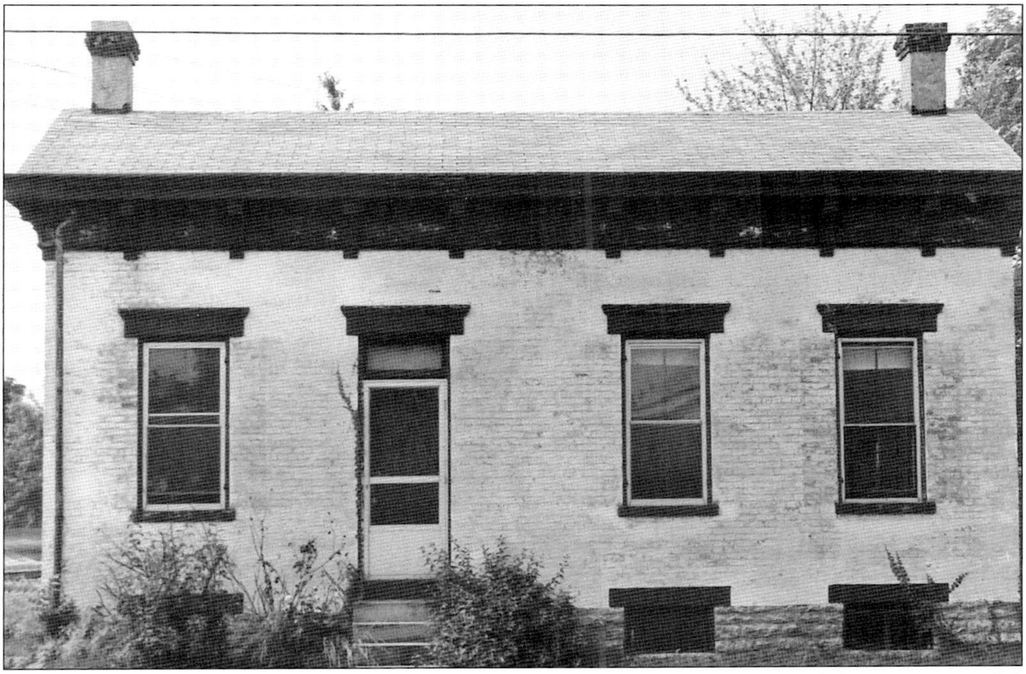

The Christopher Boehm home was on Clay Street across from the mule barns and the Broxterman(n) boatyards, next to the Miami and Erie Canal. Christopher worked with Frank Broxterman(n) excavating sand and shipping on canal barges. One of his children became a St. Bernard mayor.

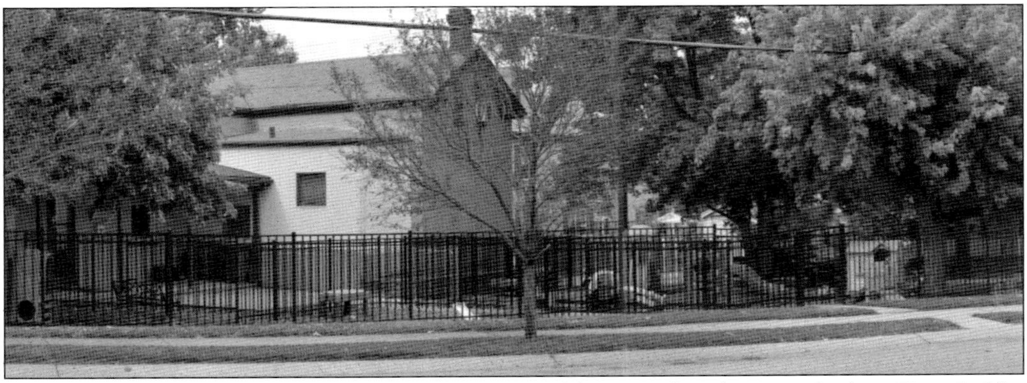

Presently, the former Boehm home is known as Kiddie Korral, a day-care facility. Founded by Sue Kathman and Virginia Foley, today Sue manages a special staff that provides a setting for learning enrichment for children. (Courtesy of JoAnne Niesen.)

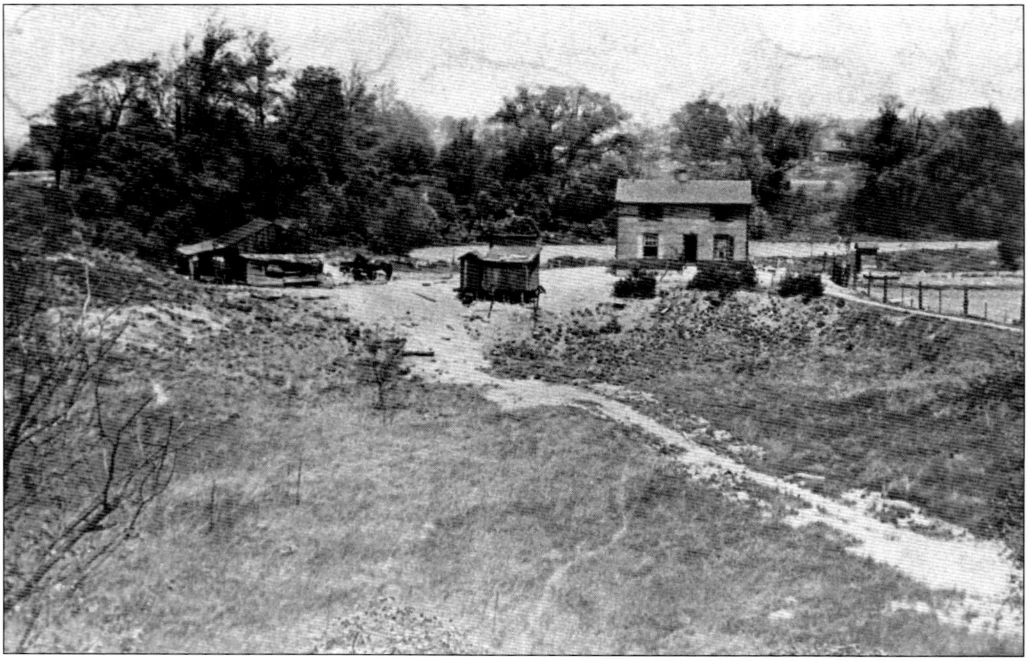

The Kemp homestead was located behind Broerman Avenue before streets were cut through the property. A log cabin was located there into the mid-1900s. When Broerman was cut through, the larger house was moved there.

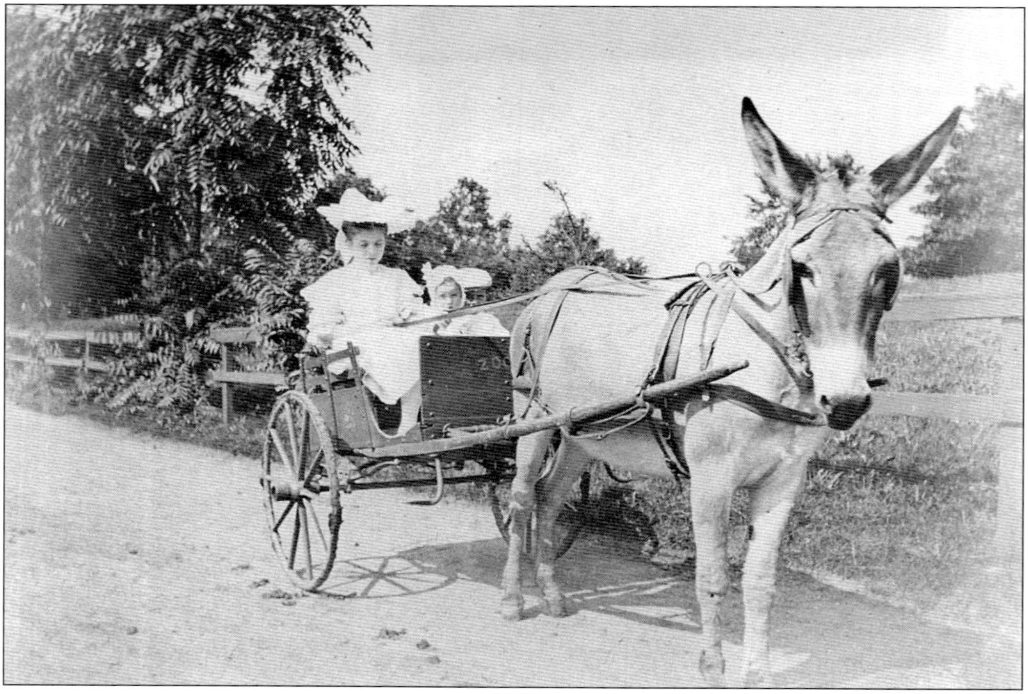

Primitive transportation before roads was more than pathways, as shown with this young girl, her donkey, and cart.

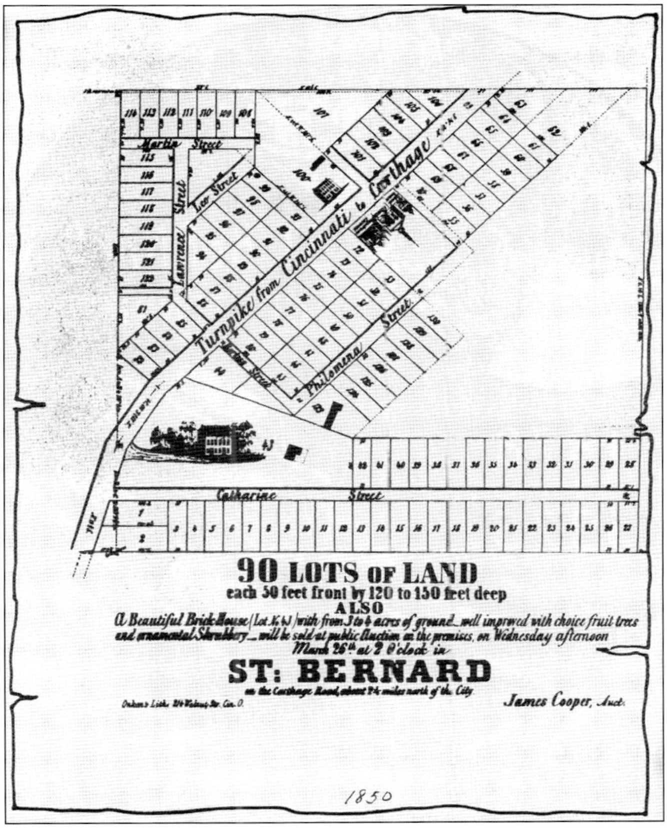

John Bernard Schroeder, founder of St. Bernard in 1850, subdivided property on Carthage Pike and named the area St. Bernard. This map by Denis M. Moran appeared in *A Survey of a Century*, published in 1951 by St. Clement Church.

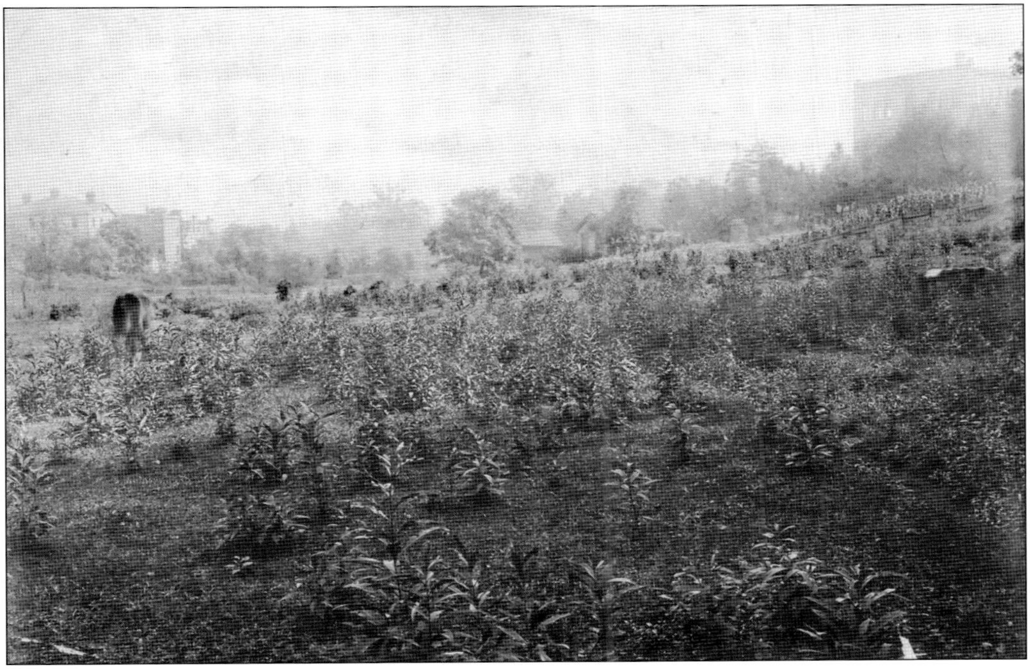

Property at the hilltop was used as pasture. When the Franciscans had the boy's school there, they raised grapes for wine on the hillside that currently leads to Vine Street Park. The public school is located on Tower Avenue.

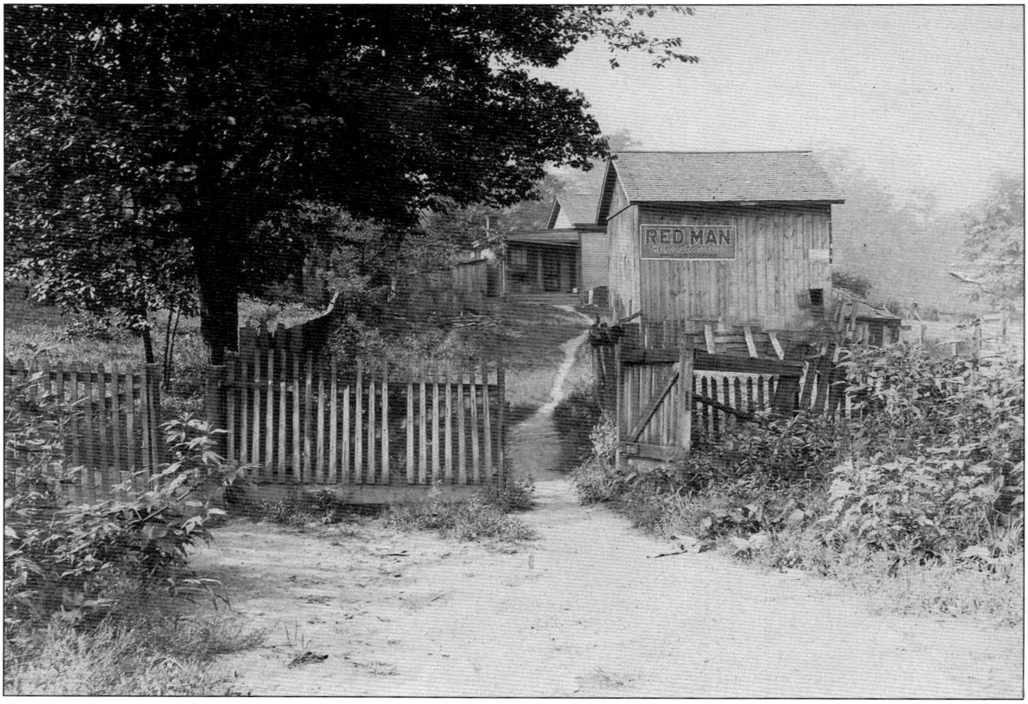

This farm was located at the top of today's Tower Avenue Hill. Formerly a small holding, Mayor Rott constructed a large home here. Initially this was a site for a Franciscan boys' school building, which became the Rott Estate, and today is home to St. Bernard Elementary School, which is part of the St. Bernard-Elmwood Place School District.

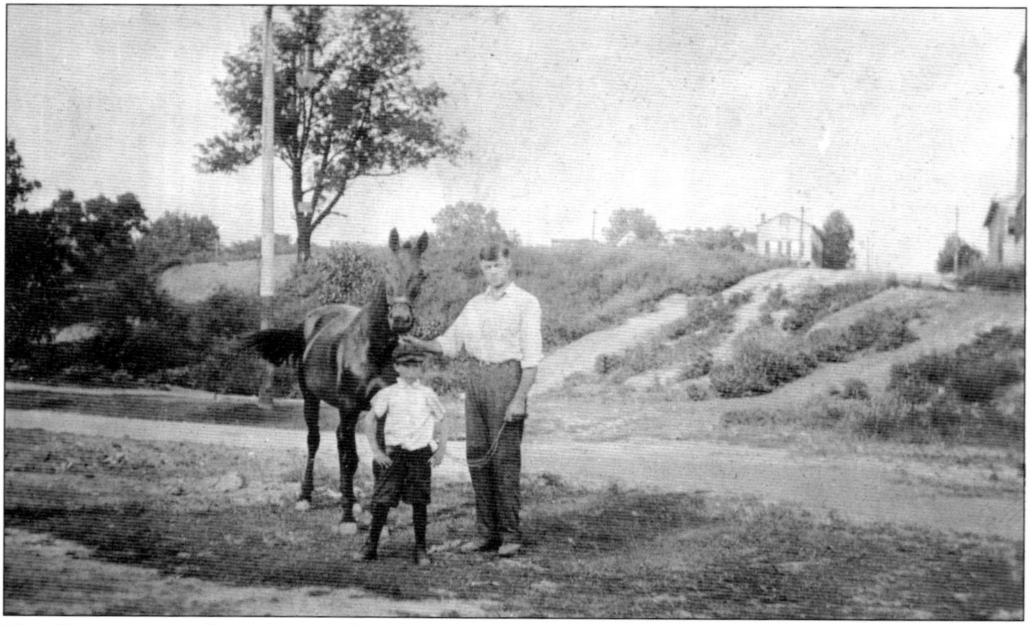

The Hennels raised produce and sold it in a shop on Vine Street. Seen here are Frank Hennel and a young boy with their horse Dolly. Note the hilly terrain on this St. Bernard farm.

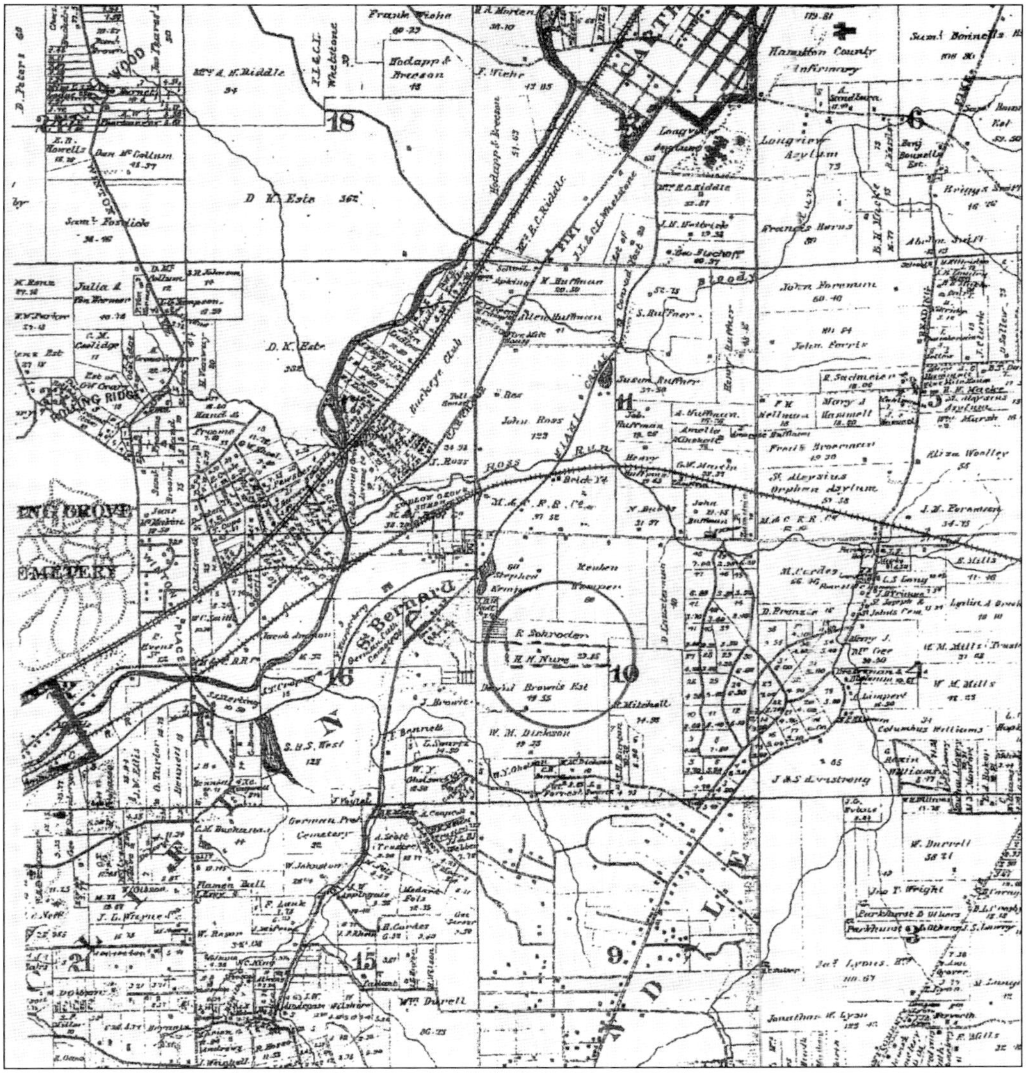

This map shows Buckeye Trotting Park from 1800 to 1900 in the area along Mill Creek where the militia was located between White's Station in Carthage and Ludlow's Station in Cumminsville. The militia would race their horses where fairgrounds were constructed. In 1860, the site of the US Fair was located here. In 1861, the military used the grounds to drill Union soldiers for the Civil War, at which time it was named Camp Harrison. Circled in the middle of the map is the Nurre farm property. (Courtesy of Daniel Nurre.)

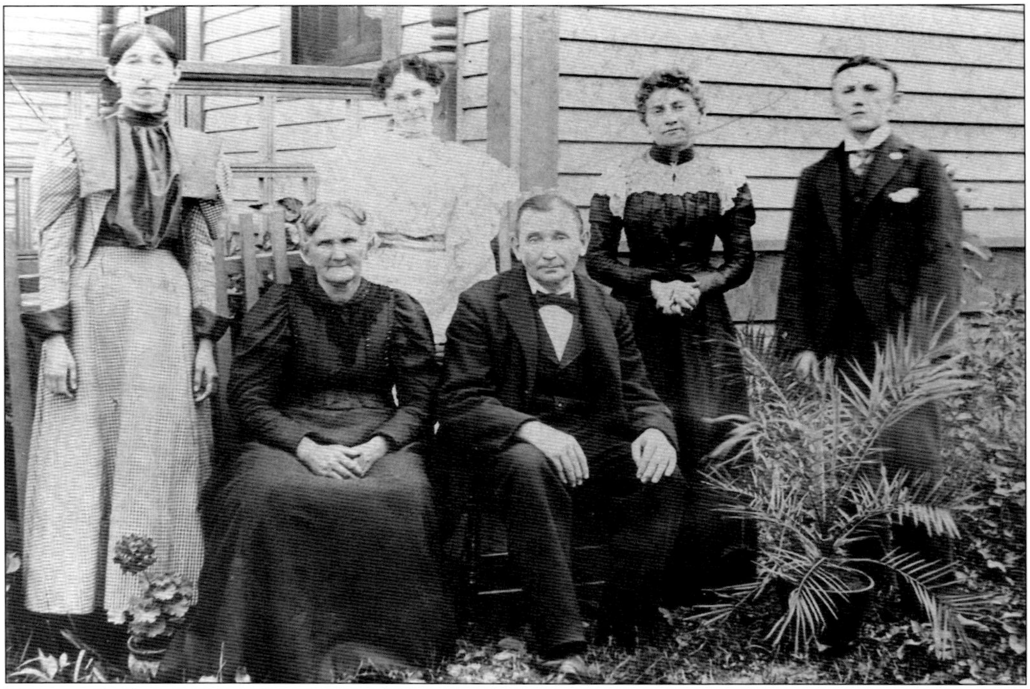

Here is Catherine Brockmann and her family. She served as a midwife keeping records of all births when doctors were scarce.

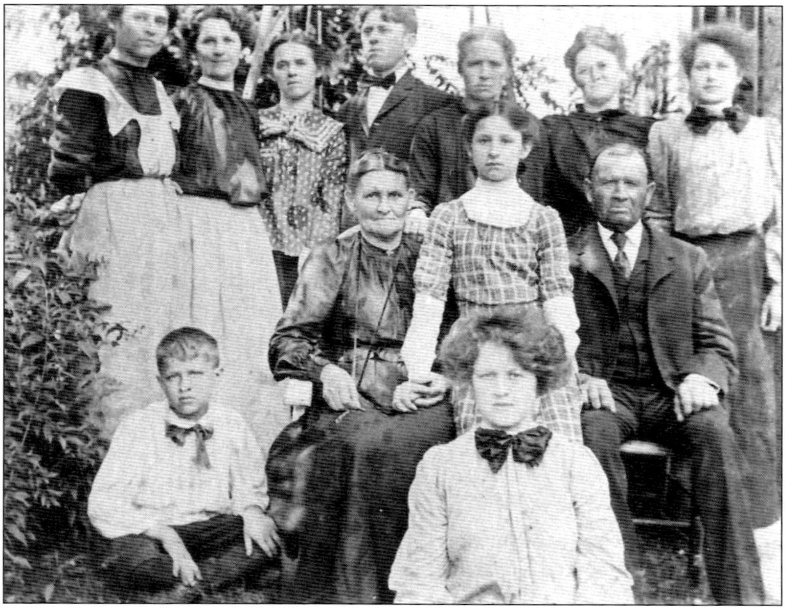

Mary Boehm is shown with her large family. She also was a midwife, and at one time it was reported she had a home on Vine Street, easily accessible to those in need.

Two

Ways and Means for Settlement

Wild animal tracks through dense forests south to the Ohio River and north to Indian villages created pathways for Shawnee, Miami, and other tribes along Mill Creek. The pathways in the 1700s became dirt roads that turned to mud when widened by the passage of militia and equipment for battles. Eventually, they became the Carthage Turnpike toll road and now present-day Vine Street and Spring Grove Avenue. Moving goods, services, and people along the Ohio River was critical to central and northern Ohio, but it also made it almost impassible for wagons and stagecoaches to travel the same areas.

From 1820 to 1825, the Miami and Erie Canal construction presented a solution. It provided open markets and provided jobs for Irish and German immigrants, who then became permanent residents. Procter & Gamble and other companies soon joined the National Starch Works, which was the first company. John Bernard Schroeder of Kleine & Schroeder purchased and auctioned 90 lots at the crest of the Carthage Pike in Millcreek Township in 1850; he named this St. Bernard. Barton, Brewster, and Folz subdivided Ludlow Grove, and Noah Babbs subdivided near Ross Avenue. Kemper, Attemeyer, Witte, Brown, Broermann, Broxterman(n), Boehm, and Nurre purchased large plats of land for farming and cattle, horses, and hogs for Cincinnati's Porkopolis. Transportation improved with the railroad development in 1851. Centrally located, St. Bernard had three railroad depots by 1880, including a passenger station near the Pike, the Broerman Avenue station for stockyard-bound animals, and a passenger station at Procter & Gamble Ivorydale. Railroads put the canal, which froze in the winter, out of business. Paving of the streets was gradual, followed by streetcars and trolley buses. Those improvements, especially on Spring Grove Avenue and Vine Street, also known as the Pike, came first, serving commerce and businesses before neighborhood streets were cut through original farms.

Mr. Wagenhals, the general manager of the Cincinnati Incline Plane Railway Company, constructed an automobile in the early 1900s in a streetcar barn on Eastern Vine Street. Vine and Tower Avenues, formerly very steep roads, were cut back to make it easier for horses to pull loads uphill. Cobbled streets that replaced mud roads became concrete. After World War I, more autos were seen, requiring passage of an ordinance limiting speeds to 10 miles per hour. After World War II, car ownership multiplied. By the 1950s, Millcreek Expressway's exit ramp was at the southern boundary at Mitchell Avenue. The expressway bisected the community but provided easy access to the Mill Creek Valley.

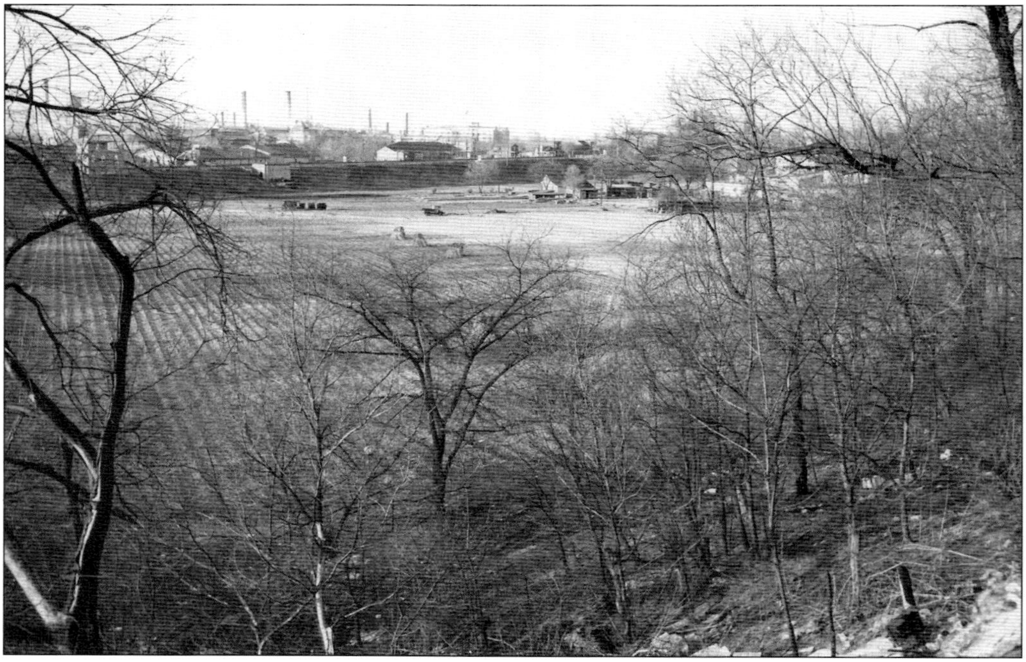

Broxterman(n)'s sand basins were located where Ross Park is today. Excavation of sand by a pick and shovel in the 1800s for construction of buildings in Cincinnati was done here along the Miami and Erie Canal. Sand was transported by canal boats and was pulled by mules at four miles per hour. This enabled delivery to customers, and return trips included merchandise from sellers in the city.

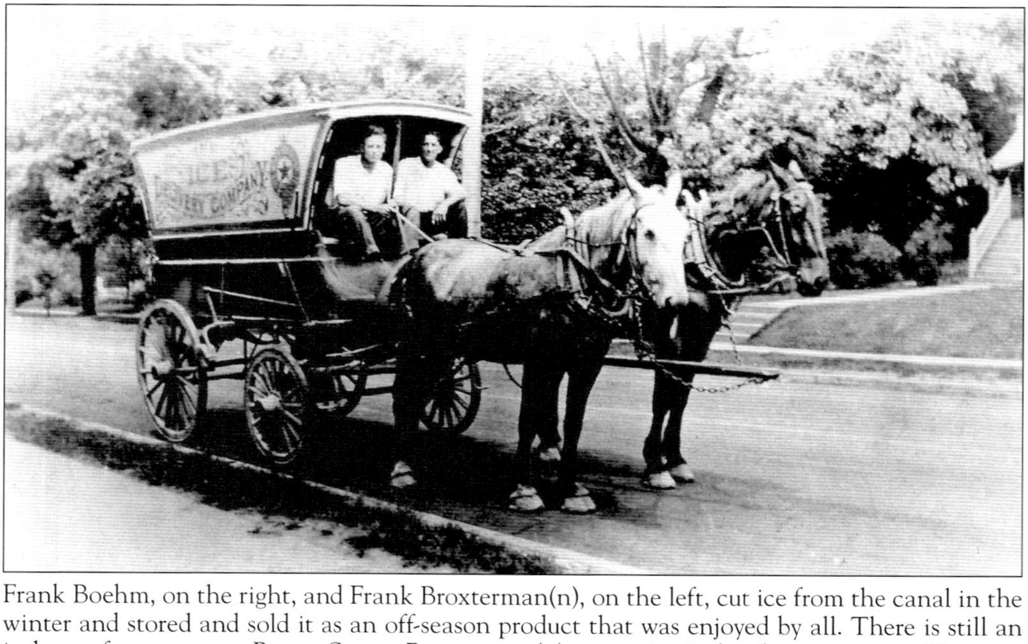

Frank Boehm, on the right, and Frank Broxterman(n), on the left, cut ice from the canal in the winter and stored and sold it as an off-season product that was enjoyed by all. There is still an icehouse for storage on Bertus Street. Broxterman(n) was active in local government. (Courtesy of Tom Boehm.)

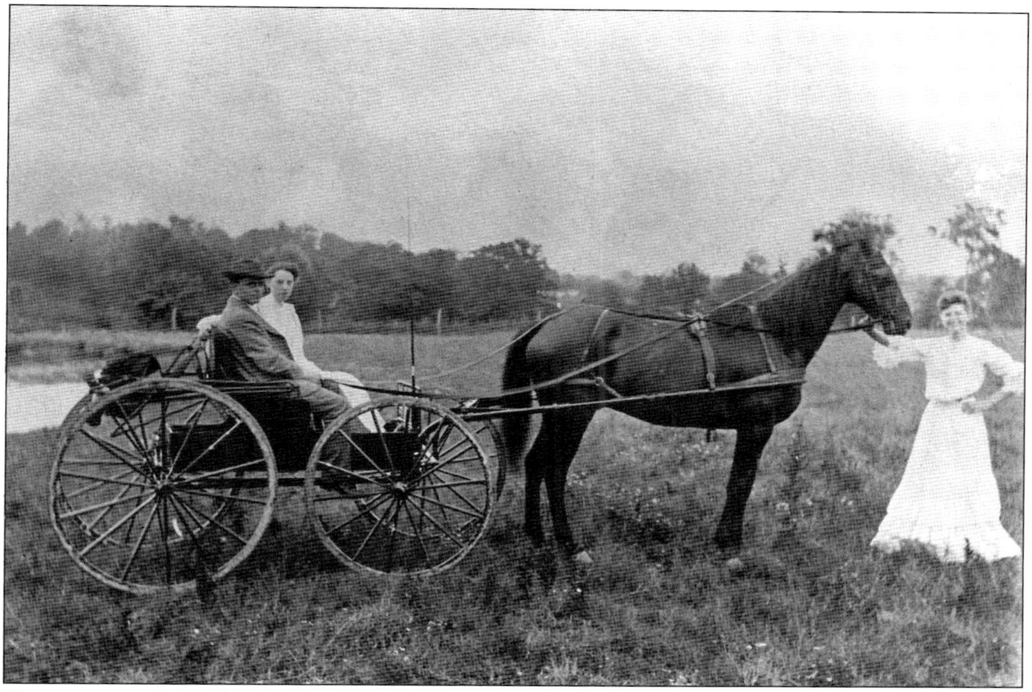

Here are visitors to the Ross Lake area out for a horse-and-buggy ride.

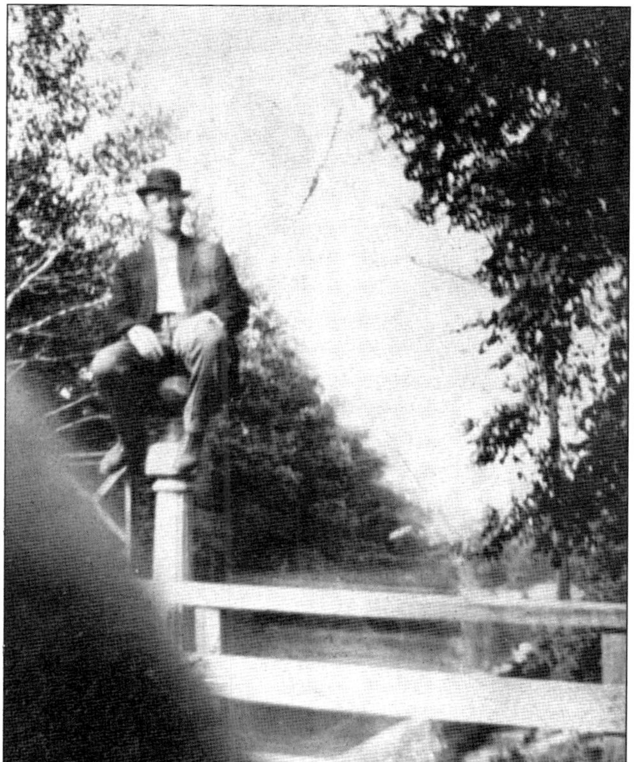

The tollgate keeper, a Mr. Schwab, collected 5¢ from anyone who entered St. Bernard at Carthage Pike (present-day Vine Street). Funds were used for road construction. On Sunday, if one carried a prayer book or a Bible, the fee was waived.

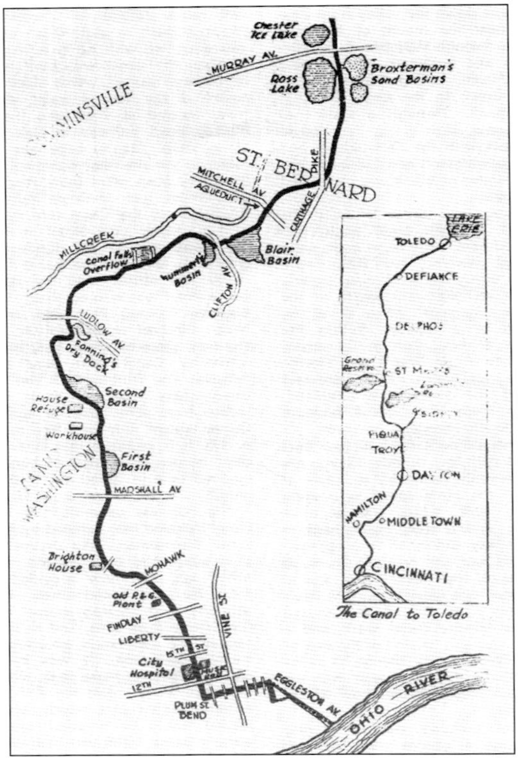

This is a map of the Miami and Erie Canal from the Ohio River through St. Bernard and Mill Creek Valley North that eventually arrived at Toledo. The writing "St. Bernard" is at the site of the water-filled aqueduct, where mule-drawn canal boats could be seen traveling overhead. Here, pedestrians and buggies passed on the Avenue underneath. Bridges over the canal were located at Vine Street and Ross Avenue, as well as a swinging bridge at Murray Road. Mr. Dieterle charged boats before letting them pass through. This new transportation venue was a boon to all. Dug with pick, shovel, and wheelbarrow, Irish and German immigrants were the labor force for the canal. (From *Playmates of the Towpath.*)

This sign on Vine Street, where a bridge over the Canal was located, shows water levels and locks en route. Water was provided by man-made lakes, such as Ross and Chester Lakes at today's Vine and Murray Roads. By 1906, railroads replaced canal travel. (Courtesy of Jan Boylan.)

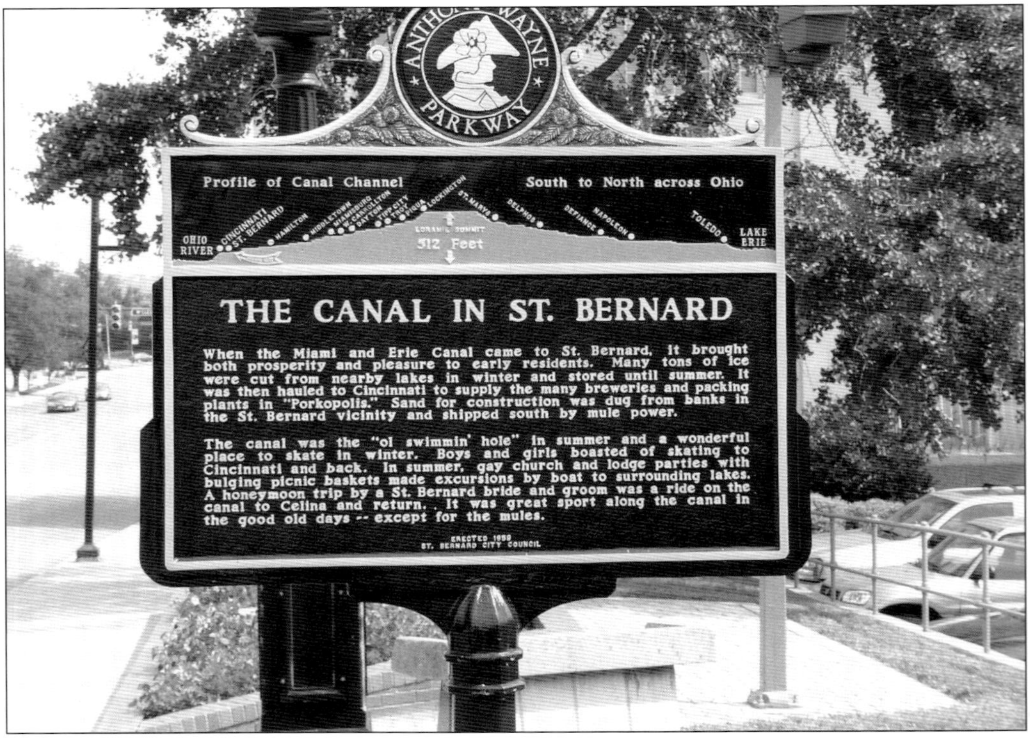

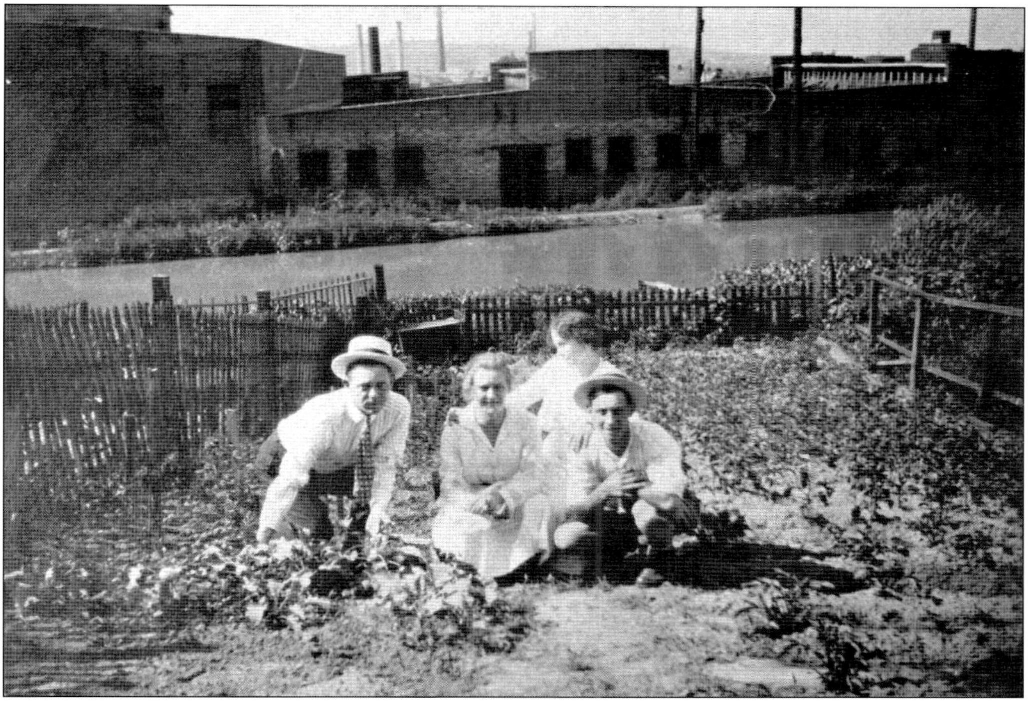

Edna McCann (second from the left) and friends are seen here at their yard on the Canal. Behind them is the National Starch Works building. Founded by Andrew Erckenbrecher, the cornstarch produced here won international awards. For a short time, the street to the factory was named Starchtown Road, now Bank Street. Water levels had to be maintained to keep boats afloat, and artesian wells and an abundant supply of water from springs and streams here made St. Bernard a hub.

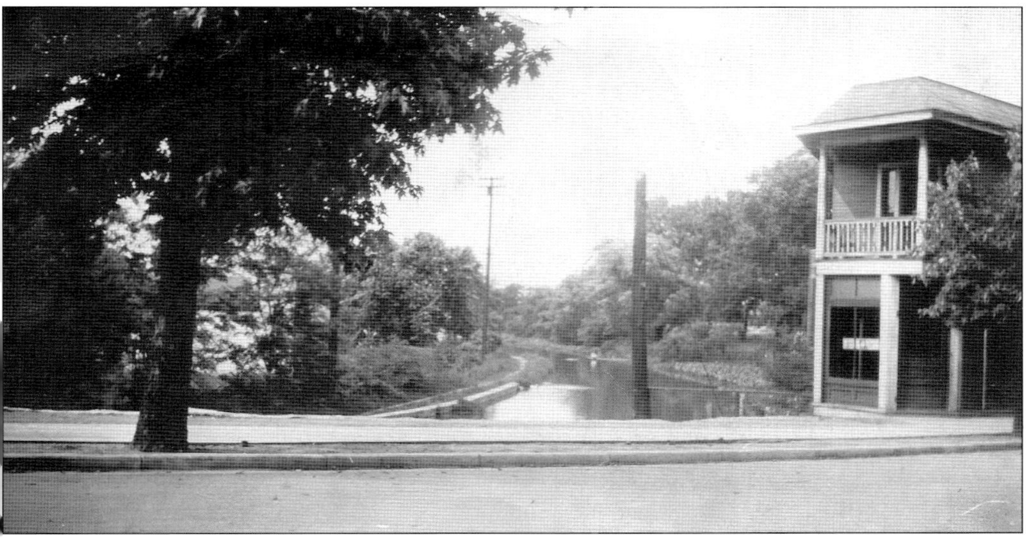

The canal bend near Vine Street is seen going out of the Mill Creek Valley. This is present-day Vine Street, where Washington Avenue has not been cut through yet. The building on the right is still in use as of 2011. (Courtesy of Mary Lynn Hinnenkamp Mayborg.)

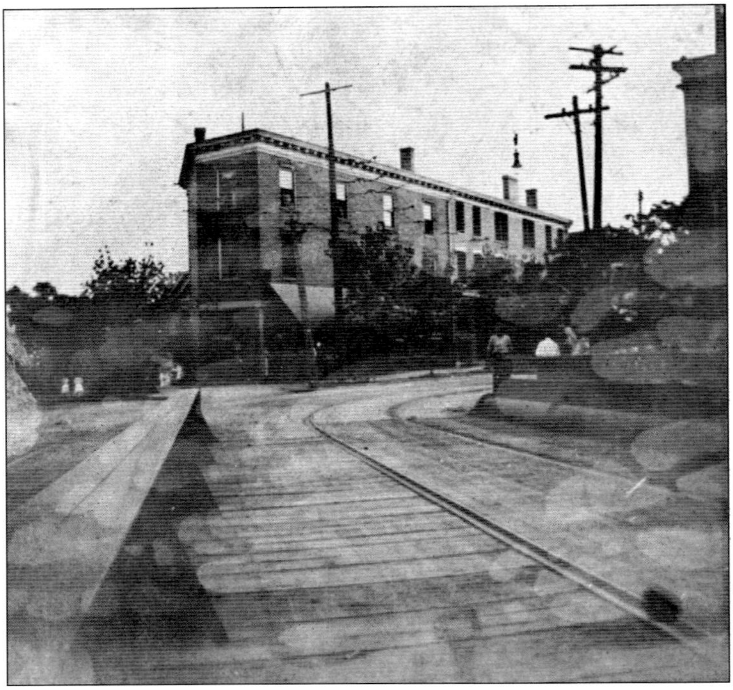

Pictured here is the Vine Street Bridge over the canal. Transportation has improved, and there appears to be trolley tracks in this c. 1900 image. Vine Street remains an artery for daily commuters in St. Bernard.

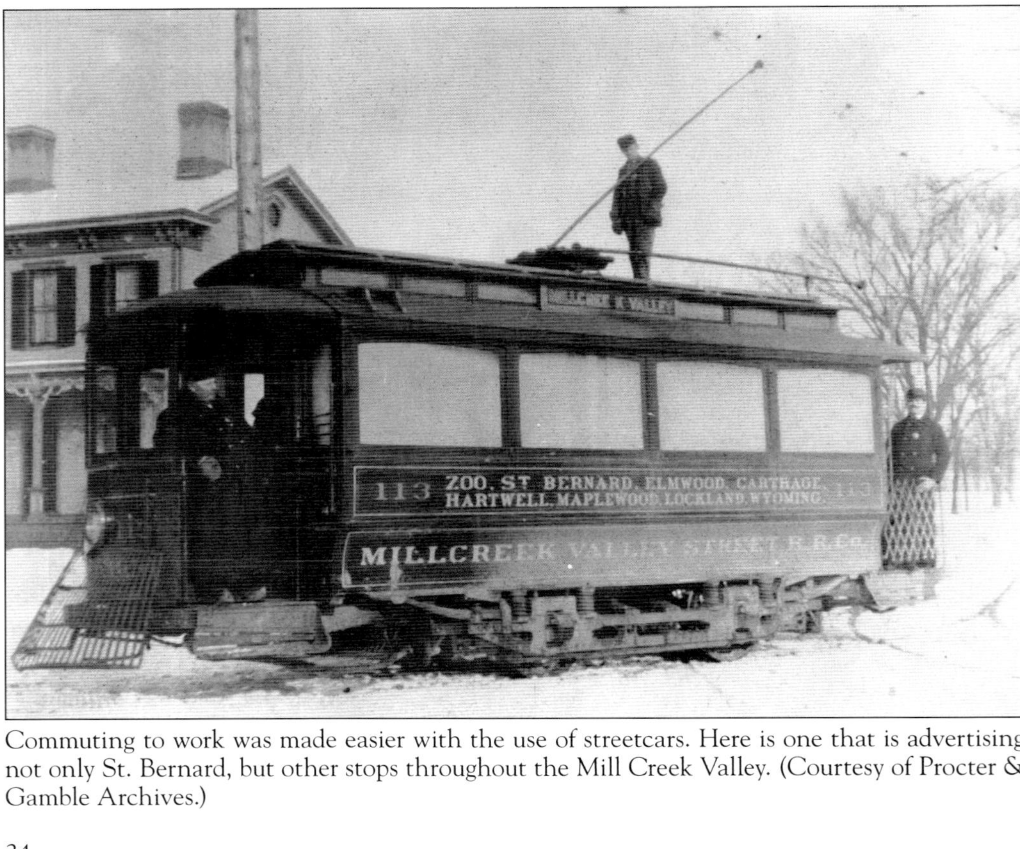

Commuting to work was made easier with the use of streetcars. Here is one that is advertising not only St. Bernard, but other stops throughout the Mill Creek Valley. (Courtesy of Procter & Gamble Archives.)

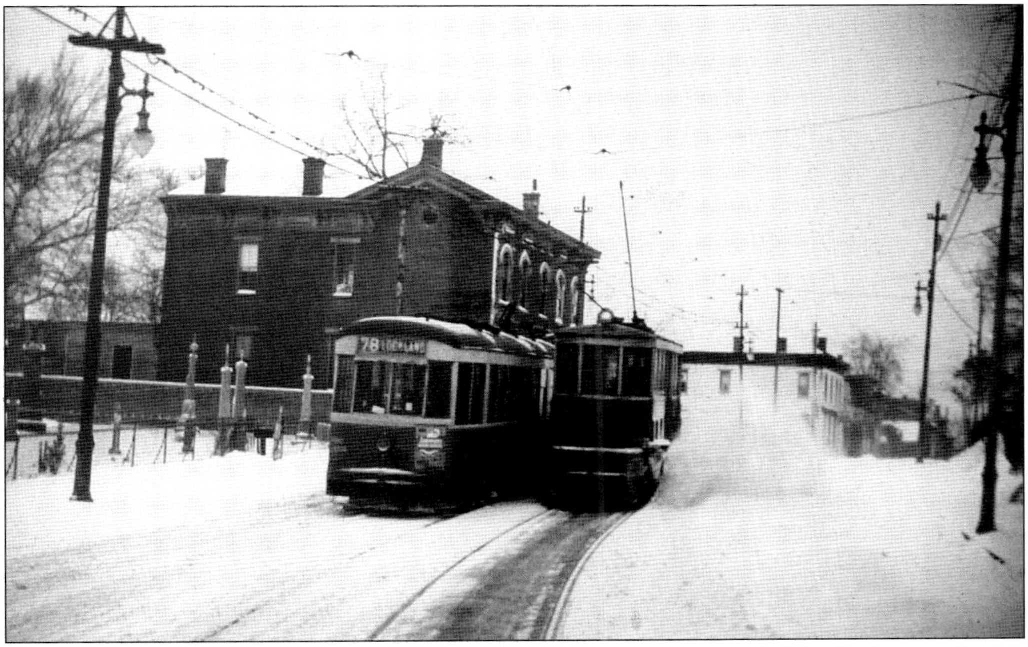

Streetcars became the commuting venue of choice as routes improved. The 3¢ fare made this affordable, especially in the 1890s. City council discussed tearing up tracks or blocking them when the streetcar company wanted to raise the fare to St. Bernard to 5¢. Millcreek Valley car barns were located on Vine Street across from Railroad Avenue. Imwalle Funeral Home and others rented out horses and wagons for those who needed individual transport prior to streetcars.

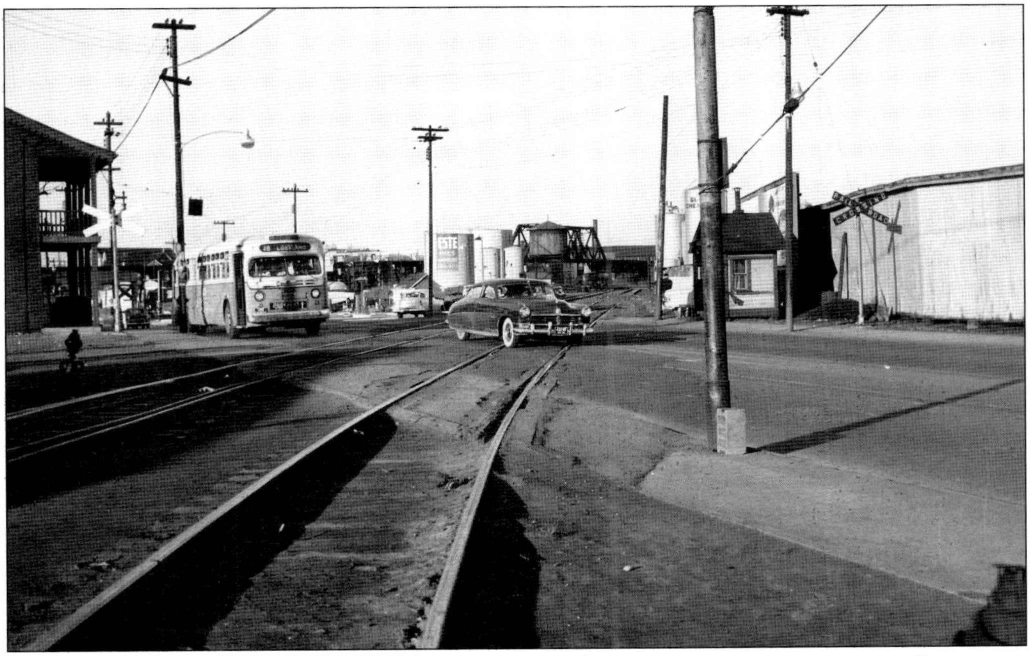

Clark's Crossing at the northern border of St. Bernard on Vine Street shown here reflects auto, bus, and train methods of transportation around 1950.

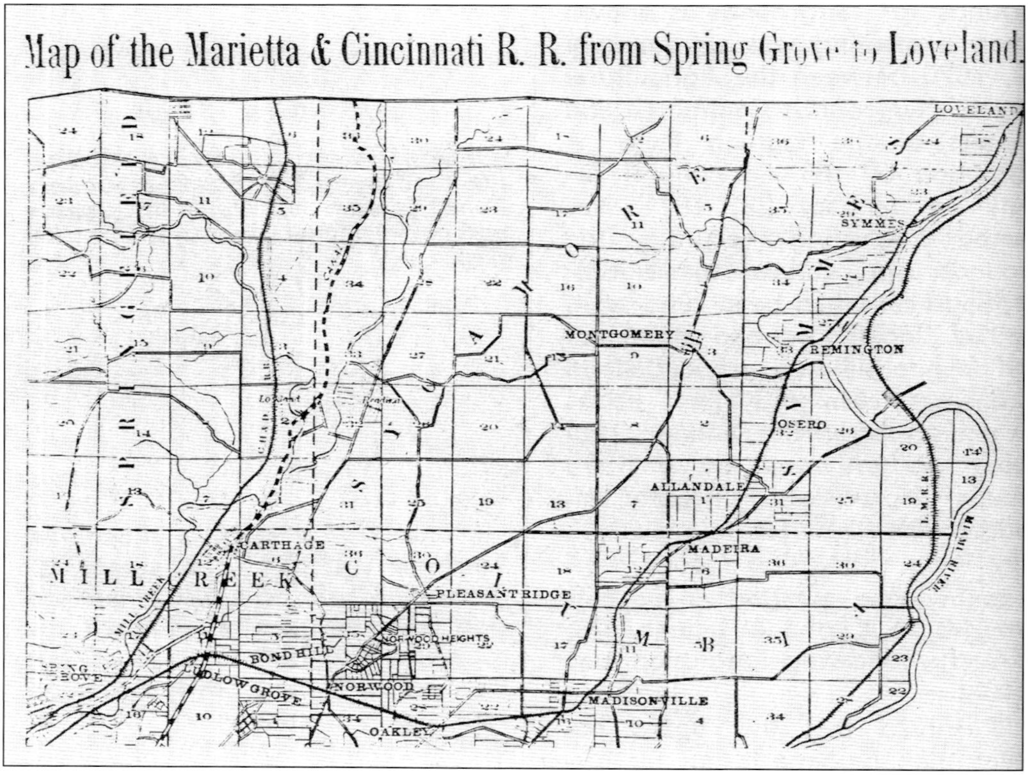

In the 1850s, railroads became competition for the canal and in St. Bernard, primarily because of its location near downtown Cincinnati. Many lines were constructed through here, which enabled industry to grow and prosper.

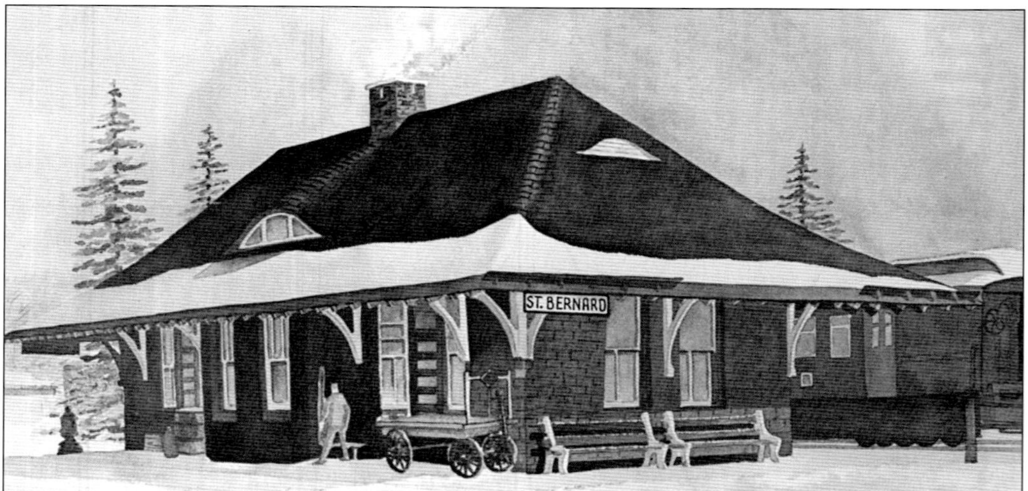

One of three railway depots in St. Bernard, this was one of the first in the suburbs of Cincinnati. It enabled commuting to a workplace elsewhere from St. Bernard. It was also was the area's first post office.

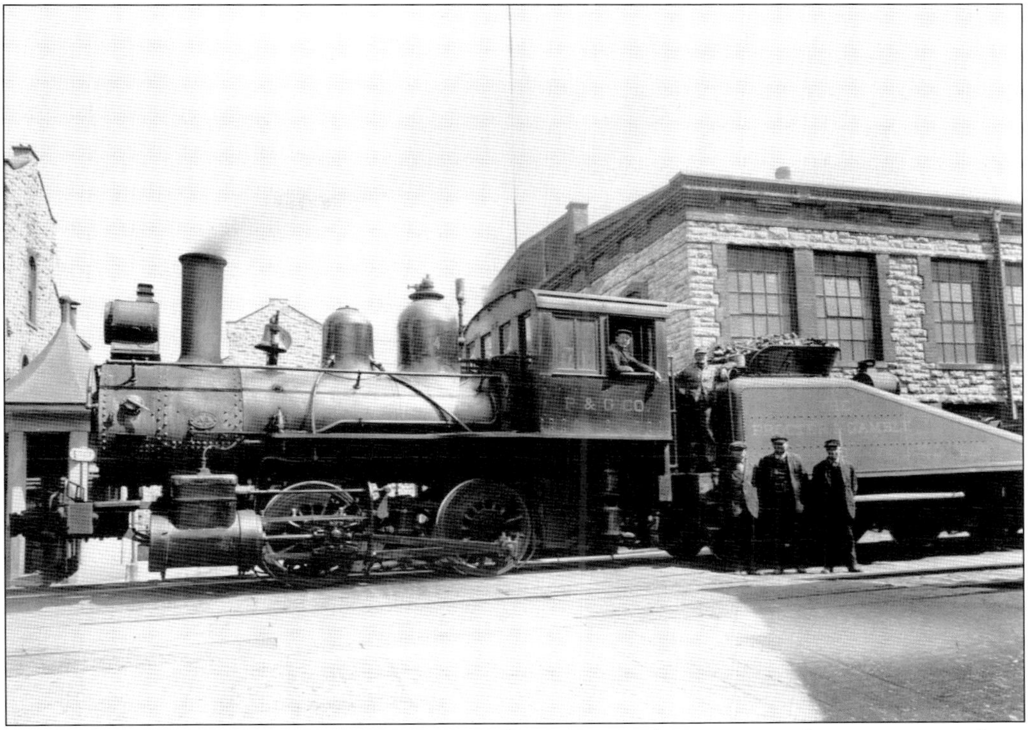

One of Procter & Gamble's own locomotives, the company also maintained its own repair shop. This is just one of the logistical advantages of St. Bernard's location that P&G effectively utilizes. (Courtesy of Procter & Gamble Archives.)

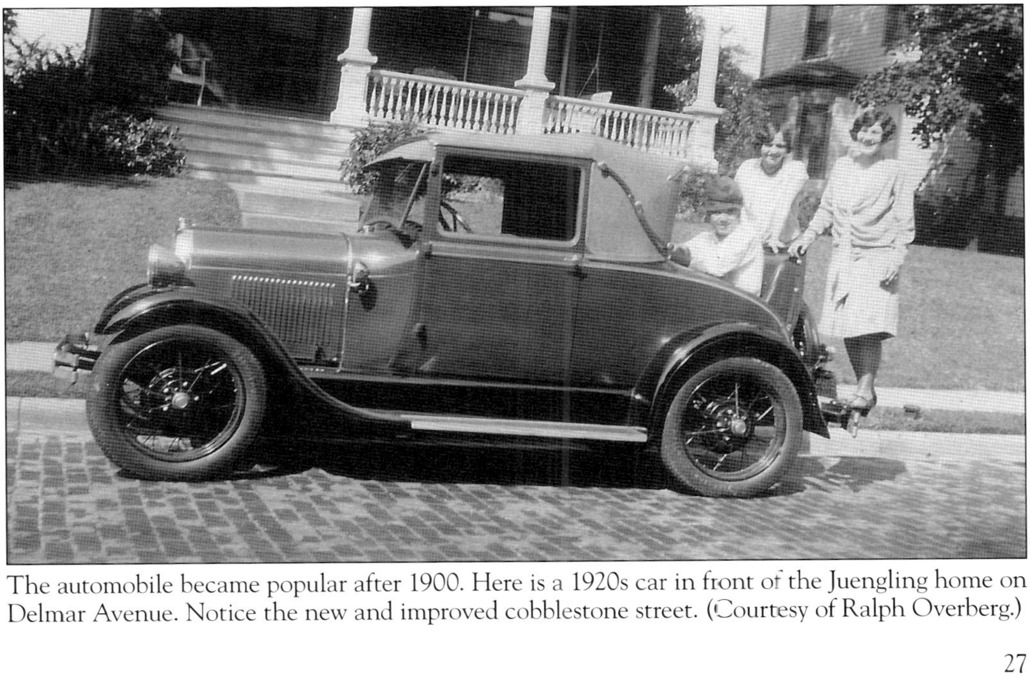

The automobile became popular after 1900. Here is a 1920s car in front of the Juengling home on Delmar Avenue. Notice the new and improved cobblestone street. (Courtesy of Ralph Overberg.)

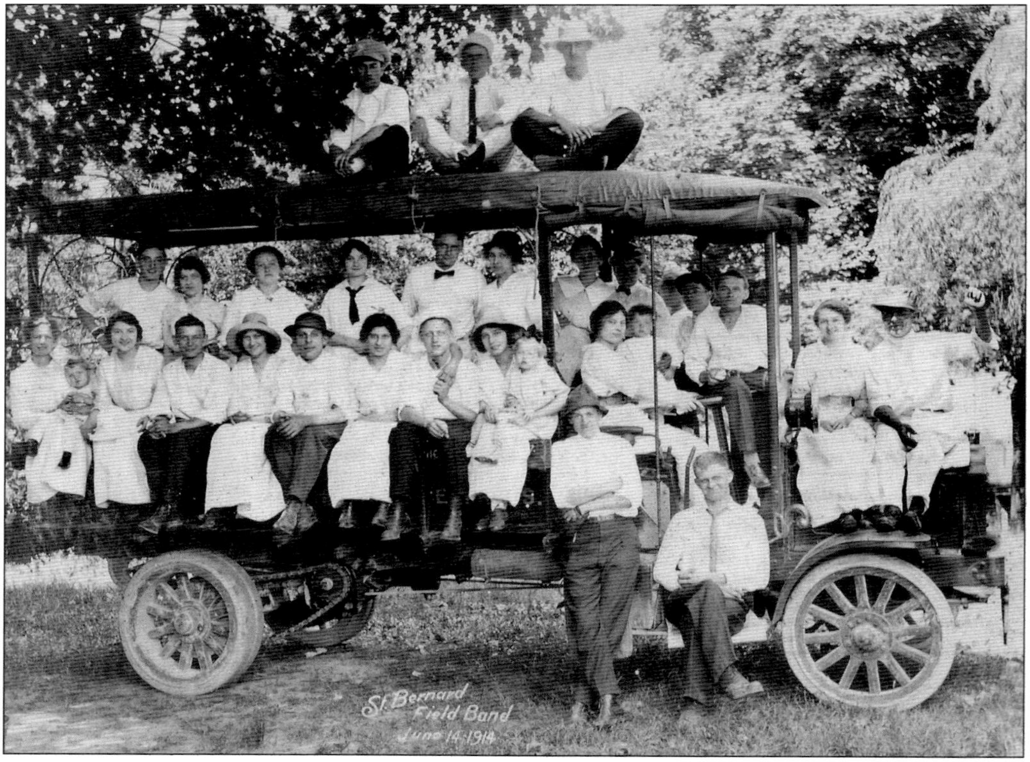

Motorized vehicles like this Henke truck improved transportation locally for transporting goods as well as people. Seen here is a large group during an outing.

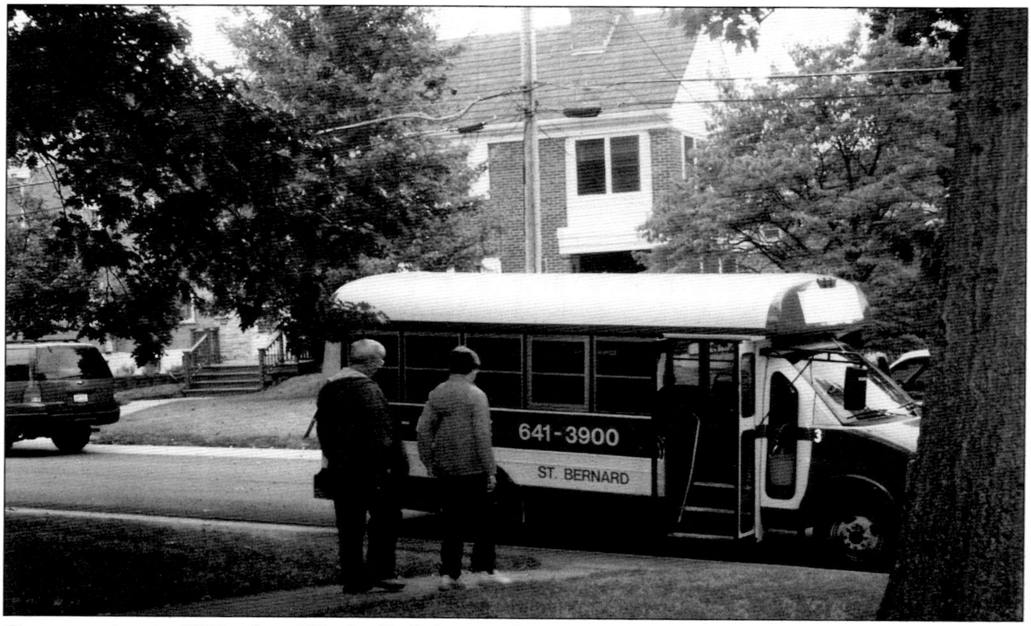

Commencing in 1970, a local Dial-a-Ride bus made easy transportation possible within St. Bernard for a nominal fare. It is a lifeline around the city for residents to this day.

Three

The Spirit Moved Them

Horseback-riding circuit preachers performed baptisms, marriages, and funerals for the scattered settlers where the Bible was home taught. Primarily Methodist Episcopal in 1810, less than 100 of Millcreek Township residents belonged to one church. John Ludlow's son William collected 30¢ per parishioner for minister's maintenance at his church near Carthage. In 1830, the Campbellites or Millerites provided some baptisms in the Miami and Erie Canal by Reverend Scott. Storefront churches were short-lived. Some such as the Cathedral of Compassion at the Andalus Theatre lasted longer.

John Bernard Schroeder, in his 1850 plat for the hilltop property he named for St. Bernard, set aside land for a Roman Catholic church and school. With 10 Catholic families' financial assistance, the Order of St. Francis of Assisi (Franciscans), from the province of Tyrol in Europe, came in 1851. A German foreign mission named the church for Germany's patron, St. Clement. Earliest services in Schroeder's home moved to a temporary frame structure in 1850 and then a completed brick building in 1851. Today's church, completed in 1871, was renovated after a 1962 fire.

As a Sabbath schoolroom over a saloon on Vine Street, Ms. Kaylor, Ms. Kemper, Ms. Long, and Ms. Hoffman started the Wilson Memorial United Presbyterian Church. Named for Rev. Theopholus Wilson, in 1874 they moved to Ross Avenue School until being forbidden to worship in a public school by an 1882 law. Resident Stephen Kemper donated funds from the sale of the Walnut Hills land for the church on Clay Street. In 1905, Sullivan and McClelland Avenues became the church site.

In 1883, Rev. John Heckmann, pastor of the German Protestant Church of Mount Auburn, organized the Immanuel United Church of Christ with 24 members. Minerva Kaylor helped found both Wilson and Immanuel Churches. For 36 years, Wilson Presbyterian and the Immanuel Church of Christ shared the church on Clay Street. Rev. Anton Seyring was the first pastor in 1885. Since 1924, the church site has been on Jefferson and Tower Avenues.

Because of deaths due to Indian wars, losses of mothers and infants to childbirth, and the occurrence of numerous epidemics, in 1849 the German Catholic Cemetery Society purchased Mathias Schulhof's farm for St. John's Cemetery. Forming part of the western boundary with the Miami and Erie Canal, this 60-acre site is the burial place for some of the first families, including John Bernard Schroeder's family. In 1877, as St. John's Cemetery was filling, 111 acres of Kemper's farm was purchased to form St. Mary's Cemetery.

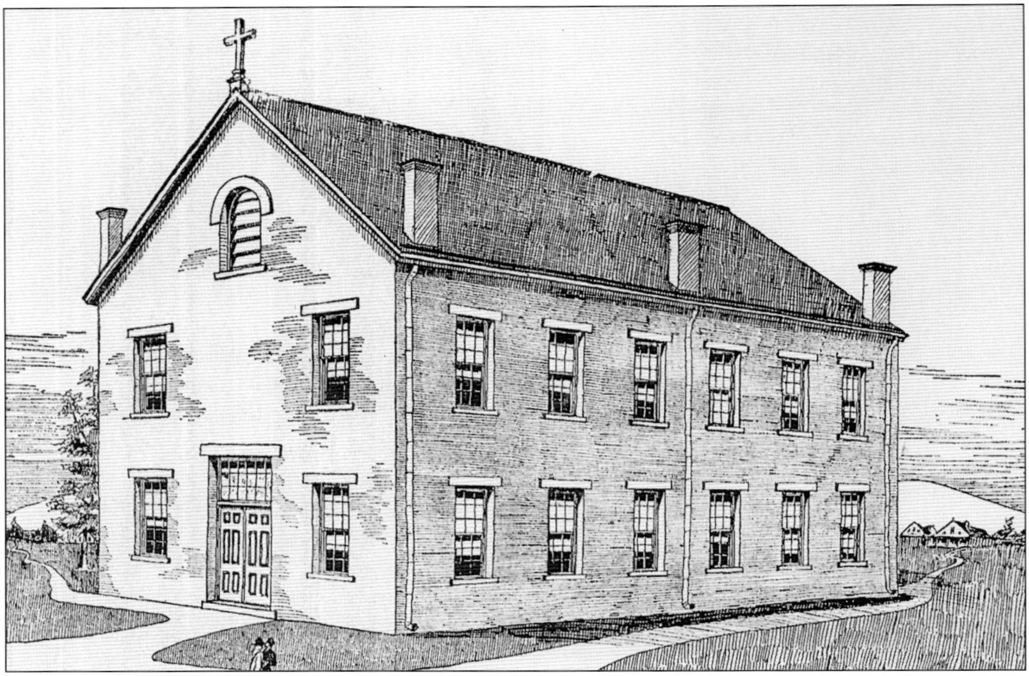

Mass was held in local homes, including the Schroeder's, until this first St. Clement Church was constructed. Church was on the second floor and school on the first floor until a newer church was constructed. Today's church was built in 1871, and seating was increased to 1,200 in 1897. In the 1970s, the church was renovated to repair damage from a fire. Today's pastor is Fr. Fred Link, OFM, and the associate pastor is Fr. Jim Van Vurst, OFM, with assistance from Fr. Louis Bartko, OFM. (Courtesy of St. Clement Church.)

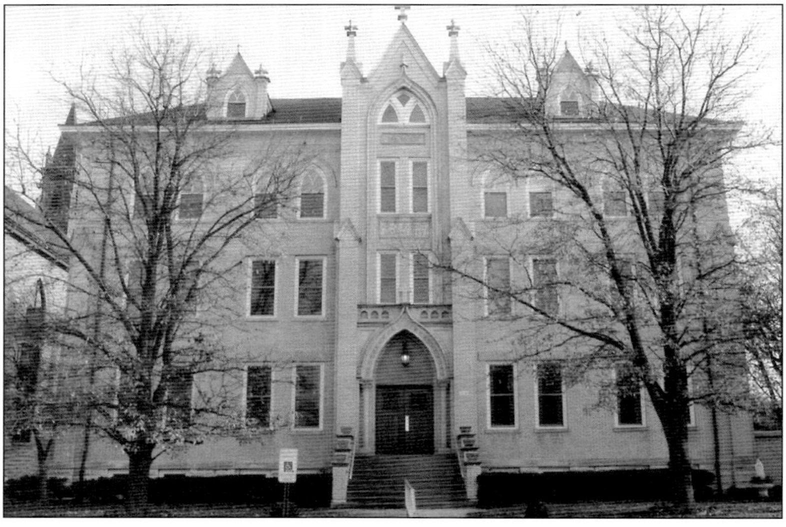

St. Clement Friary has provided priests and brothers ministering to the parish, as well as teaching at St. Clement School and the parochial high schools. Today, 17 brothers and priests live here. (Courtesy of Brother Chris Meyer, OFM.)

The Building Committee of Diamond Jubilee of St. Clement Parish included Henry Nunlist, Frank Koepfle, Aloysius Nurre, Louis E. Doepke, and Joseph Broxterman(n). (Courtesy of St. Clement Church.)

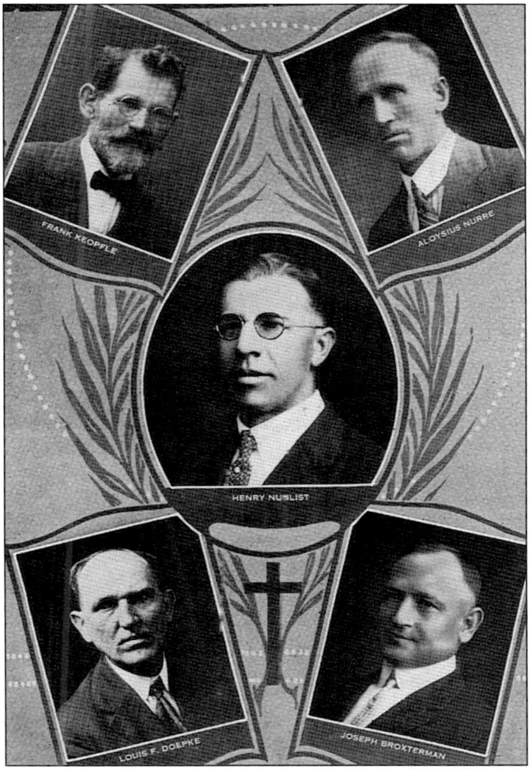

Seen here is Field Mass at Vine Street Park as well as St. Clement Church in the background. Especially in the early years and during war years, people came from the Greater Cincinnati area to take part in these events.

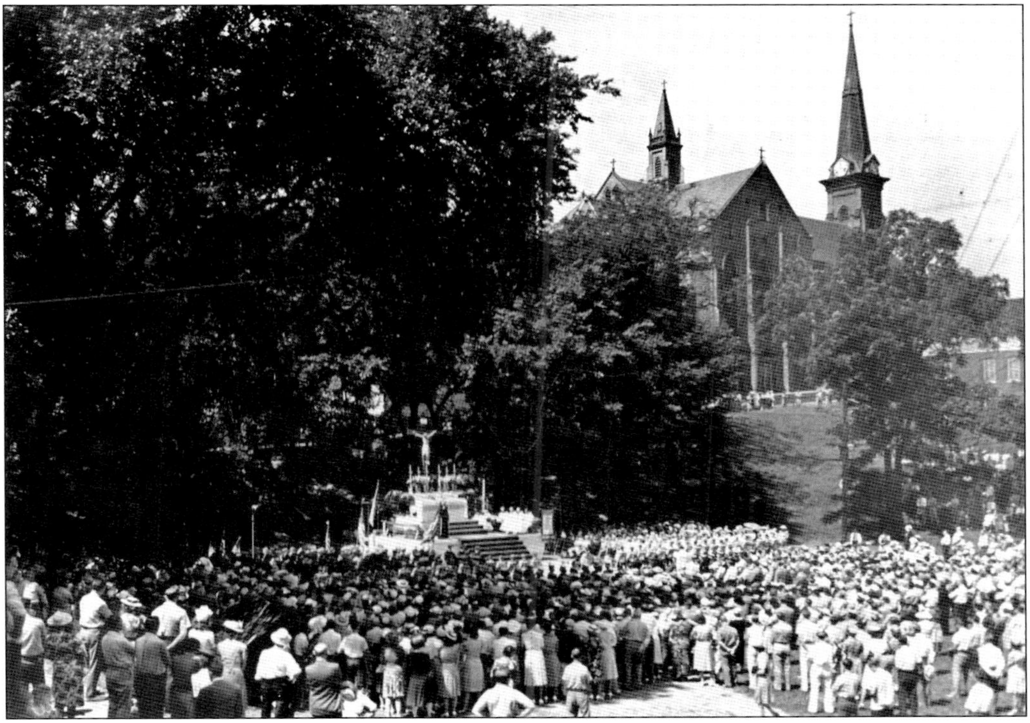

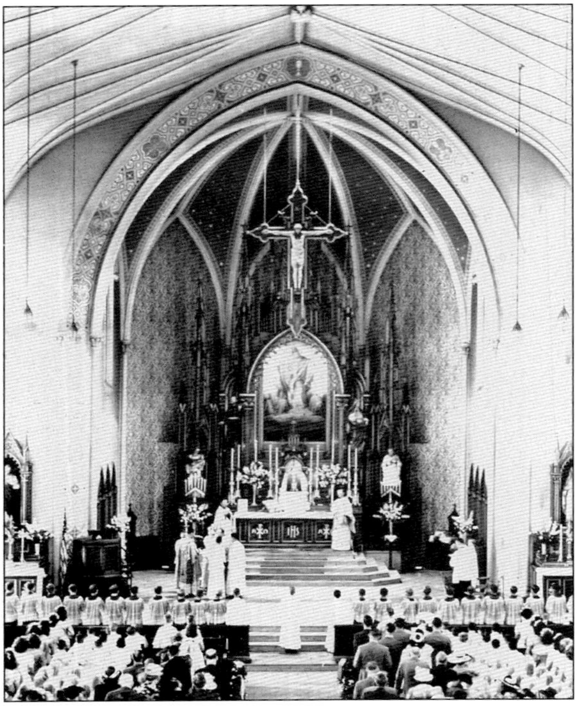

This is the St. Clement Church interior before the fire in 1962, with the original Gothic interior and painting of St. Clement behind the cross over the altar. This painting was lost in the fire, but local artist Clara Doerger was able to do a likeness that is used today in the renovated church. Clara and her husband, Urban Doerger, restored Stations of the Cross that were painted on copper.

A special honor was to be the girl chosen to crown the Blessed Mother at the annual May Crowning. With processions and beautiful Marian hymns, it is a very special, prayerful event.

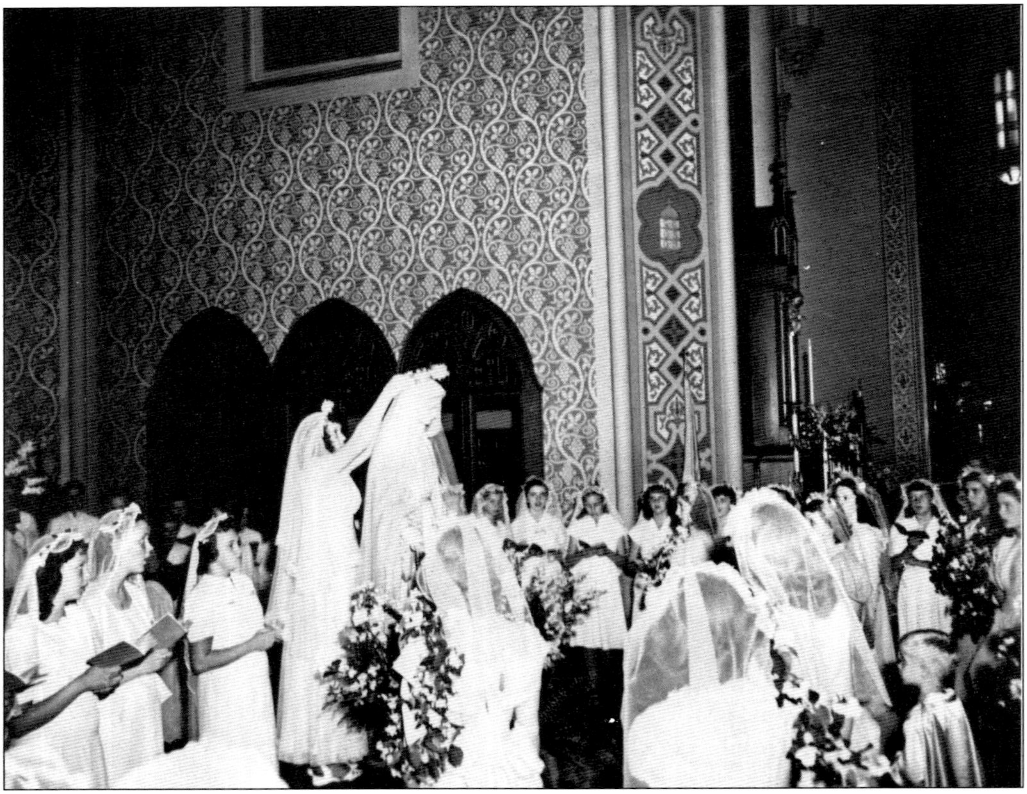

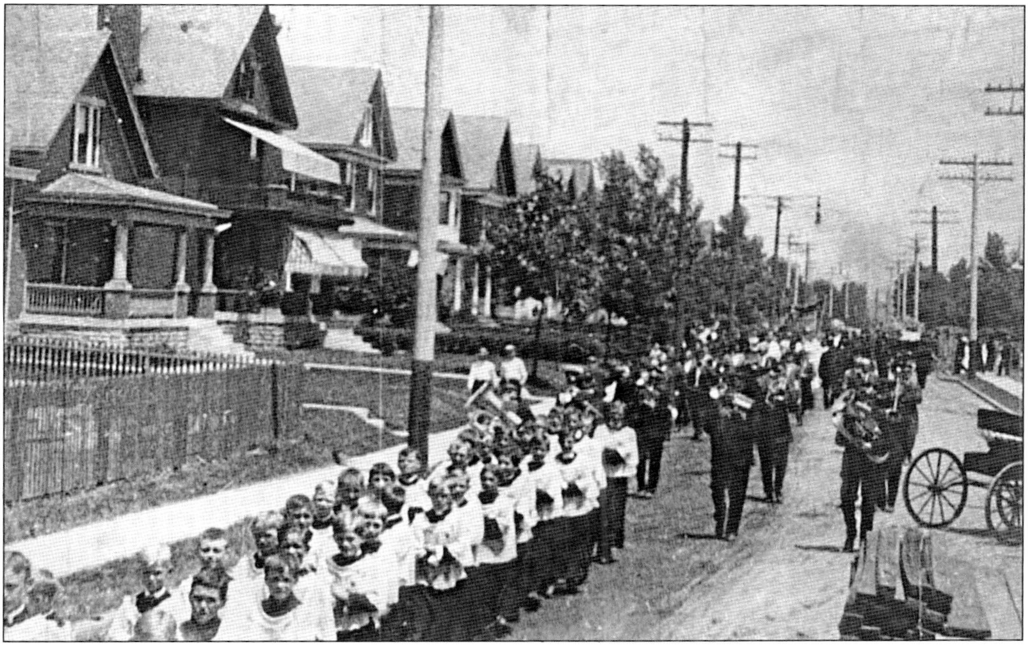

Corpus Christi Procession through the streets of St. Bernard was an annual tradition, with prayers and singing by residents and visitors alike. Three altars were set up at residences. A procession took place from St. Clement to the Nurre residence, as well as Our Lady of Angels and Roger Bacon High Schools, before returning to the church for a final blessing.

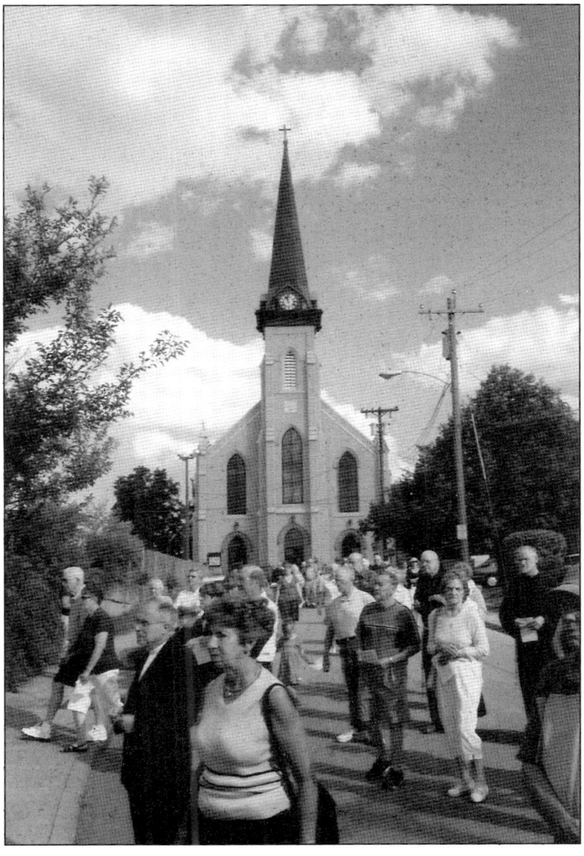

This is the Corpus Christi Procession in 2010. It went from St. Clement Church to altars at the Stella Brannen home on Martin Street, the Lorraine Brunner home on Lawrence Street, the St. Clement School, and it closed with a benediction at St. Clement Church. (Courtesy of Brother Chris Meyer, OFM.)

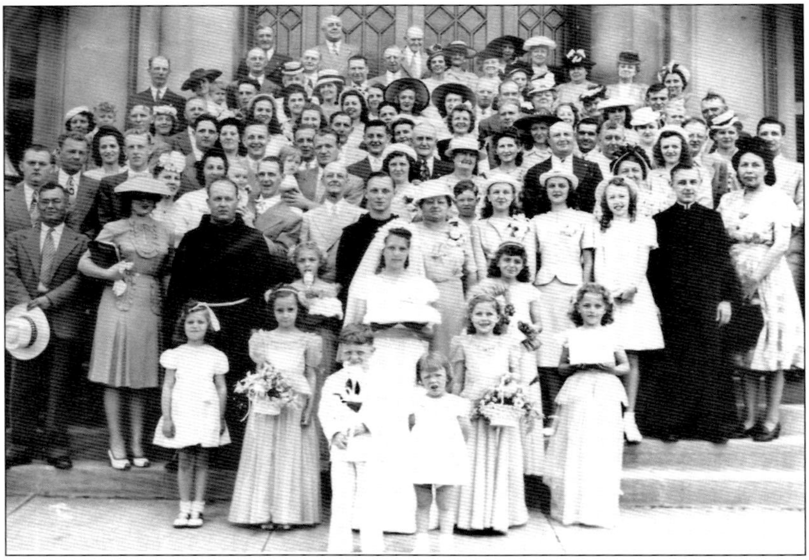

Von Hagel's first Mass at St. Clement was important to the entire parish, family, and friends who came to celebrate.

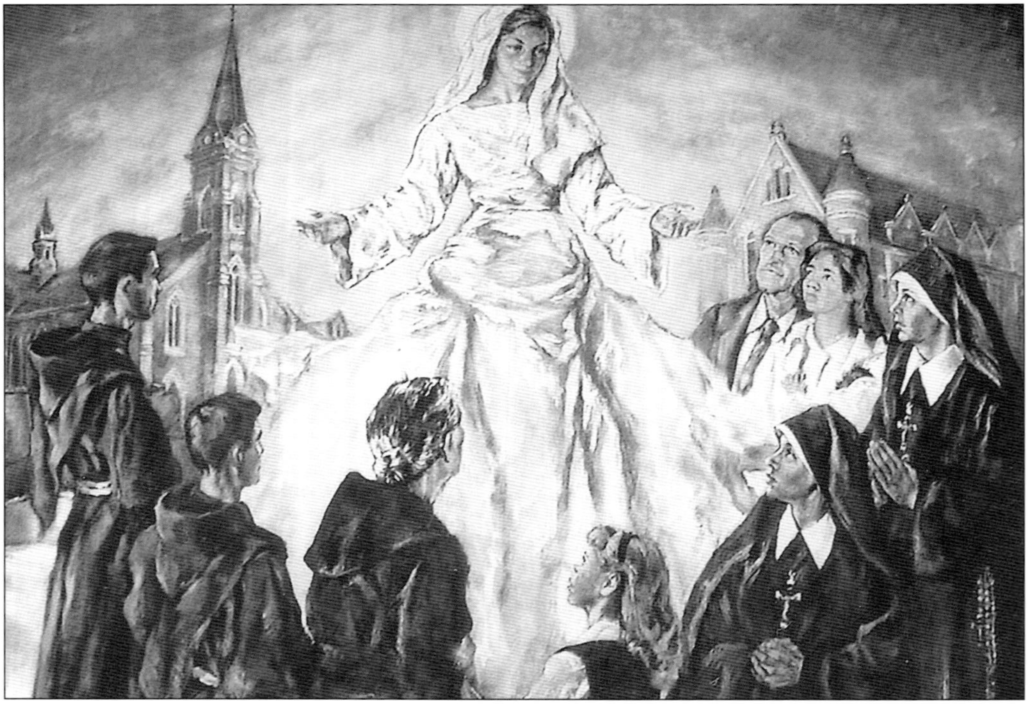

Our Lady of Lourdes Grotto was constructed in 1900 beneath St. Clement Church and was renovated in the 1950s. Here German artist Carl von Volborth painted this picture he named Our Lady of St. Clement in St. Bernard. He used a friend as model for the Virgin Mary. Brother Ambrose Beam, OFM, and Brother Thomas Flahie, OFM, were the clergy. Rosa Geiser represented the elderly, Colleen Vogeler represented a child, and Joan Koetters and Patricia Ballard acted as sisters since religious sisters were not permitted to pose. Mary Ann Schlotman represented the mothers, and John Baur represented the fathers. The Virgin Mary is reaching out to embrace all, and the church and town hall of the community is in the background. (Courtesy of Patricia Ballard.)

Pictured is the first Presbyterian chapel on Clay Street that was built in February 1882 for $1,649.85. German settlers donated a large portion to cover the cost, so German services were permitted before noon and English services in the afternoon.

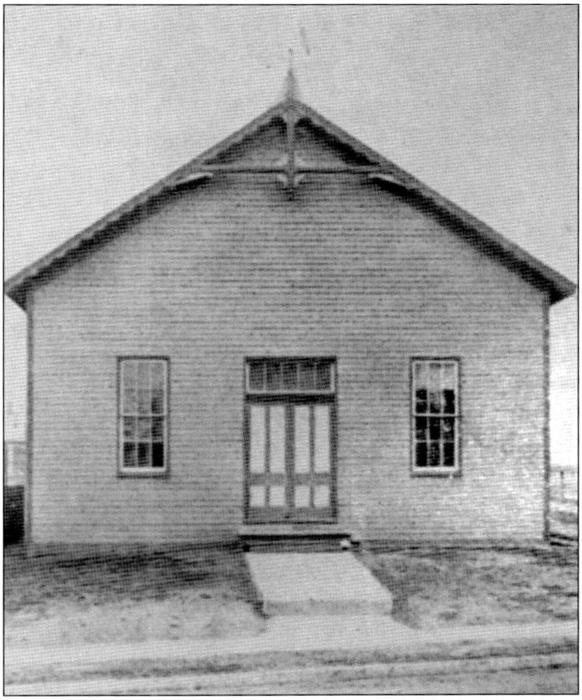

Serving as a commercial building following the departure of the congregations to larger quarters, businesses purchased and modified the property. One such business was the Palmer Thermometer Company. Today, this is the location for Crane Heating and Cooling.

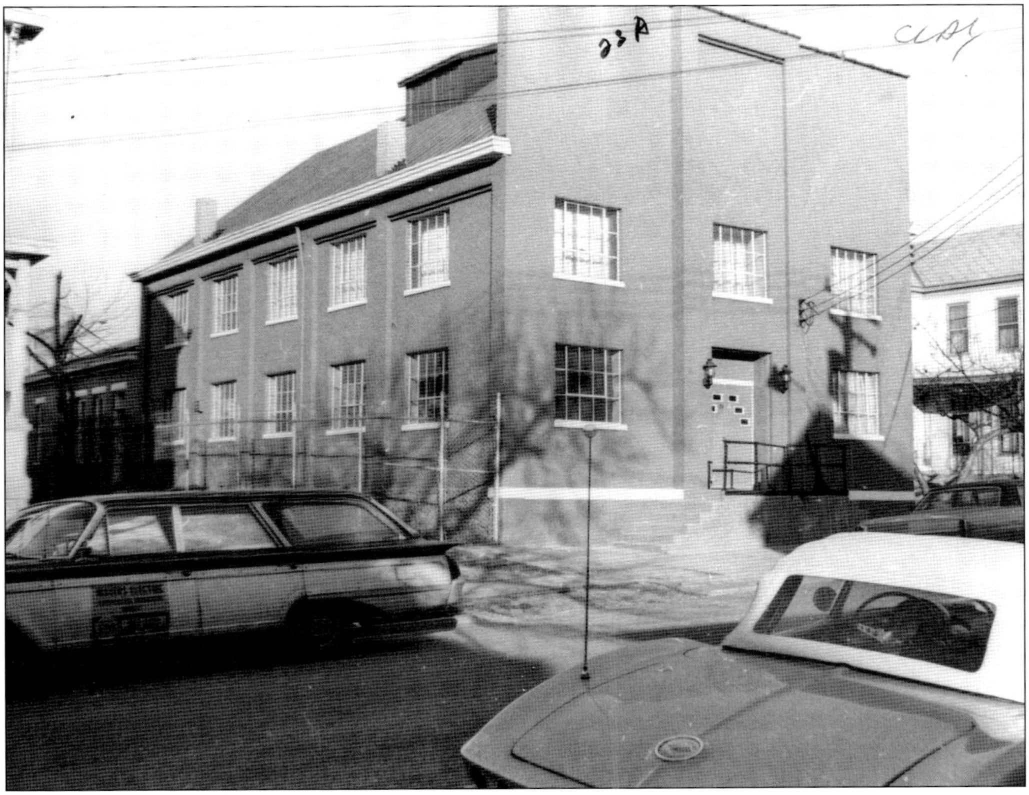

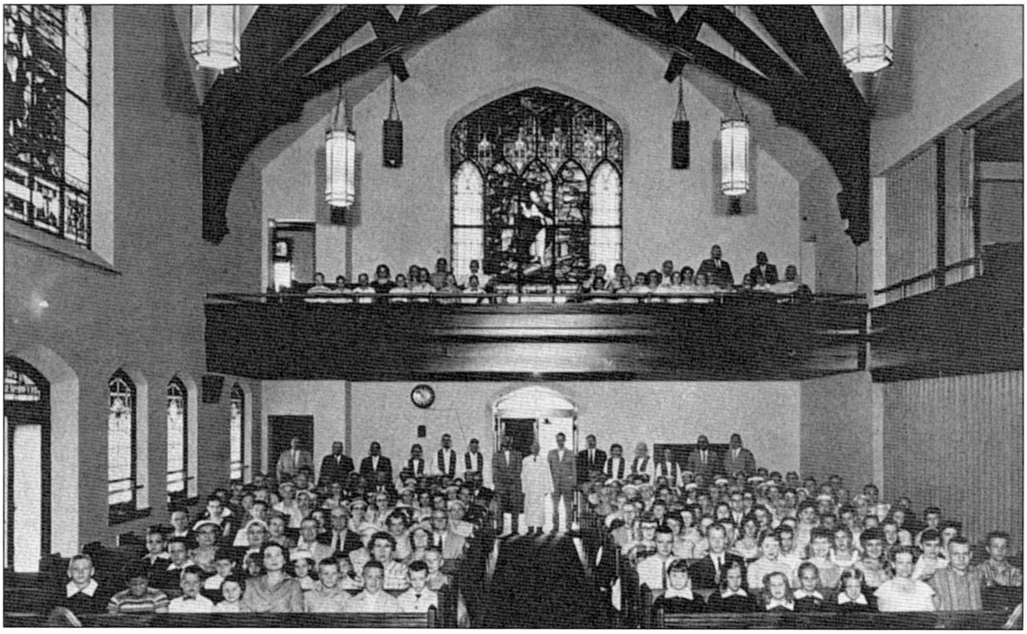

Immanuel United Church of Christ constructed their church on the corner of Jefferson and Tower Avenues, with Sunday school rooms and beautiful stained-glass windows. (Courtesy of the Distler and Willenbrink families.)

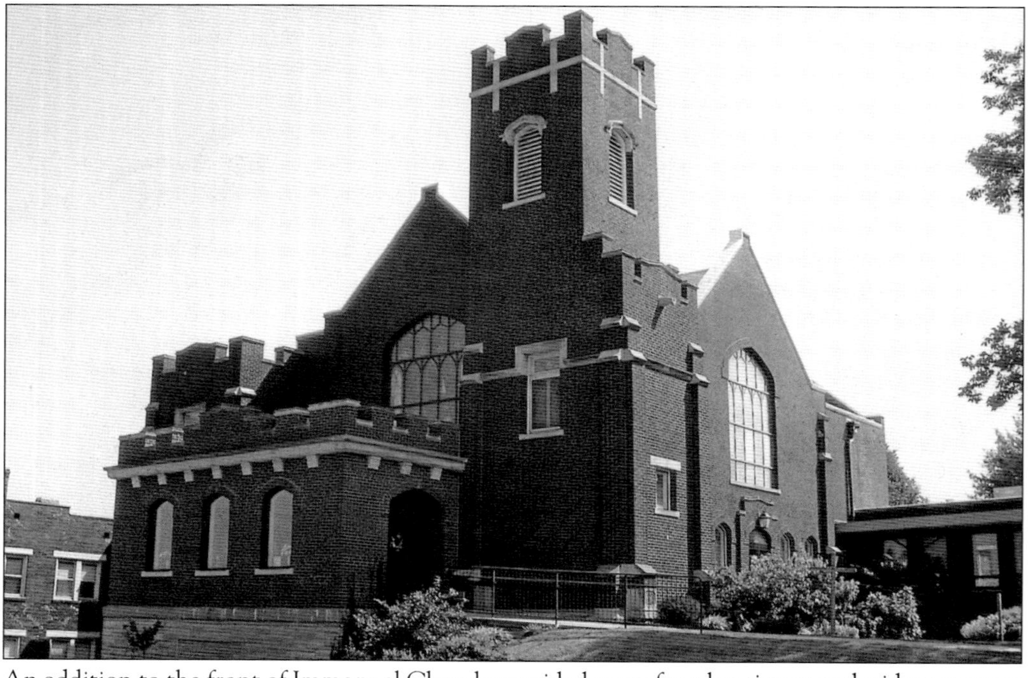

An addition to the front of Immanuel Church provided room for a baptistery and wider entrance vestibule. Throughout the years, more classrooms have been added. Vacation Bible school has been important to the community here. The current interim pastor is Rev. Nancy Millwater. (Courtesy of Jan Boylan.)

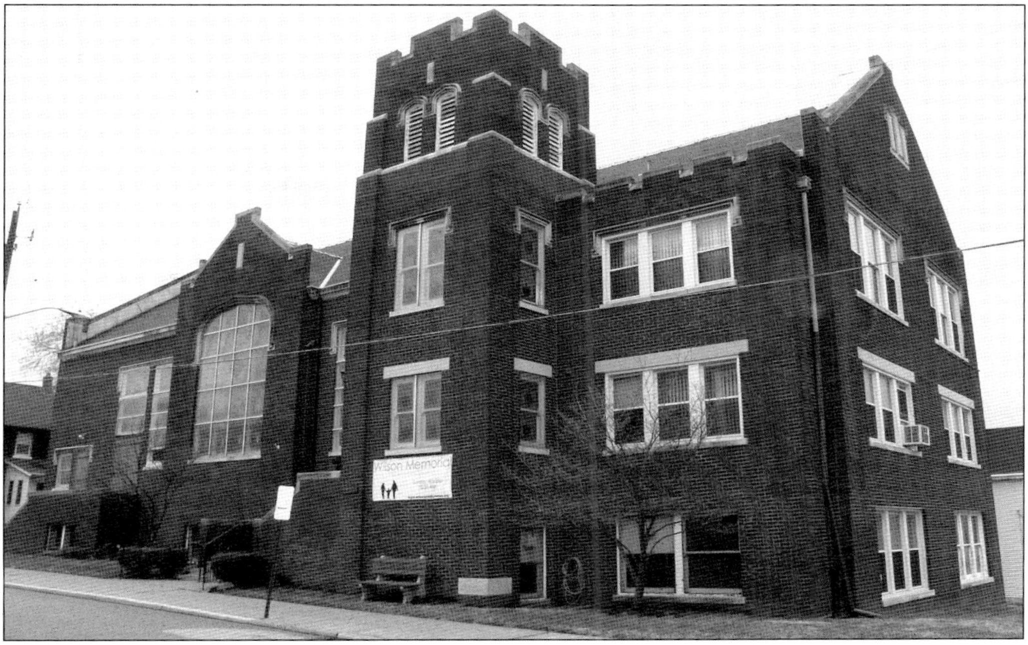

Wilson Memorial Presbyterian Church, located on the corner of McClelland and Sullivan Avenues, also has Sunday school. Dawn Sarchet was the first woman minister to preach here. The current pastor is Rev. Bill Westmoreland. (Courtesy of JoAnne Niesen.)

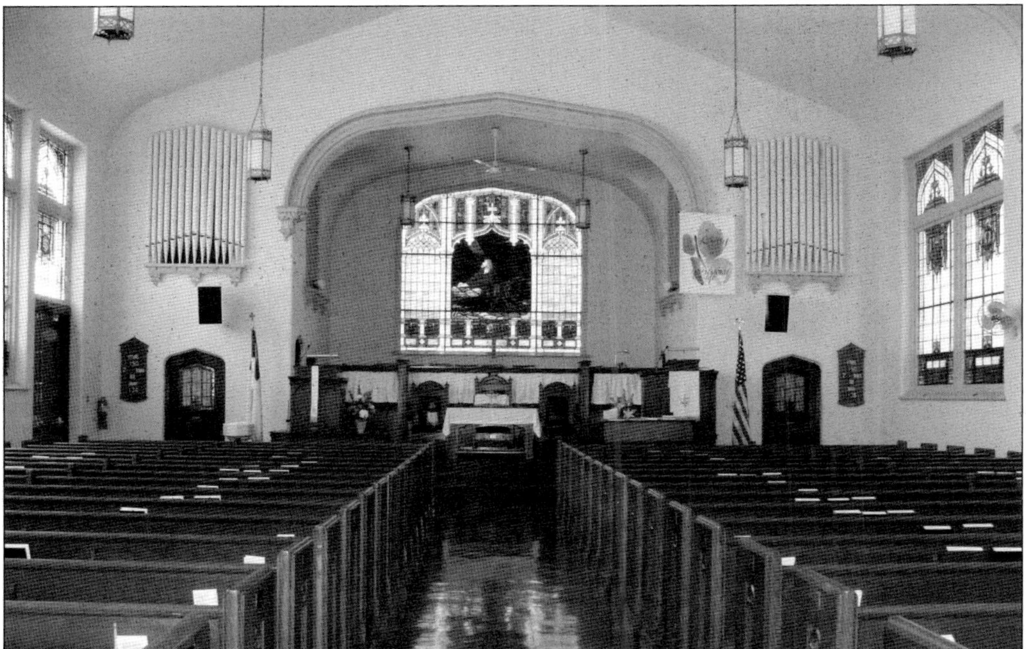

The interior of Wilson Memorial has room for a large congregation, and for many years Ruth Jones accompanied the church choir, as well as for ecumenical groups when there was a shared community service. (Courtesy of JoAnne Niesen.)

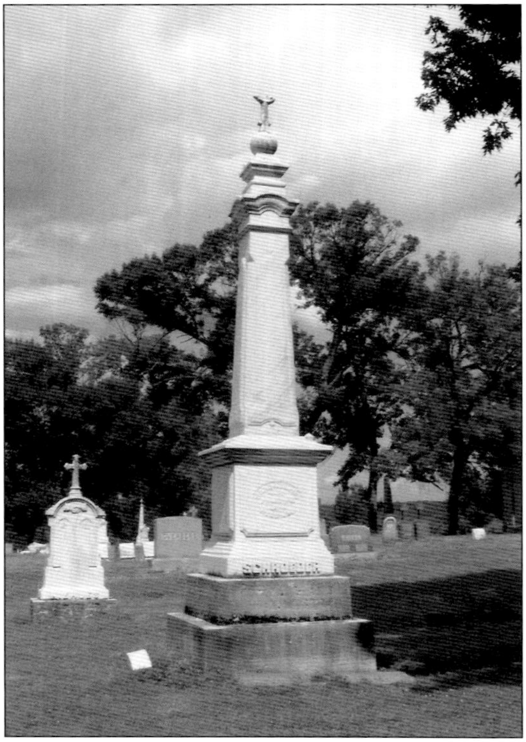

The founder of St. Bernard, John Bernard Schroeder, and his family are buried at St. John's Cemetery. When he passed away in his 50s, his wife continued to raise their children and run their successful lock business. (Courtesy of Jan Boylan.)

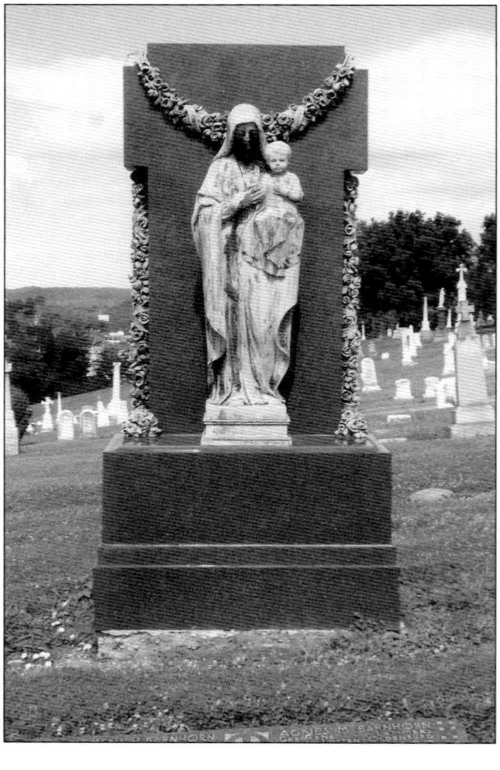

This bronze statue, created by Clement Barnhorn, can be seen at his parents' grave site at St. John Cemetery. (Courtesy of Jan Boylan.)

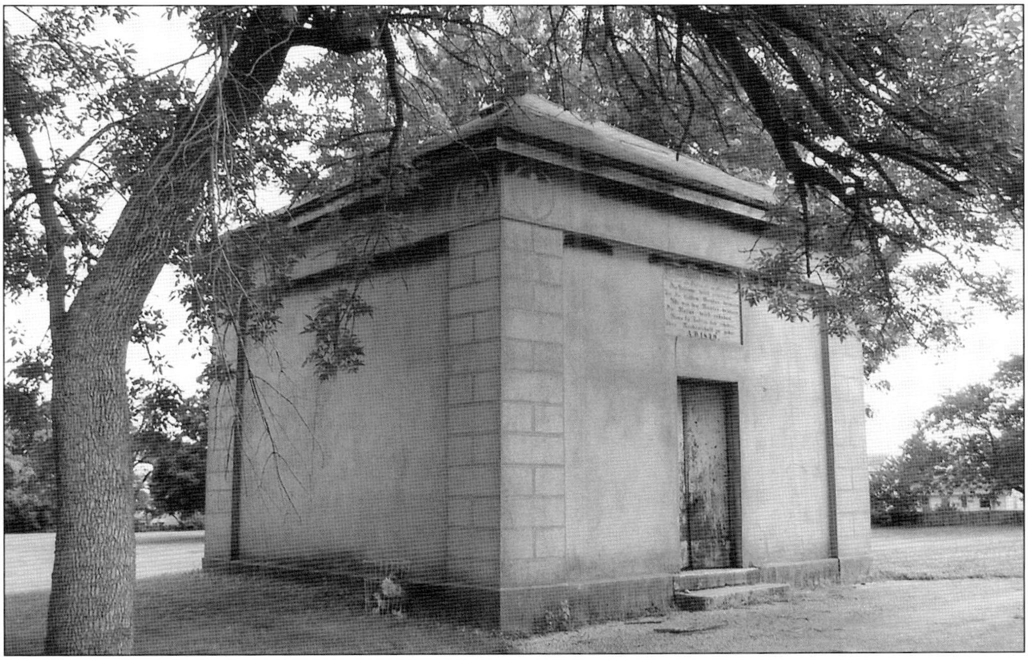

This mausoleum was constructed at St. John's Cemetery. (Courtesy of Jan Boylan.)

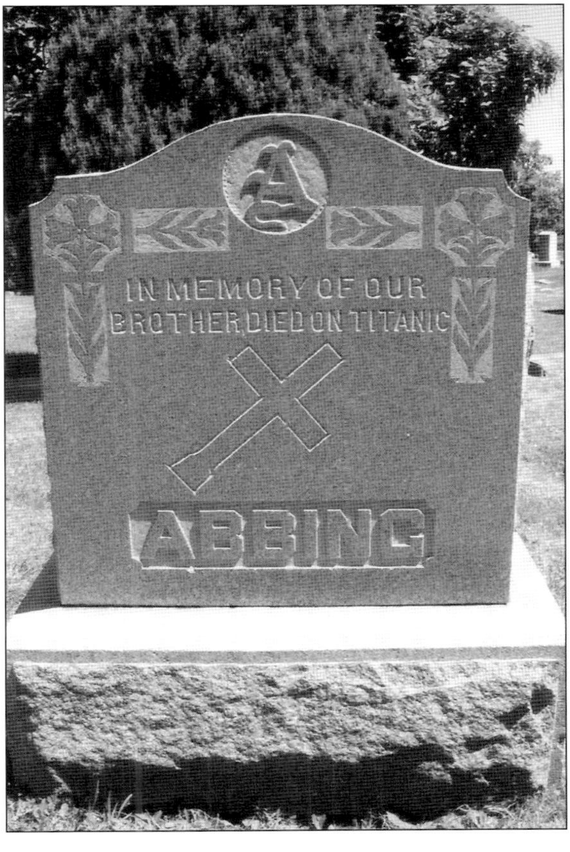

At St. Mary Cemetery, a memorial to a lost family member on the *Titanic* in 1912 is pictured here. (Courtesy of Jan Boylan.)

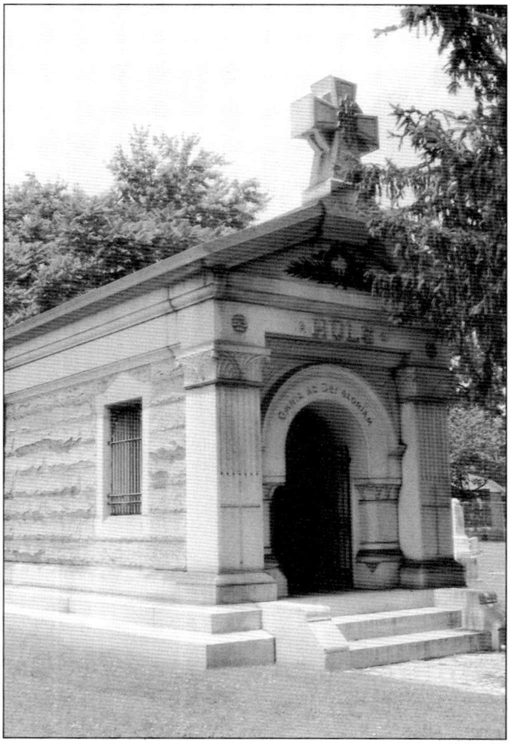

The Huls family mausoleum is located at St. Mary's Cemetery. (Courtesy of Jan Boylan.)

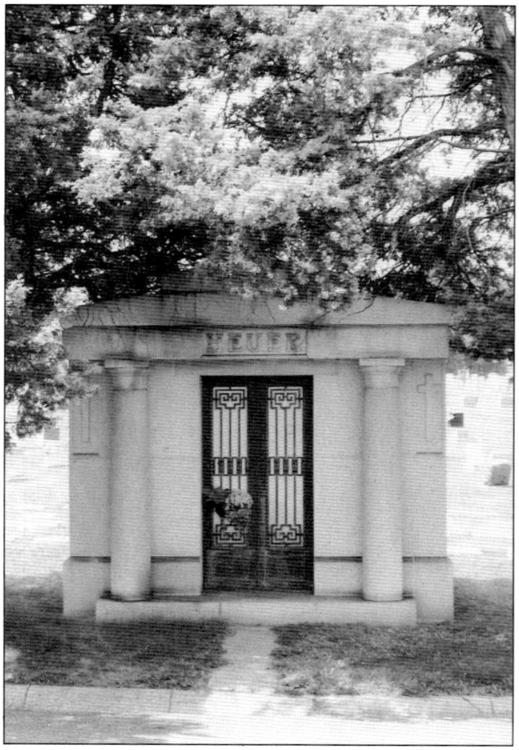

Here is another beautiful mausoleum showing a classical design at St. Mary's Cemetery. (Courtesy of Jan Boylan.)

This St. John the Baptist statue was rescued from a downtown Cincinnati parish and placed in St. Mary's Cemetery. (Courtesy of Jan Boylan.)

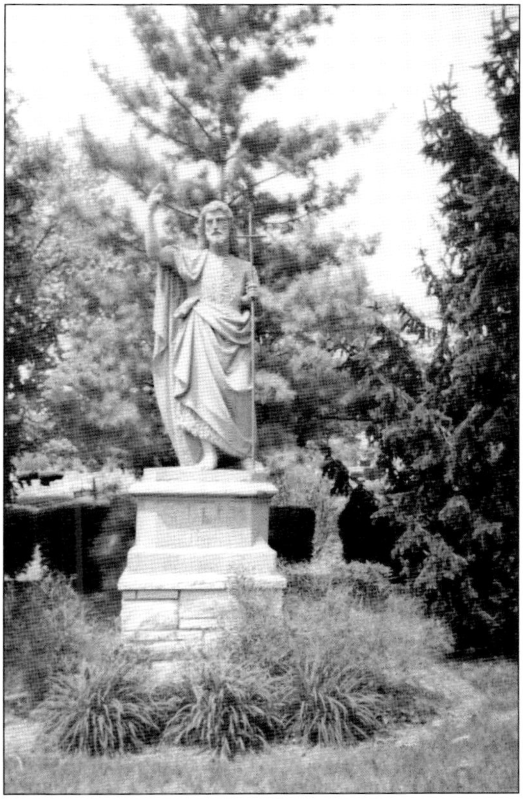

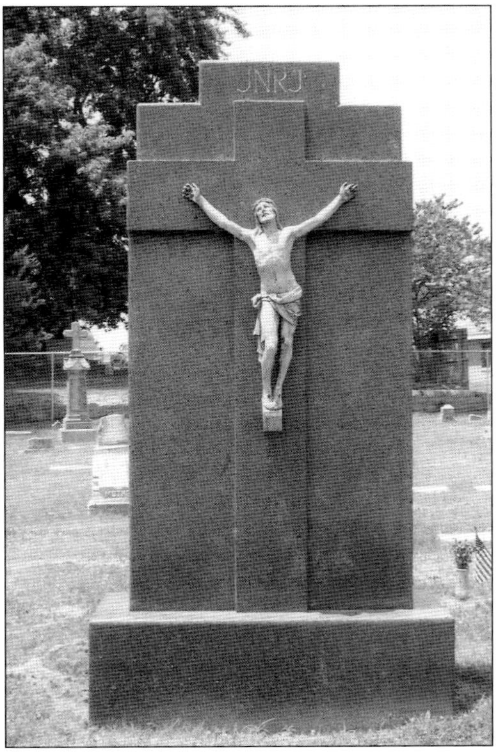

This is the Clement Barnhorn Crucifixion sculpture at his grave site in St. Mary's Cemetery. (Courtesy of Jan Boylan.)

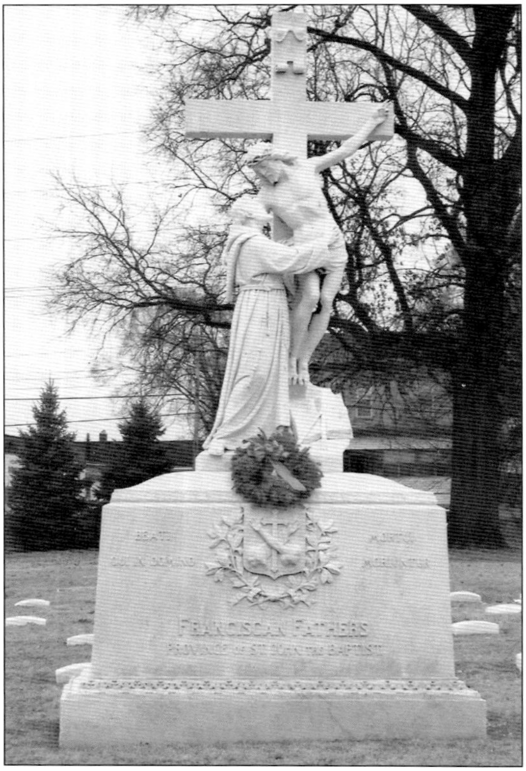

This St. Mary's Cemetery monument was constructed for the Franciscans, many of whom were born in St. Bernard and lived, worked, and died in the city. The community has been truly blessed. (Courtesy of Jan Boylan.)

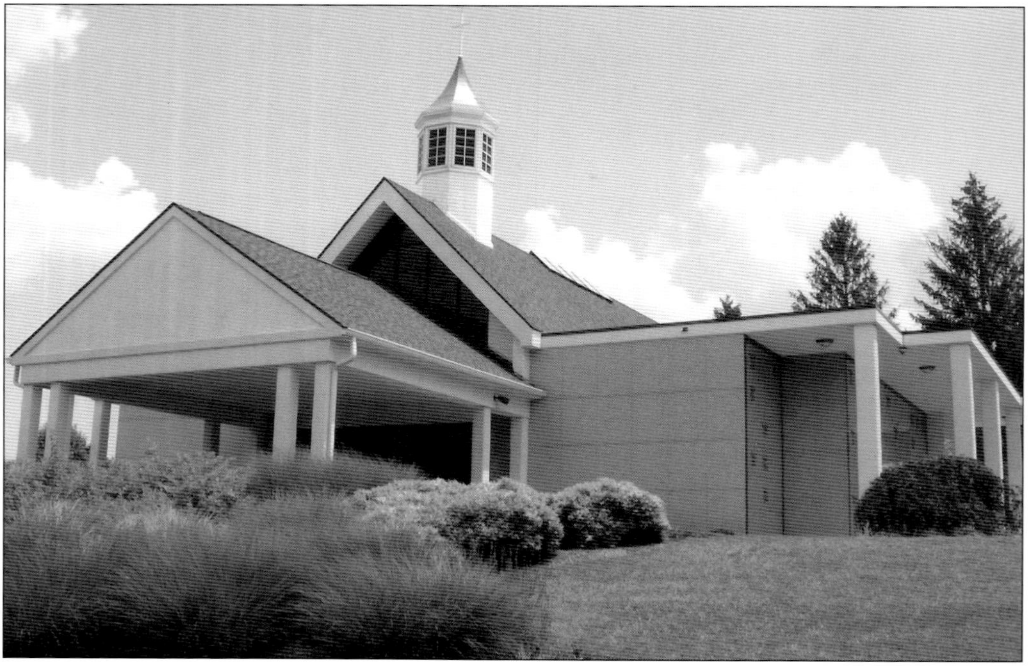

Here is one of two new mausoleums at St. Mary's Cemetery. (Courtesy Cincinnati Catholic Cemetery Society/Stephen Bittner.)

Four

Some Came to Get an Education

Home Bible schooling preceded Elm Tree School in North Ludlow Grove. This primitive cabin school in the early 1800s closed after two children drowned in the canal. In 1839, Anthony Cook's property housed classes for families in lower Millcreek Township with students named Ludlow, Kemper, Huffman, Kaylor, and Spangler. Public education at Ross Avenue School District No. 4 was on Kemper's corner near Vine Street in 1869. In 1893, four classrooms were added and 277 students by 1900. Financed by $30,900 in bonds, the purchase of lots in 1900, between Jackson and Burnet, provided for Tower Avenue School. Students north of Washington Avenue attended Ross, and students south of Washington attended Tower Avenue. The nearest high school was in Norwood or Cincinnati, where tuition was $40. From 1903 to 1910, St. Bernard experimented with the addition of ninth and tenth grades. In 1911, grades 11 and 12 were created, with the first four-year graduation in 1912. In 1918, a separate high school was constructed. Buildings were replaced in 1974 to respond to current needs and teaching methods. When school districts were restructured, award-winning St. Bernard-Elmwood Place School District incorporated both communities for educational efficiency. Today, they are guided by Superintendent Dr. Mimi Webb.

In 1923, St. Clement Elementary included an auditorium of main floor seating for 800, with 200 more seats on balconies. It also had three floors of 18 classrooms for 800 pupils. Today, tuition is charged, and the curriculum includes computer labs and instructors in addition to core classes. The principal is Jeff Eiser. Our Lady of Angels High School merged with Roger Bacon High School but began with 350 students in 1927. Taught by the Franciscan sisters and lay personnel, the first graduating class was in 1929. Through the years, music, sports, and scholastics, with numerous curriculum updates, educated many. The convent was the former Wess homestead. In March 1984, the decision was made to close Our Lady of Angels after graduation. A small college used the building until its demolition. Now, it is St. Bernard's most upscale neighborhood called Angel's Way. Archbishop McNicholas's request to Franciscans brought construction of Roger Bacon High School for boys in 1927. Fr. Juvenal Berens, OFM, was the first principal. Today, the principal is Rick Sohlmann. The president, Fr. Bill Farris, OFM, ably serves as a religious guiding hand to this contemporary school. Known for scholastic excellence, students continually show proficiency in athletics, music, and art. Today, the Our Lady of Angels and Roger Bacon traditions share ideals and ideas of a Franciscan education to meet the future. These ideas have been coeducational since 1985.

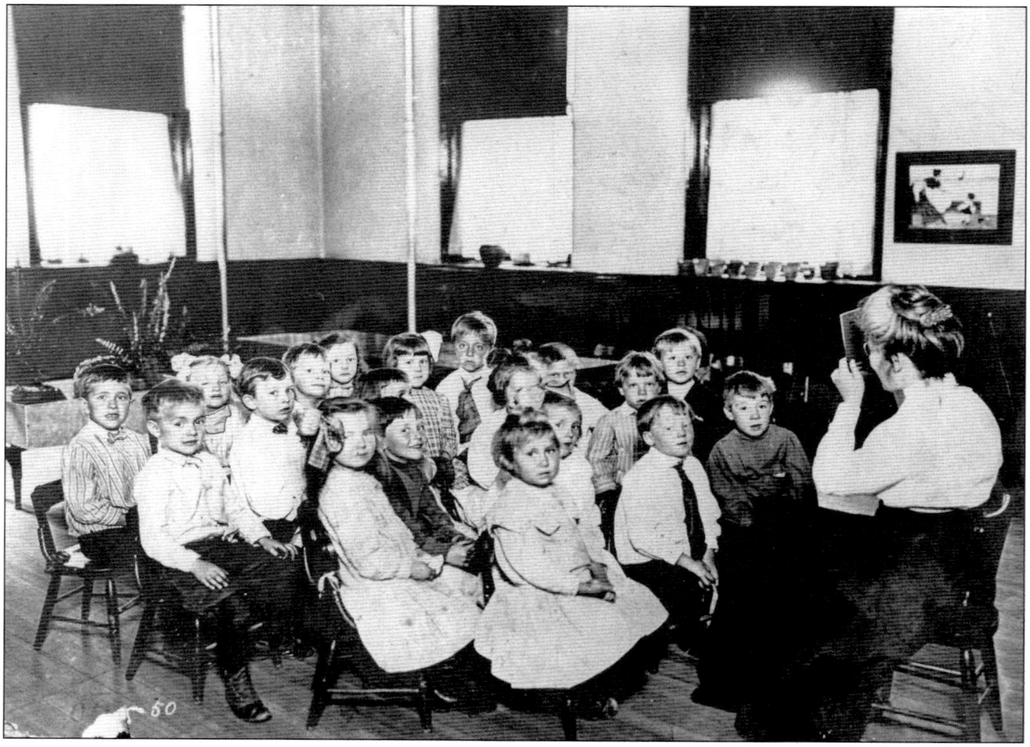

The first public school was at Ross Avenue and consisted of four classrooms, which later were increased by four more. Eventually, danger of nearby railroad crossings and noise of the trains forced the closing of this school in favor of Tower Avenue School.

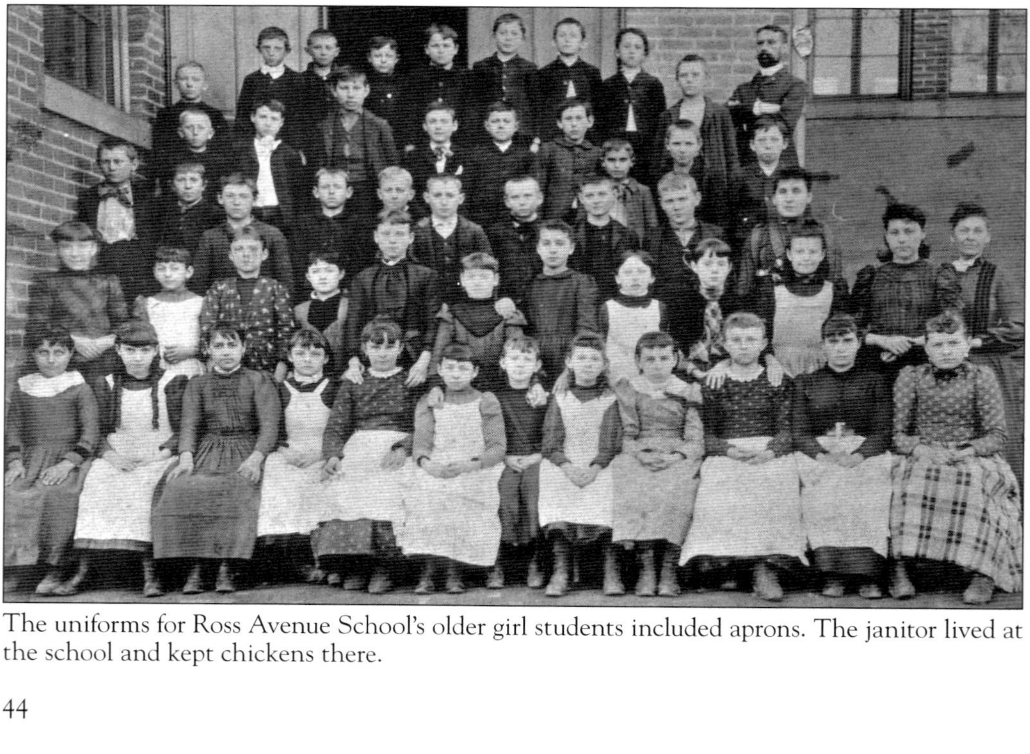

The uniforms for Ross Avenue School's older girl students included aprons. The janitor lived at the school and kept chickens there.

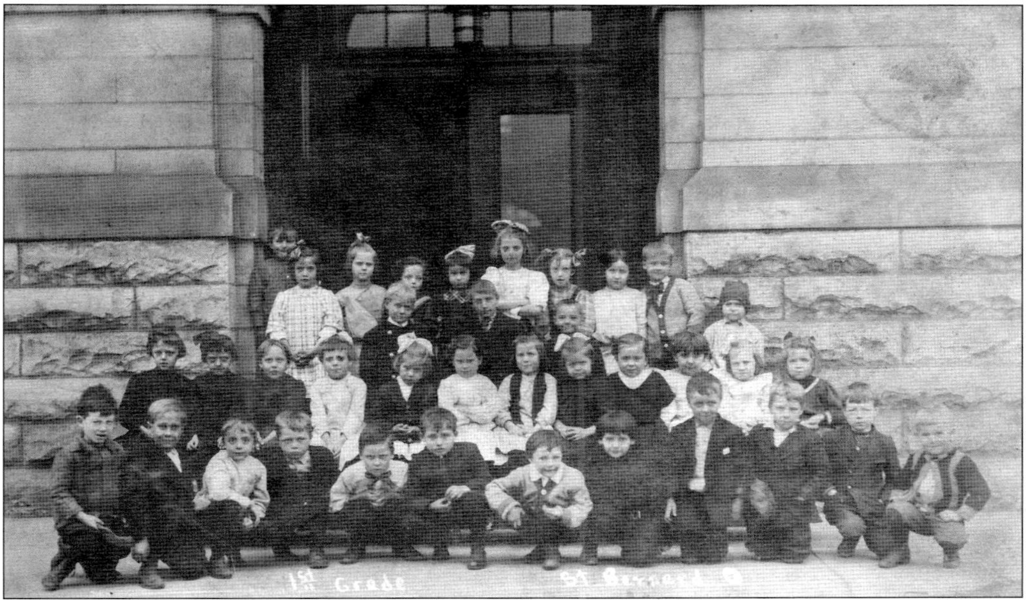

When Tower Avenue School opened, it gave more students the opportunity to receive an education, as Ross Avenue School was crowded. Those living south of Washington Avenue attended Tower Avenue School.

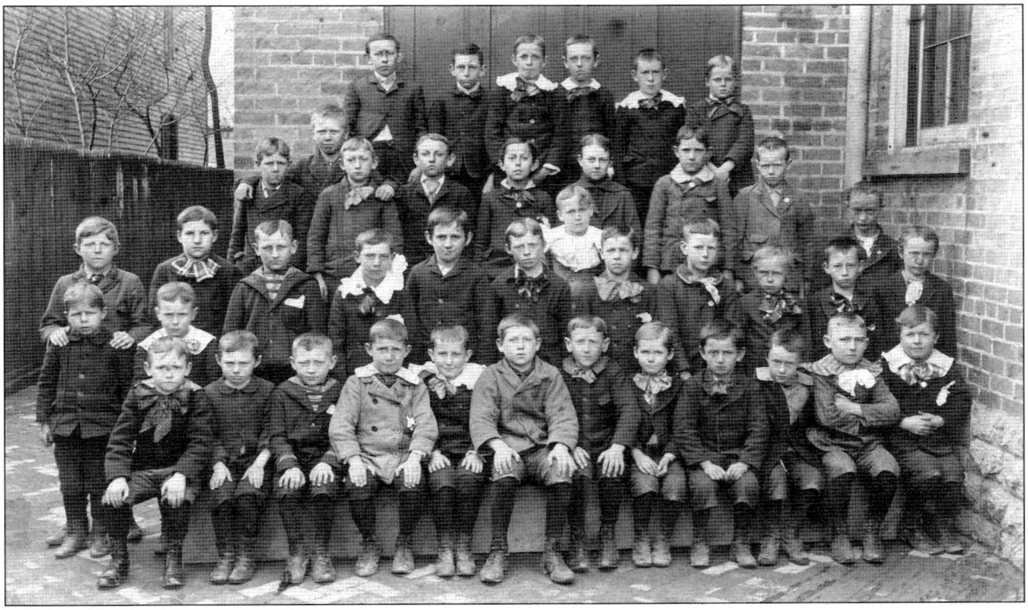

This is the St. Clement boys' class around 1890. As a rule, classes were segregated by gender, and boys and girls were taught in separate classrooms.

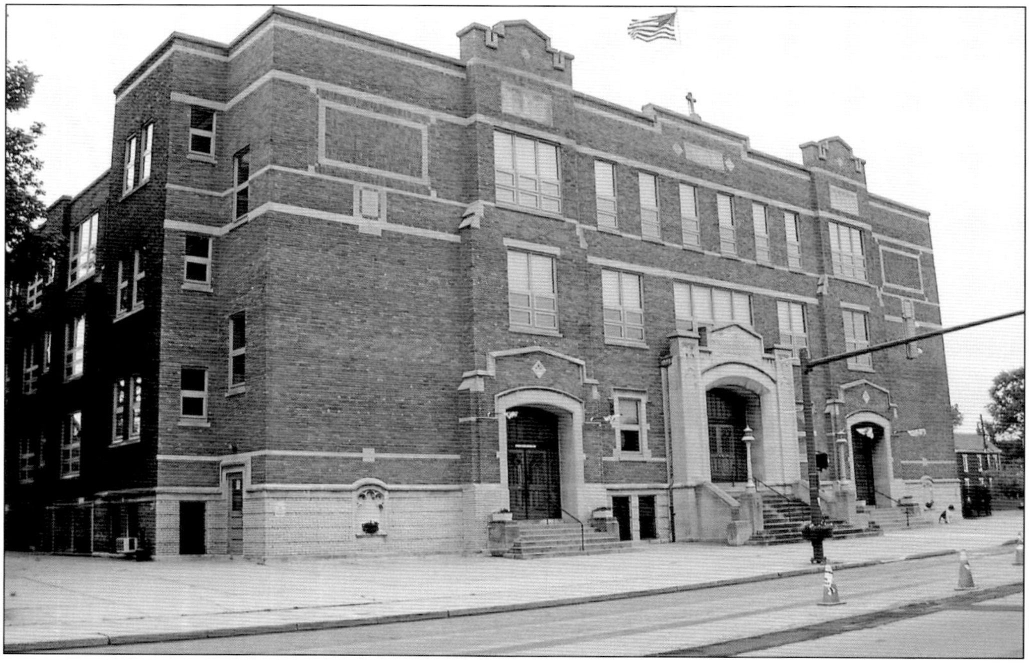

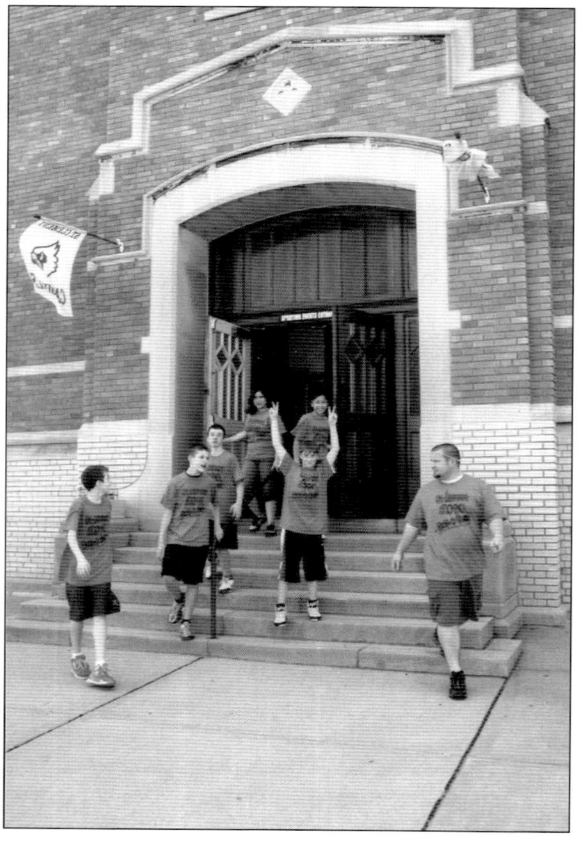

St. Clement Elementary was constructed in 1923 and had special amenities, including a large auditorium, three floors of classrooms, and a balcony. This school was annexed to the public school system due to financial problems from 1936 to 1951. (Courtesy of Jan Boylan.)

Today's students of St. Clement are preparing for a walk-a-thon to raise money for the school. (Courtesy of Brother Chris Meyer, OFM.)

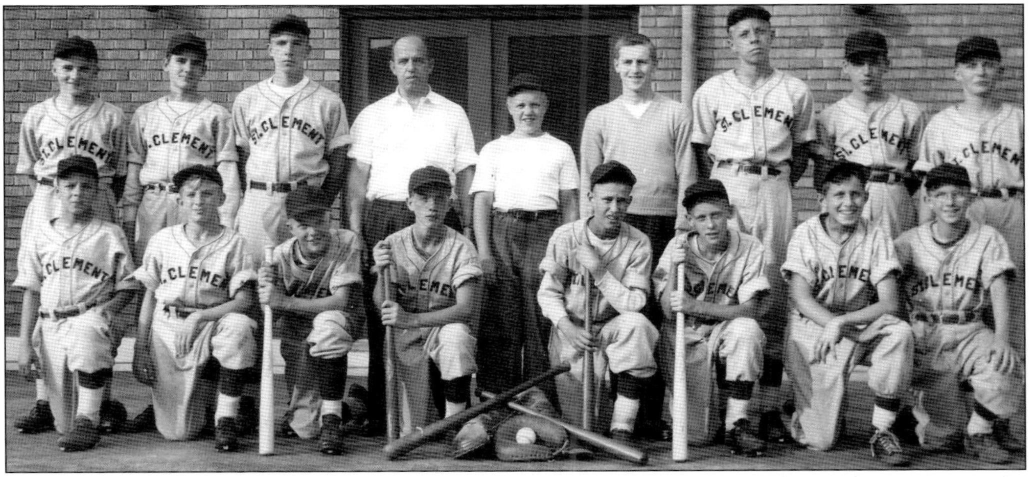

Joe Hellner coached all sports and was a mainstay and role model for the students. He taught them fundamentals as well as life lessons. His motto was "a winner never quits, and a quitter never wins." Many of his athletes went on to become successful coaches in their own right. His baseball record included 144 wins and 40 losses, 15 league titles, and five city championships. His other records include three league football titles, two track and field city championships, and third place for the swim team. (Courtesy of Jerry Doerger and Richard Doerger.)

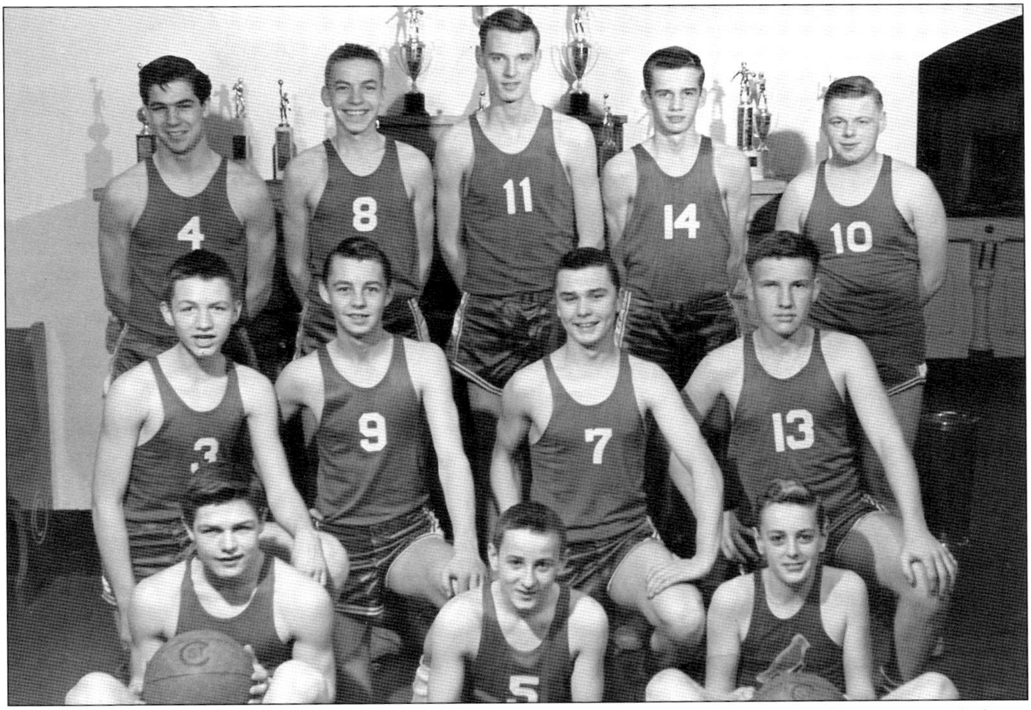

The St. Clement basketball teams have been annual contenders since Joe Hellner entered them into the Catholic Youth Organization (CYO) in 1935. Out of the 20 years that he coached, 18 out of 20 titles were won, with 502 wins and 113 losses. He also had seven city championships. The Joe Hellner Tournament was held each year at the St. Clement gymnasium and was the climax of every season.

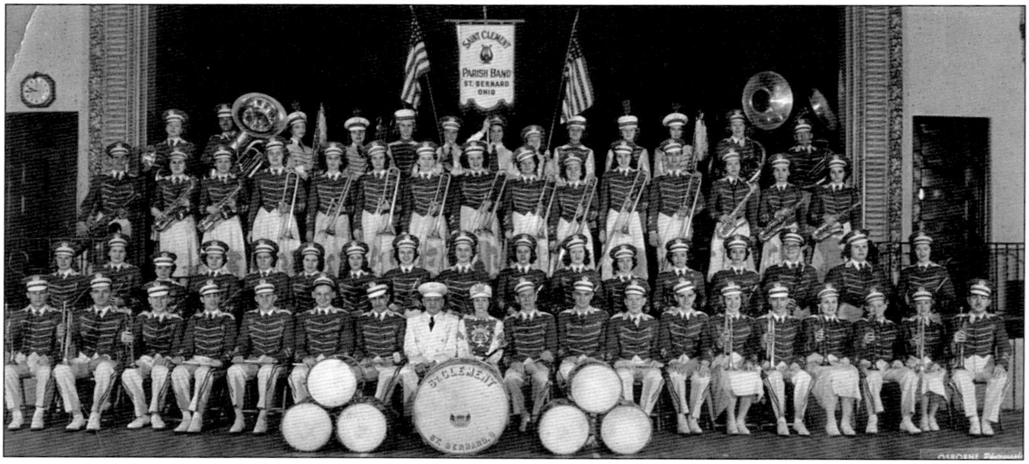

For many years, St. Clement had a large alumni band. Many members played in the school band and continued their musical interest. This is a group from 1951. (Courtesy of Carolyn Ungruhe.)

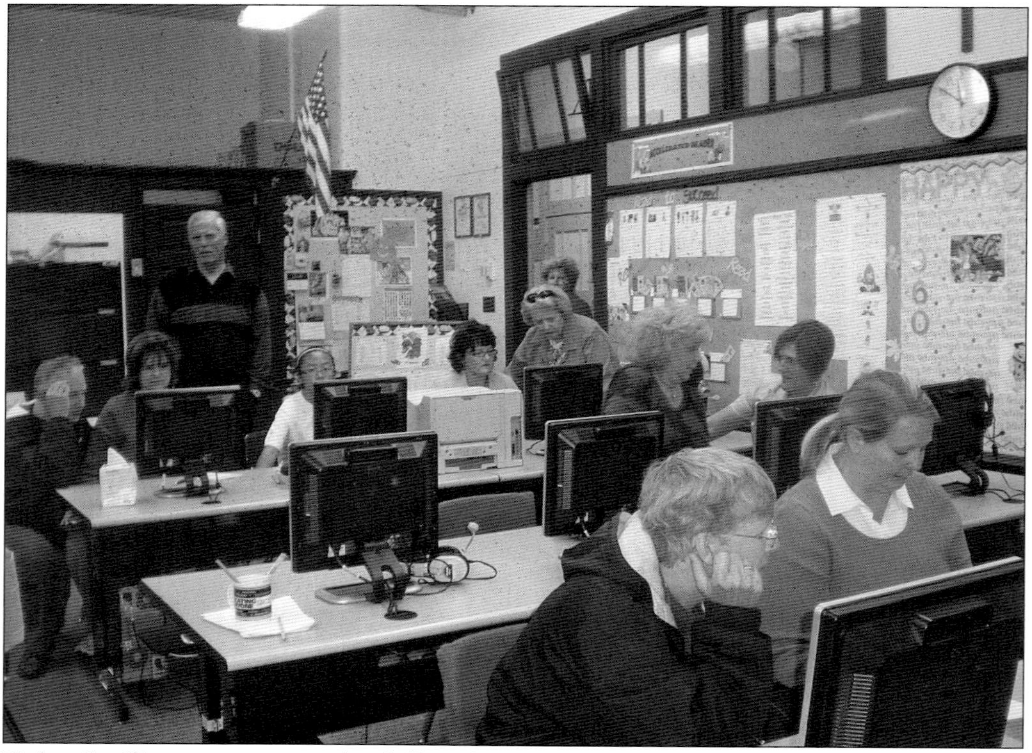

Today, St. Clement trains pupils of all grades in computer technology to assure they are well prepared for the future. (Courtesy of Paula Blessing.)

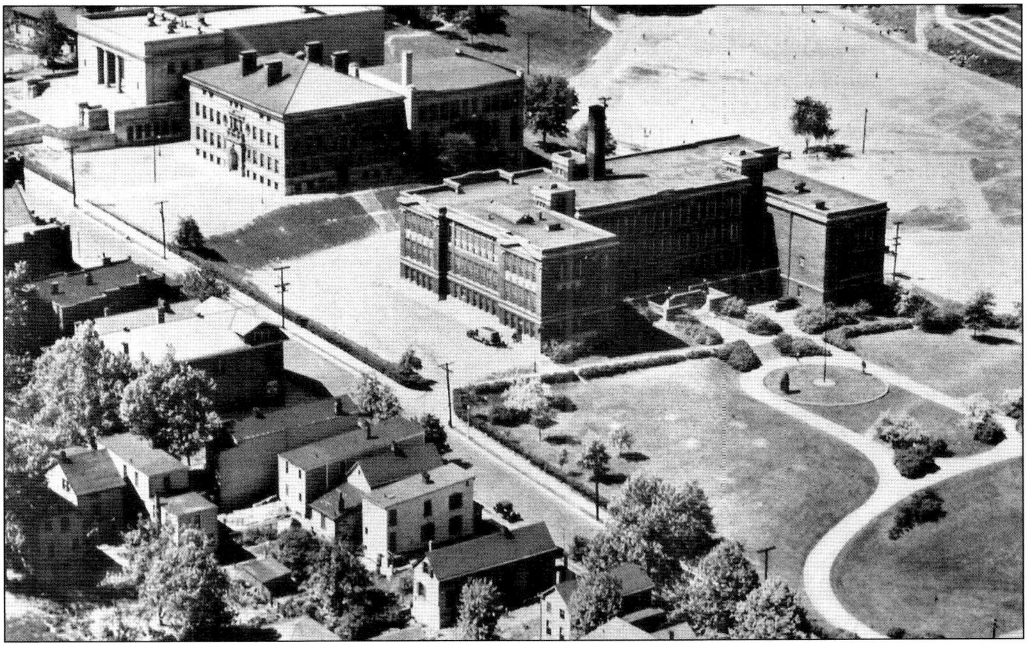

This is an overview of the first St. Bernard school complex. The gymnasium and auditorium are on the left, and the elementary school is between that and the high school on right. (Courtesy of the St. Bernard Yearbook.)

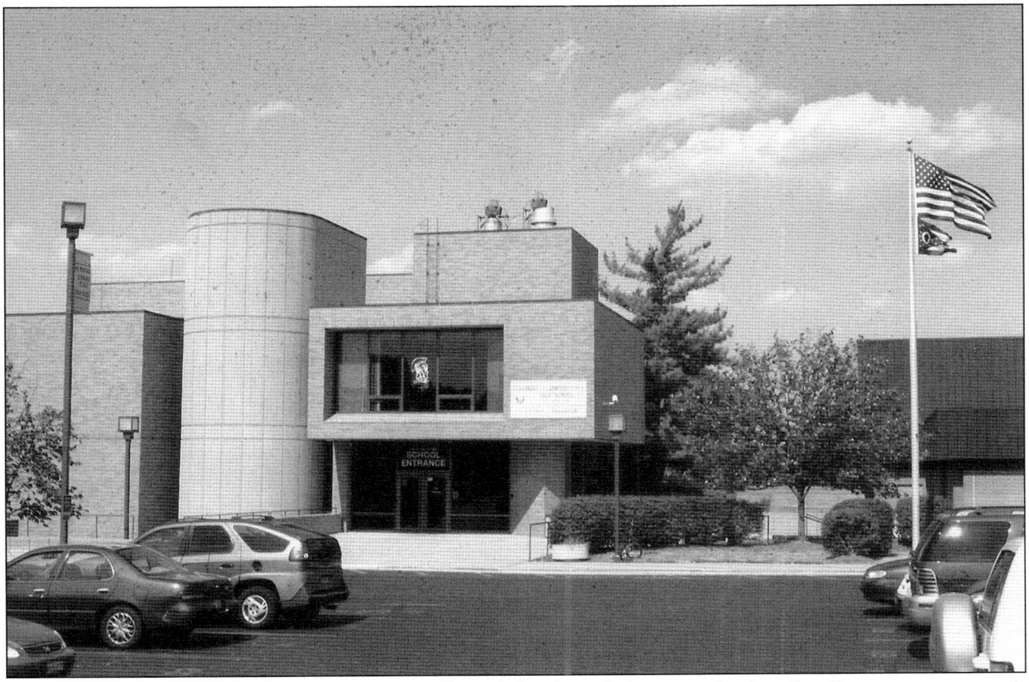

In 1974, the former school complex was demolished, and this new high school was constructed. It includes a swimming pool, a horticulture center, an auditorium, and a gymnasium, in addition to computer labs and special classes. (Courtesy of Jan Boylan.)

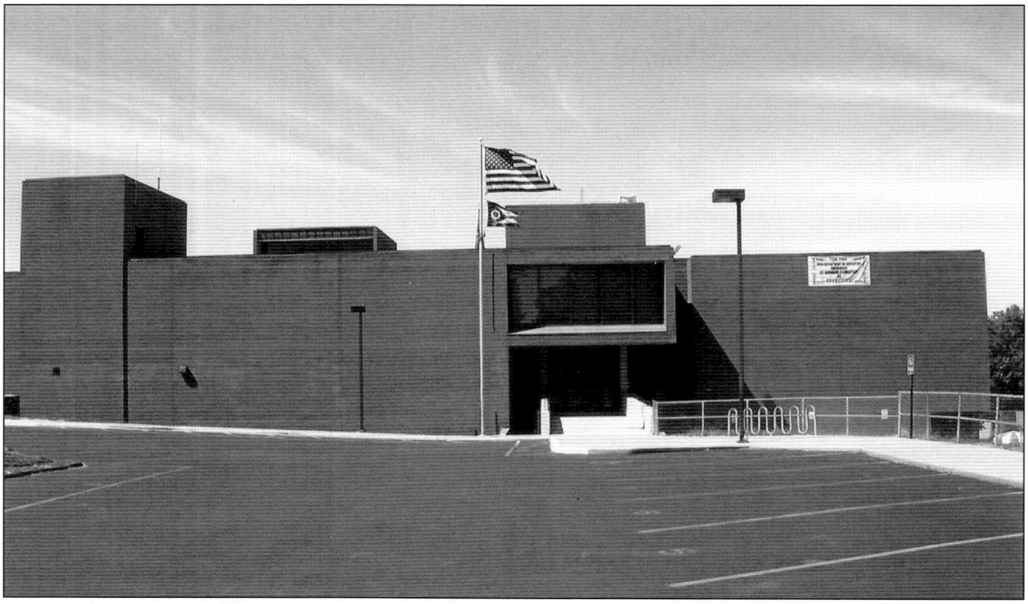

A new elementary school was constructed where the former auditorium and gymnasium had been located. Following an open classroom theory, students were challenged by this new educational philosophy. (Courtesy of Jan Boylan.)

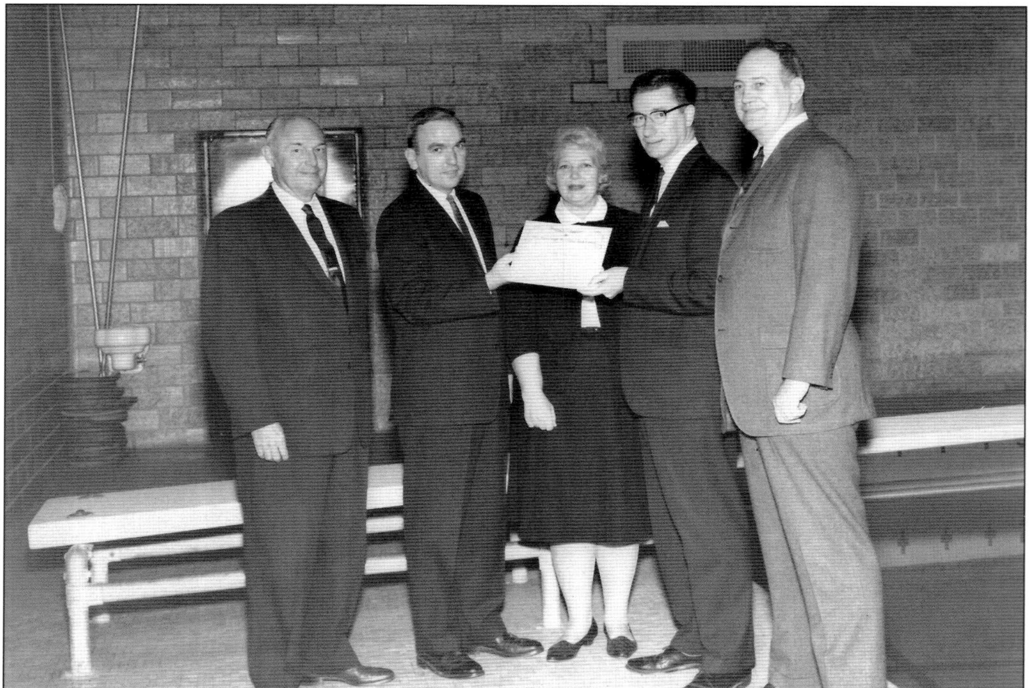

The St. Bernard School received an award from Mayor Joseph Haverland. Pictured here from left to right are Crawford Bower, the high school superintendent; George Hufford, the principal; Louise Gimms, the gym teacher; Mayor Haverland; and Coach Carl Yeager.

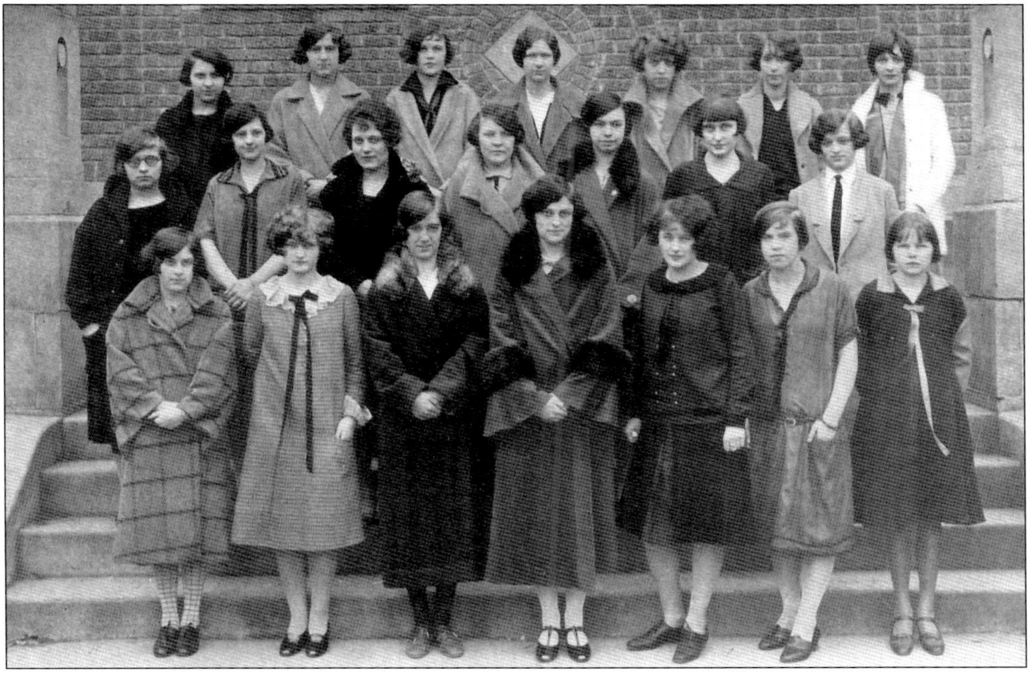

The Girls' Booster Club at St. Bernard High organized to promote high ideals and school spirit. (Courtesy of the 1926 St. Bernard High School Yearbook.)

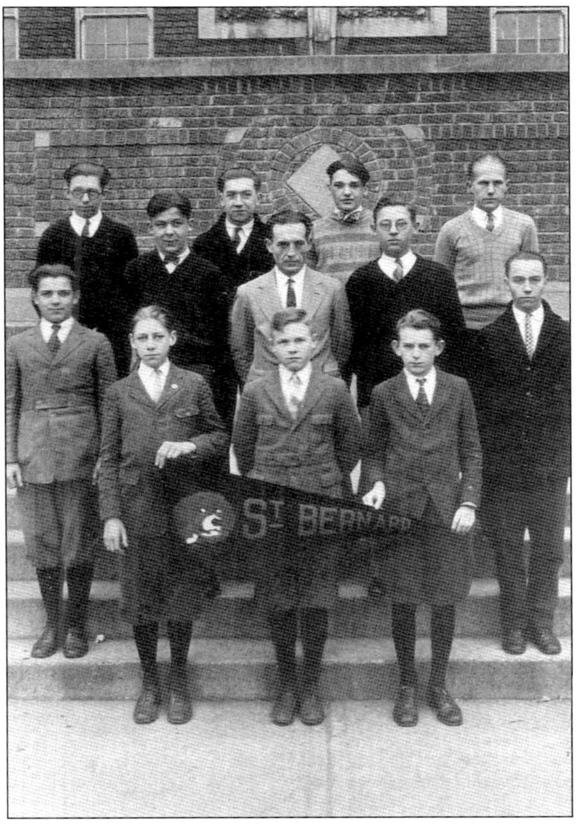

This Boys' Booster Club at St. Bernard High was organized in 1923. It promoted good fellowship, loyalty, and higher ideals of the school. (Courtesy of the 1926 St. Bernard High School Yearbook.)

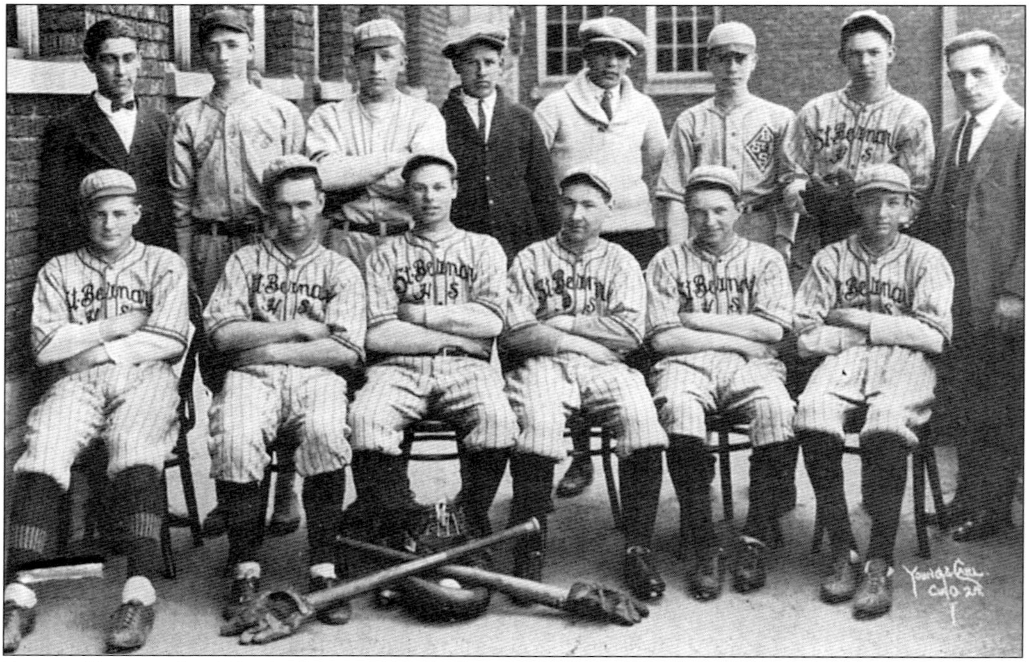

Pictured here is the 1924 St. Bernard High School baseball team. They are, from left to right, (first row) Huffman, Dorsey, Case, Buckley, Murphy, and Bauer; (second row) Strohmenger (manager), Hampel, Kalkbrenner, Easton, Hudepohl, Jones, Gustin, and A.W. Milner (coach). (Courtesy of the St. Bernard High School Yearbook.)

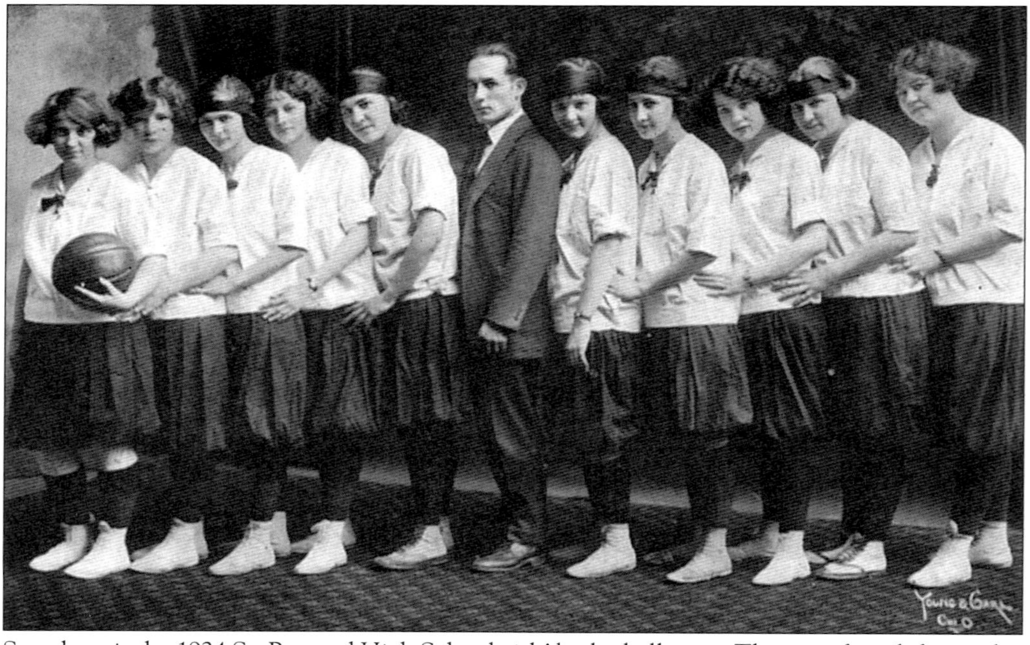

Seen here is the 1924 St. Bernard High School girls' basketball team. They are, from left to right, Mersch, Moedl, Kemper, Gustin, Macksum, A.W. Milner (coach), Mottern, Weaver, Grabbenstetter, Richards, and Herbst. (Courtesy of St. Bernard High School Yearbook.)

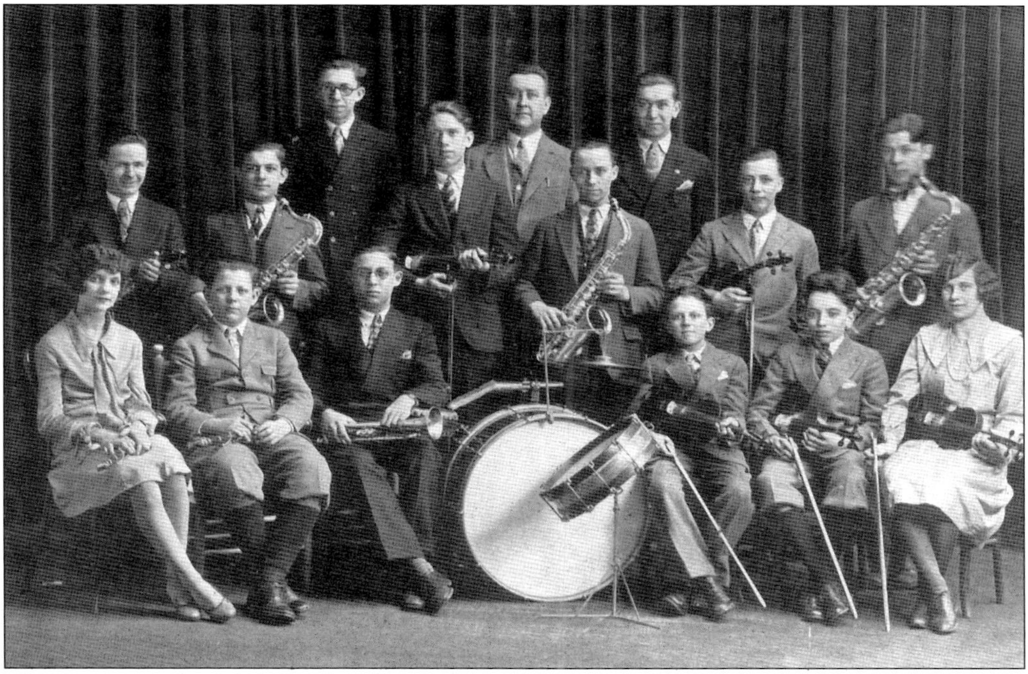

The St. Bernard High School orchestra began in 1921 under the direction of Prof. Frank A. Young. (Courtesy of St. Bernard High School Yearbook.)

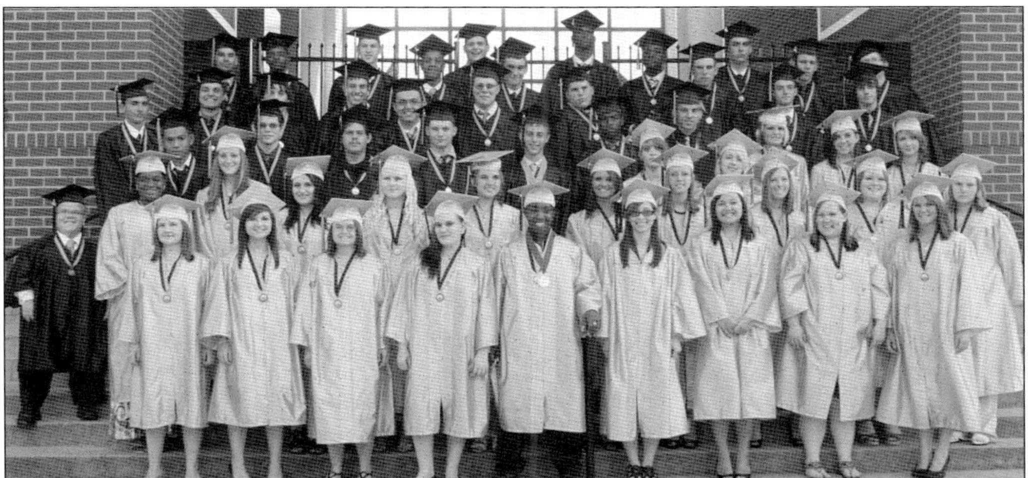

Pictured is the graduating class of 2010 of St. Bernard High School. (Courtesy of Pam Carroll.)

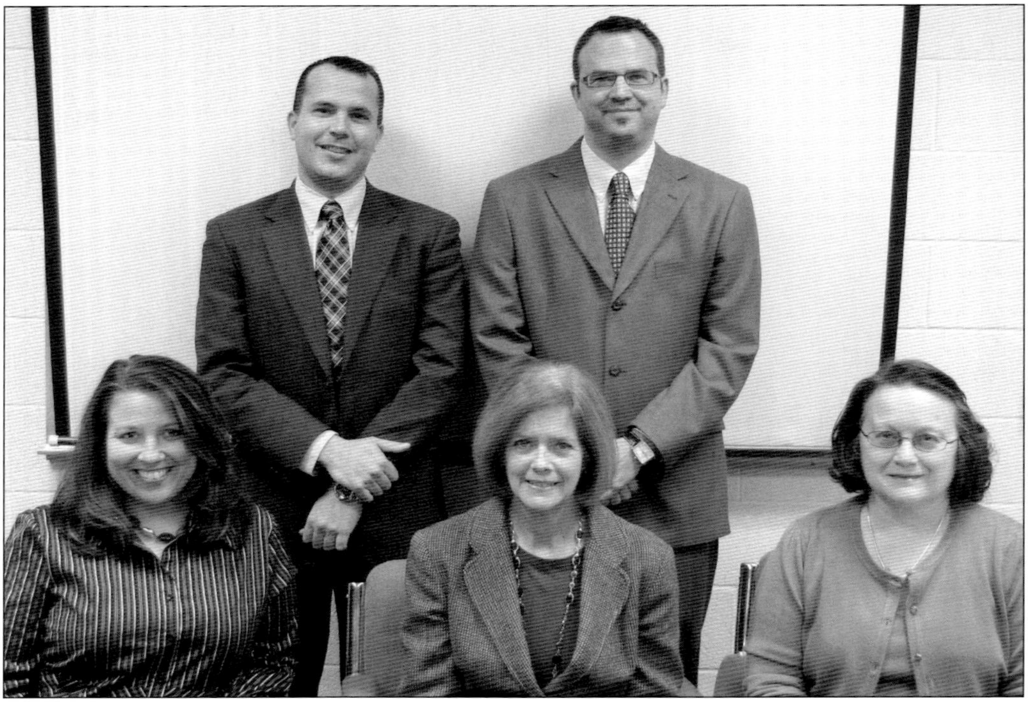

This is the St. Bernard School Board in 2011. Pictured are, from left to right, (first row) Tricia Hackney, Linda Radtke, and Debbie Steidel; (second row) Gabe Sanders and Steven Rutemueller. (Courtesy of Pam Carroll.)

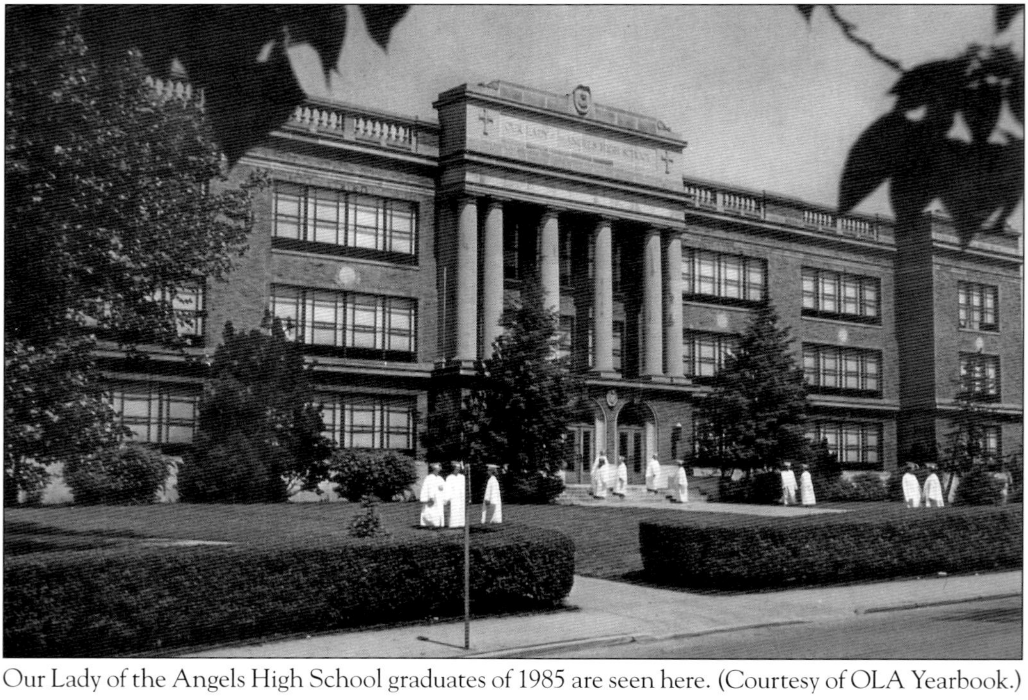

Our Lady of the Angels High School graduates of 1985 are seen here. (Courtesy of OLA Yearbook.)

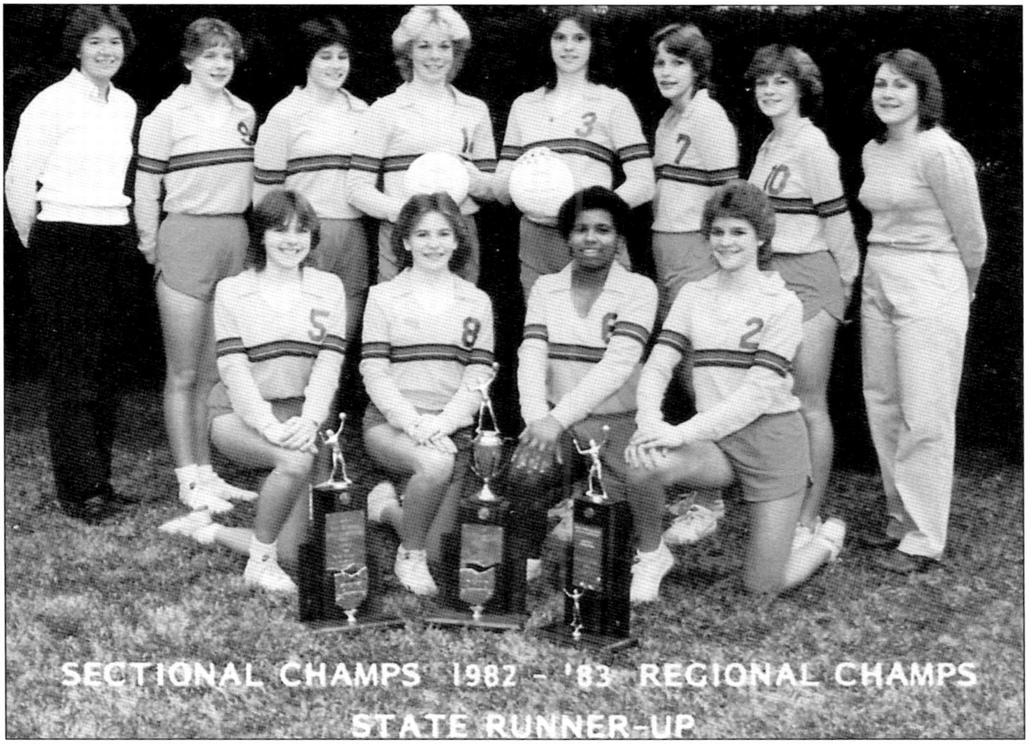

The 1982–1983 members of the volleyball team of Our Lady of the Angels High School were winners. (Courtesy of OLA Yearbook.)

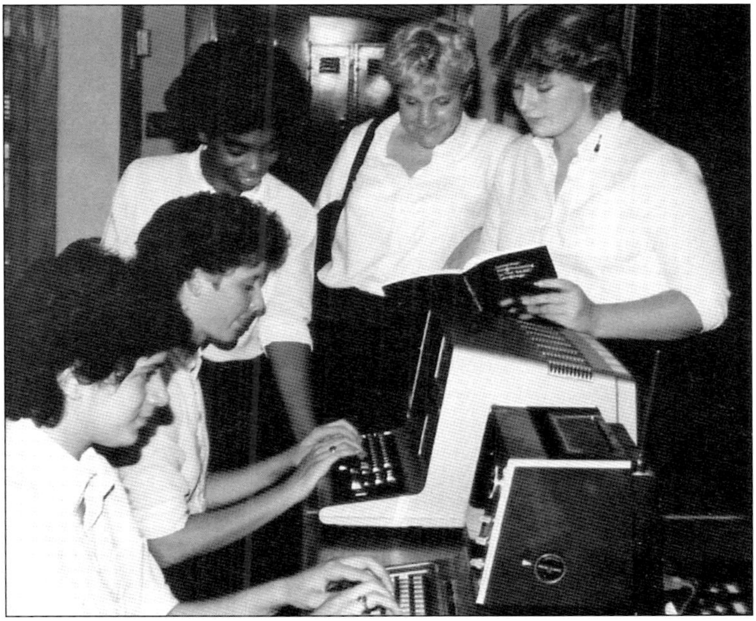

In 1984, the newest curriculum included computers at Our Lady of the Angels to give students a strategic advantage when they entered the workplace. (Courtesy of OLA Yearbook.)

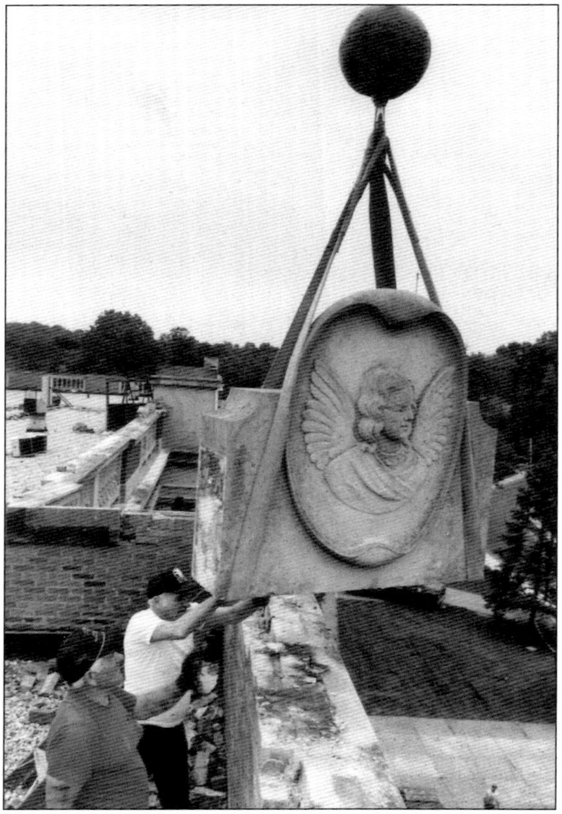

When Our Lady of the Angels High School was closed, items were rescued from demolition. Here, the emblem was saved, and it serves as part of that neighborhood's gateway, Angels Way. (Courtesy of Gerry Wiedmann.)

In response to Archbishop McNicholas's request, Roger Bacon High School for boys was constructed in 1928. Following early classes in the Witte homestead, the school has been expanded several times to include music, art, athletics, and core classrooms. In 1985, combined with Our Lady of the Angels, this became a coeducational school. (Courtesy of Jan Boylan.)

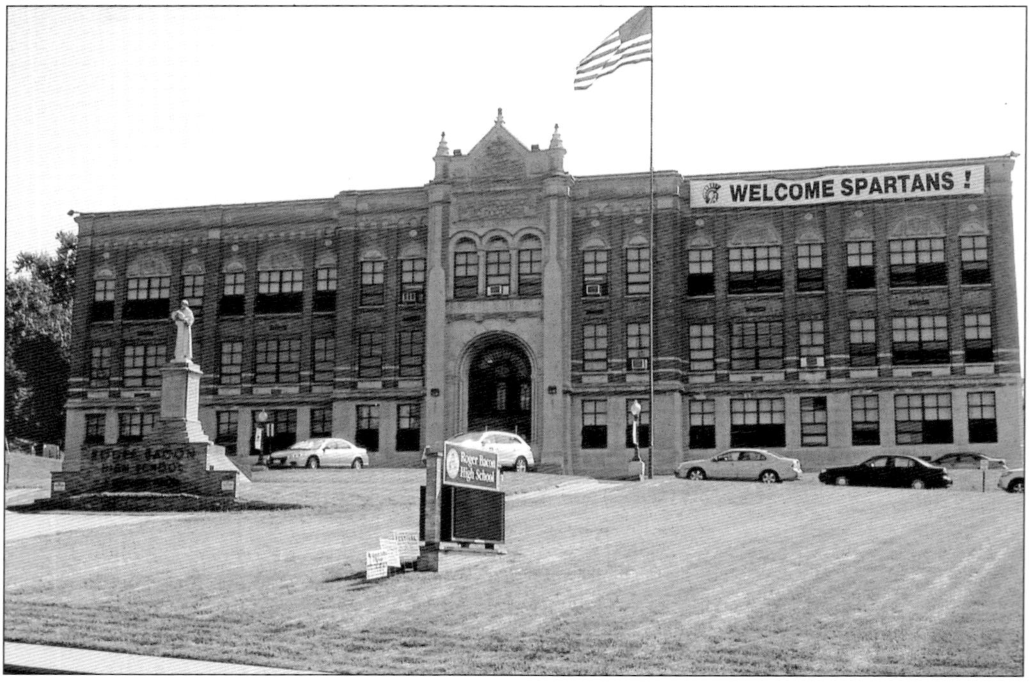

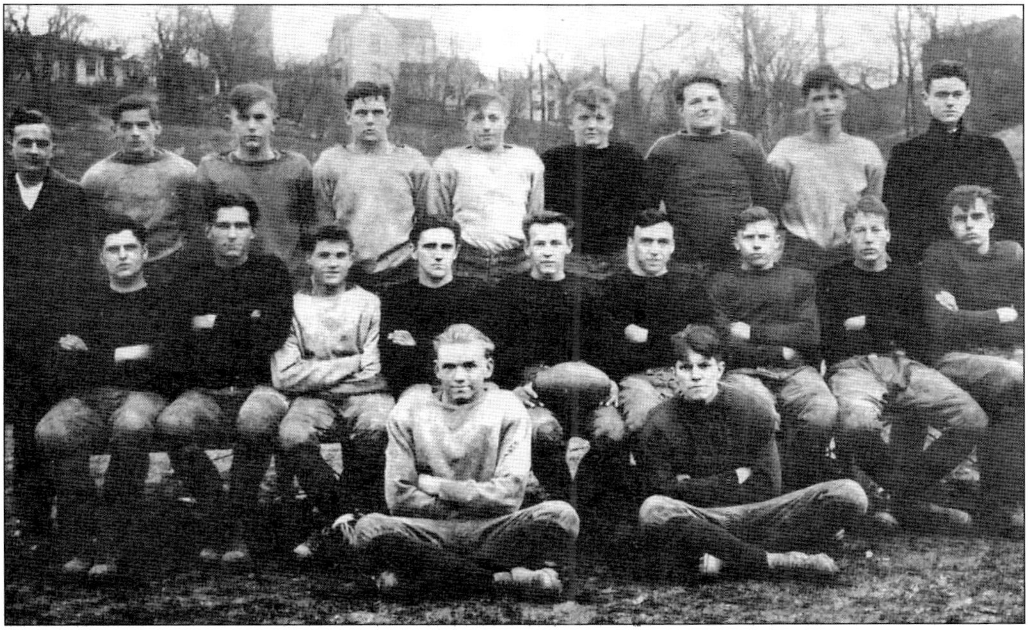

The first Roger Bacon football team in 1929 is seen here. Roger Bacon State of Ohio championship titles included boys' baseball in 1935, boys' basketball in 1982 and 2002, boys' soccer in 1989 and 1990, girls' basketball in 1995, and girls' volleyball in 2001, 2004, and 2005. (Courtesy of *Roger Bacon Alumni Quarterly*.)

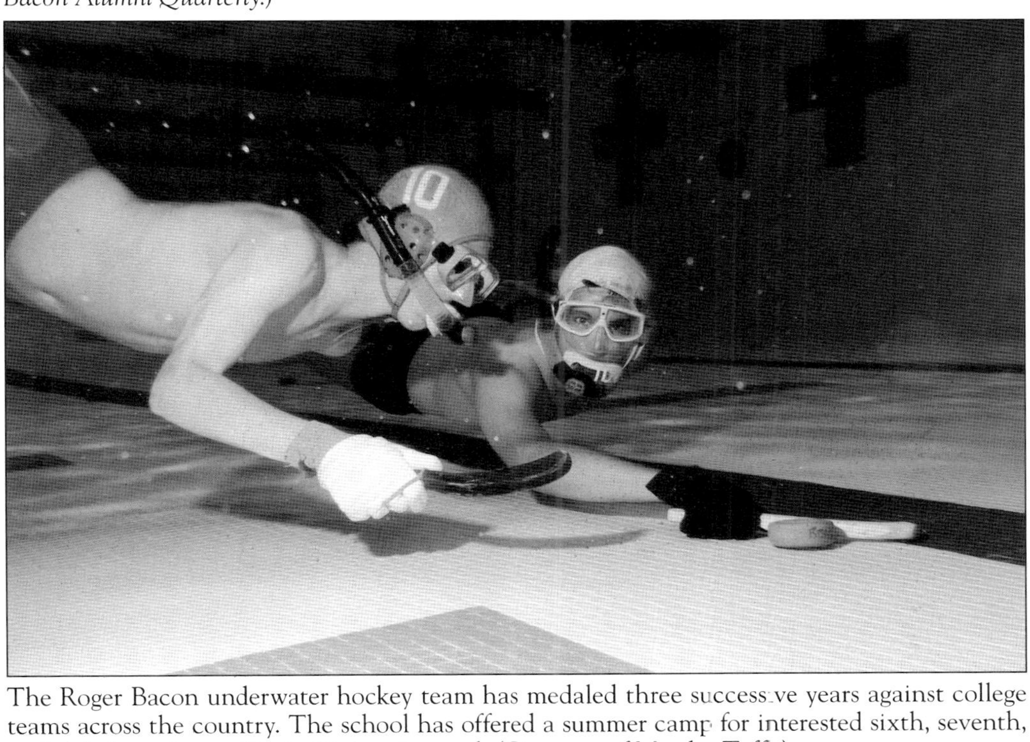

The Roger Bacon underwater hockey team has medaled three successive years against college teams across the country. The school has offered a summer camp for interested sixth, seventh, and eighth graders at Xavier University pool. (Courtesy of Marsha Tuffs.)

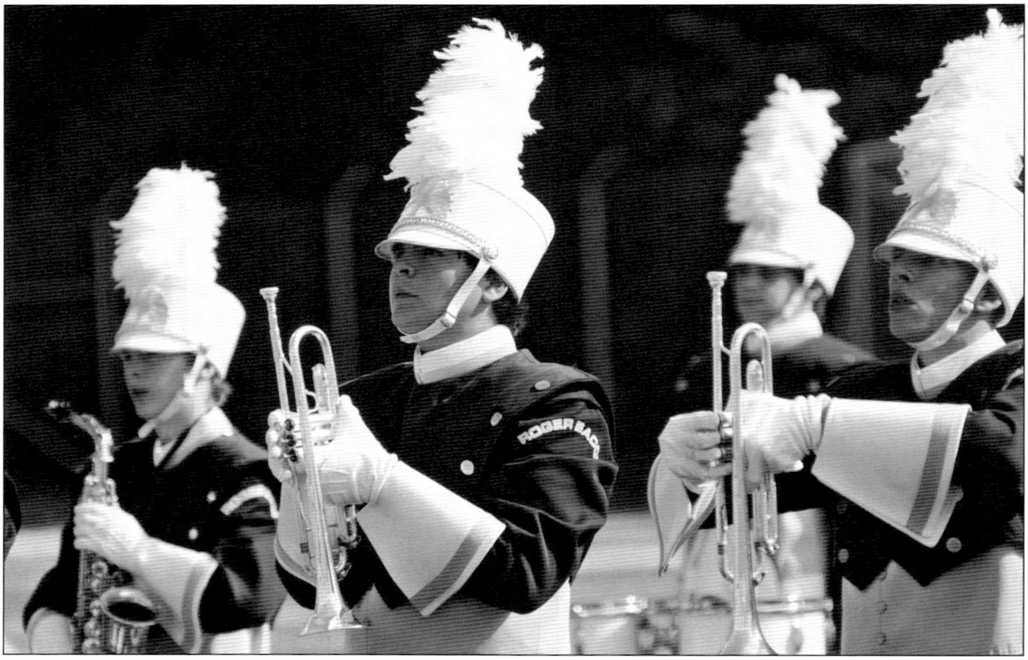

The Roger Bacon band has won competitions against bands all over the country. Some graduates have created their own bands after their Roger Bacon years. One is called Sound Body, the name taken from the school motto, "Sound Mind, Sound Body." (Courtesy of William Carey.)

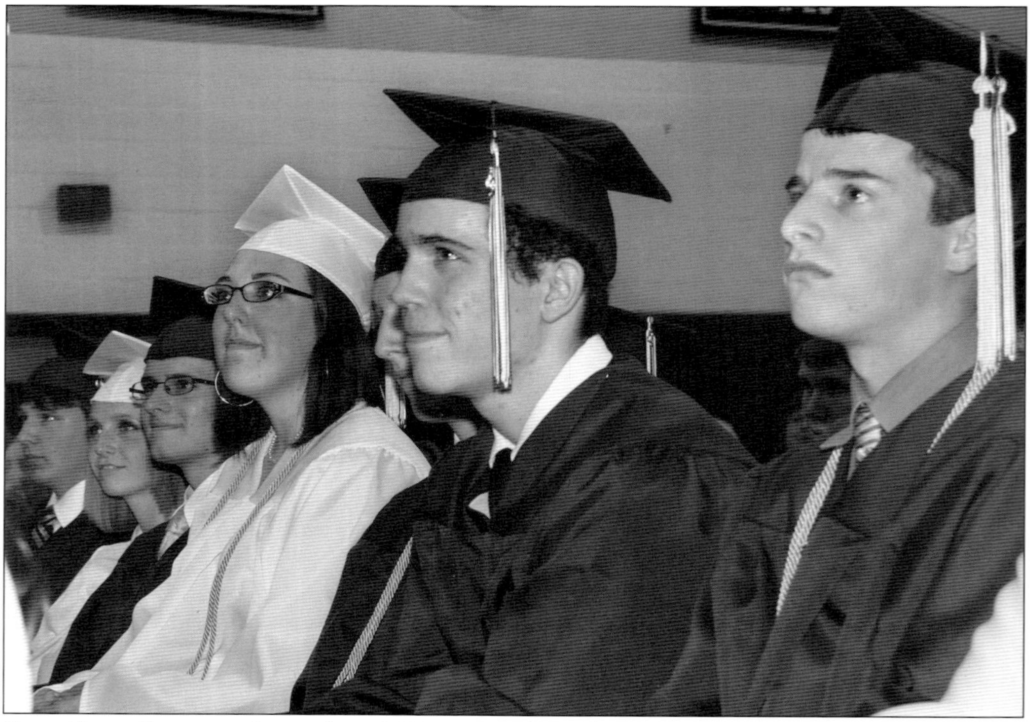

Some Roger Bacon graduates from 2010 are seen here. (Courtesy of William Carey.)

Five

Neighborhoods Defined the Community

Plat maps show names of owners of early farms who were the foundations of the neighborhoods. Attemeyer, then Witte, were right of Vine Street and north of Mitchell Avenue. In 1850, John Bernard Schroeder's land, adjacent to that of Attemeyer, was subdivided and named St. Bernard. Near the church, streets were named for family members, Philomena (Park Place), Bertus, Catherine (now Orchard), George (now Delmar), Lawrence, and Leo. Many years were to pass before all neighborhoods had roads instead of paths to and from homes.

Reuben Kemper purchased and settled on property at Ross Avenue. When the Kemper property was subdivided, newly created streets were named for some US presidents. The Kemper family sold 111 acres of land to the German Catholic Cemetery Society for St. Mary's Cemetery when St. John Cemetery had little available space. In 1960, St. Mary's Cemetery sold property for modern homes on today's Heger and Chalet Drives. Across from the Kemper home lived the Broerman family, who started arriving from Germany in 1850, with the last immigrating family member arriving in 1869. Along Ross Avenue and at the canal were the Broxterman(n) and Boehm families. Their occupations were excavating sand from today's Ross Park, as well as cutting and selling ice from the canal. Ross Park stands there today.

More centrally located, the Nurre family arrived from Germany in the mid-1850s. Today, the Nurre homestead is in the National Register of Historic Places and stands as testimony to the fact that homes are built to last. Generations of Nurres worked the farm and lived here for 123 years until the home was sold to James Royston in 1982. Originally bordered by Meadow, Rose Hill, and Tower Avenues, holdings included part of Greenlee Avenue, and many were sold in single lots.

Industry and homes developed after an auction by Barton, Brewster, and Folz in the Railroad Avenue area. Noah Babbs subdivision along Vine Street became small businesses and residences for those who wanted to live close to commerce. Baker and Philips Avenues developed along the canal. Bank Street near Vine Street developed as small homes, while the area to the west was originally a group of farms owned by Schlensker, Reckman, and others. Ross Avenue to Paddock Road and the Rose Hill subdivision at Mitchell Avenue were added as increased population created a demand for centrally located housing with access to jobs. Most recent is the Angels Way neighborhood, with more growth to be seen in the future.

Deed Transfers					
Grantor	Grantee	Date	Book	Page	Description
Shawnee, Miami & Delaware Indian Tribes & British Crown	United States	1783			Treaty Of Paris
United States/ President George Washington	Symmes, Jno C.	15 Oct 1788	S	203	Patent for Miami Purchase
Wyandot, Delaware (Lenape; several bands), Shawnee, Ottawa (several bands), Chippewa, Potawatomi (several bands), Miami (several bands) Wea, Kickapoo, Kaskaskia Indians battle Frontiersman	General "Mad Anthony" Wayne & The United States	3 Aug 1795			Treaty Of Greenville
Symmes, Jno C.	Wilson, Peter	28 Dec 1795	B-2	478	640 Ac whole sec
Wilson, Peter Heirs of	Piatt, Jno H	11 Oct 1813	M	139	334 Ac on W side of sec
Wyandot, Delaware, Shawnee, Seneca, Miami and Potawatomi Indians sign a second Treaty	General William Henry Harrison and Governor Lewis Cass & The United States	22 Jul 1814			Second Treaty of Greenville
Piatt, Jno H	Bell, Wm & Gordon, Edw	28 Apr 1819	S	587	334 Ac on W side of sec
Bell, Wm & Gordon, Edw	Bogert, Ruliff	23 Dec 1819	T	467	59 1/10 Ac N of Spinnings' tract
Bogert, Ruliff Per Shff	Howell, Stephen	Nov 1825	24	170	59 1/10 Ac on west side of sec lying next N of Spinnings' tract
Howell, Stephen & Lewis	Brown, Archibald	9 Mar 1826	24	207	59 1/10 Ac on west side of sec lying next N of Spinnings' tract
Brown, Archibald	Brown, David	11 Feb 1852	173	439	49.55/100 Ac on W side of sec next N of Chas M Brown land
Brown, David Per Sherriff	Schwegmen, Jos & Hillenbrand Wm	27 Oct 1886	625	111	
Schwegmen, Joseph	Hillenbrand, Wm.	15 Feb 1902	869	468	
Hillenbrand, Wm.	Zimmerman, Frank A.	22 Aug 1911	1049	307	
Zimmerman, Frank A.	Hunt, Oliver C.	18 Feb 1914	1099	69	
Hunt, Oliver C.	Woll, Frank A.	9 May 1919	1179	532	
Woll, Frank A.	Woll, August J.	31 Jan 1922	1243	633	
Woll, August J.	Woll, Mary E. (Leininger)	24 Mar 1952	1288	503	
Woll, Mary E. (Leininger)	Woll, Frank A., Edw W., & Ray P.	1 Apr 1952	2538	420	
Woll, Frank A., Edw W., & Ray P.	Woll, Myrtle E. (Doll)	29 Sep 1953	2639	505	
Woll, Myrtle E. (Doll)	Woll, Thomas	28 Nov 1986	4367	666	

Research of property titles from the Native Americans to the Woll family is shown here. It is interesting to see how many times properties changed hands and how many years a property remained in the same family. (Courtesy of Jean Woll.)

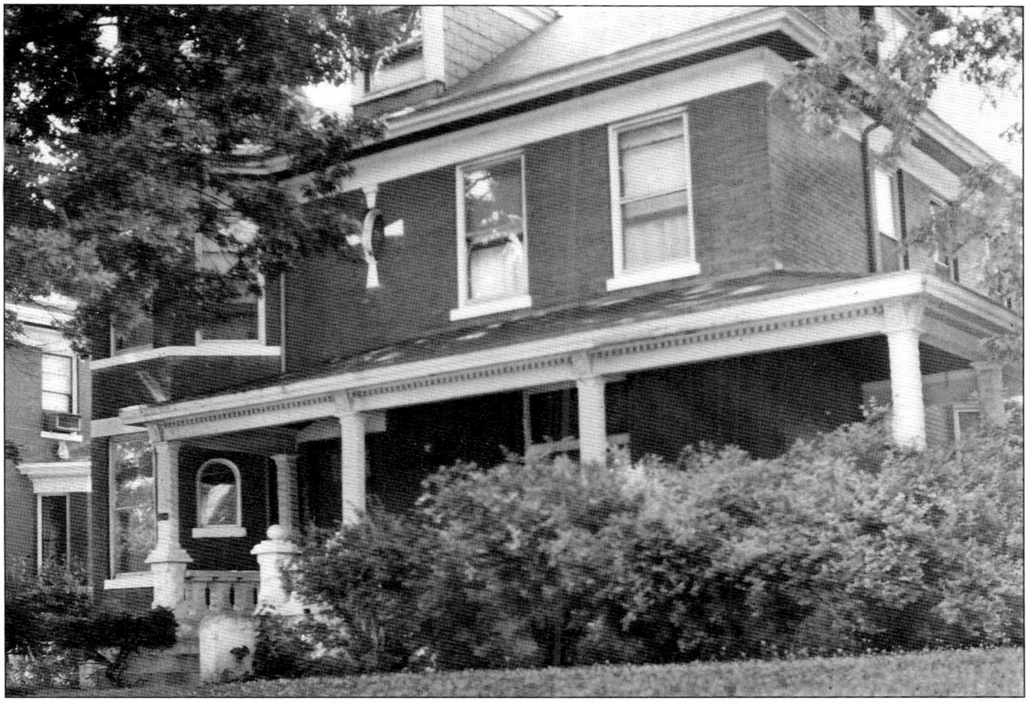

Former mayor Schwegman's home on Mitchell Avenue was originally part of the David Brown estate as shown on the previous page. He kept part of it and sold the rest of the property.

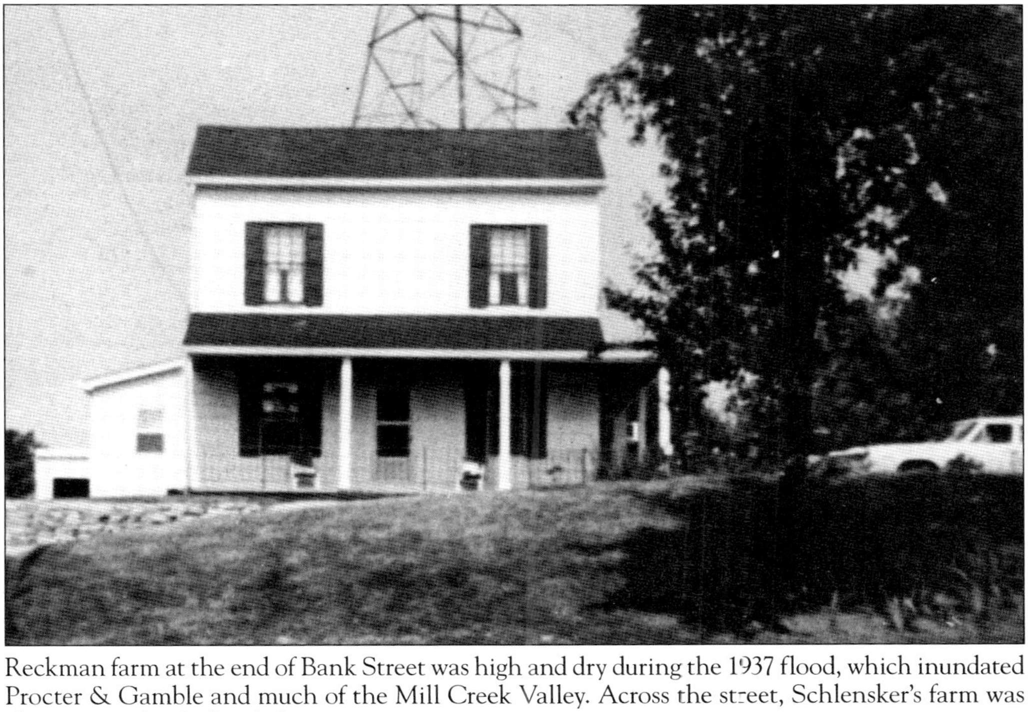

Reckman farm at the end of Bank Street was high and dry during the 1937 flood, which inundated Procter & Gamble and much of the Mill Creek Valley. Across the street, Schlensker's farm was almost completely flooded.

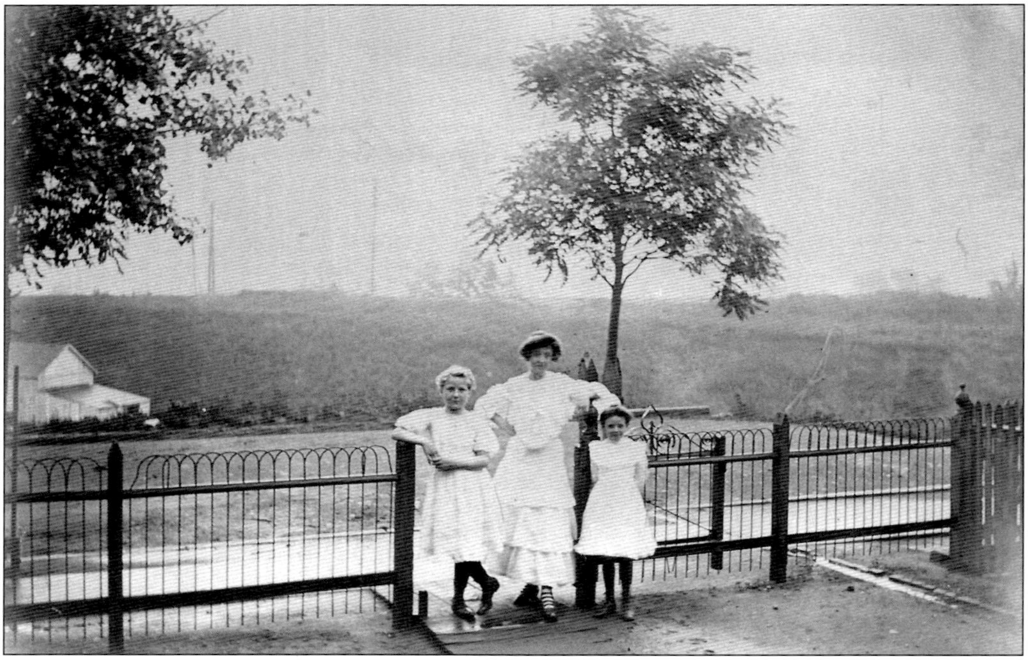

Oak Street at the canal was an interesting place in the 1800s and into the 20th century, but when Interstate 75 was put through in the mid-1900s, this neighborhood no longer supported residences.

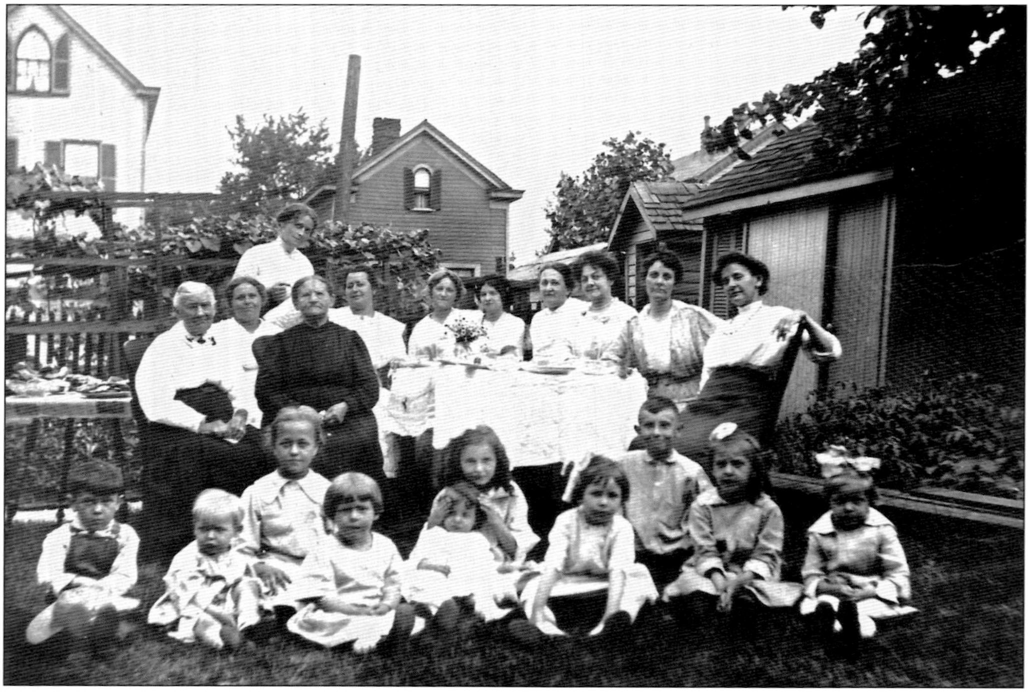

This family gathering took place on Oak Street in the good old days before the expressway was constructed. St. Bernard was known for large families like the one pictured.

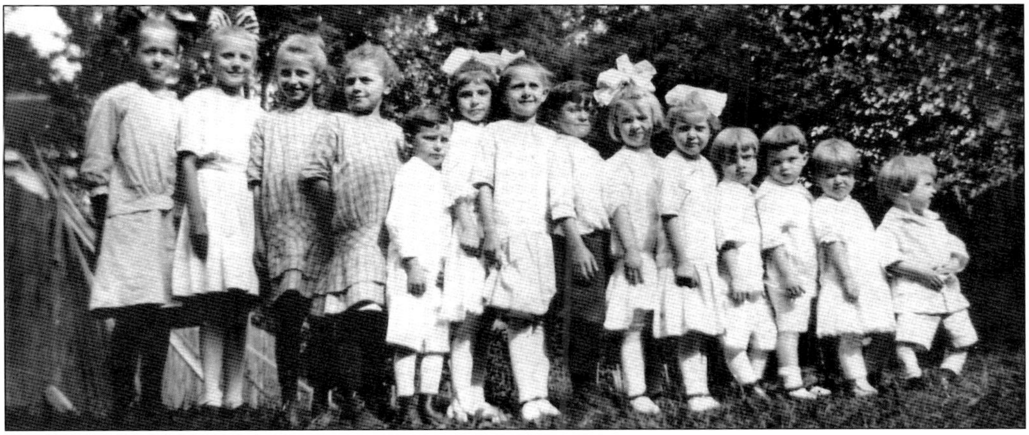

The Kennedy family provided this photograph years ago. These pictures took a while to snap, but the children stayed still for it!

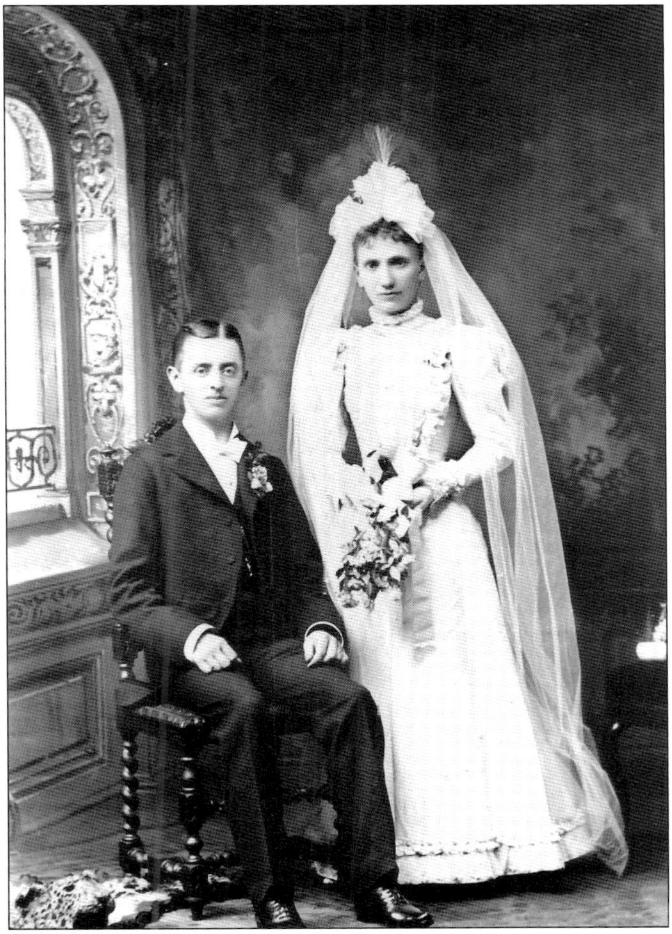

Here is a professionally taken photograph of the Mersch bride and groom around 1890.

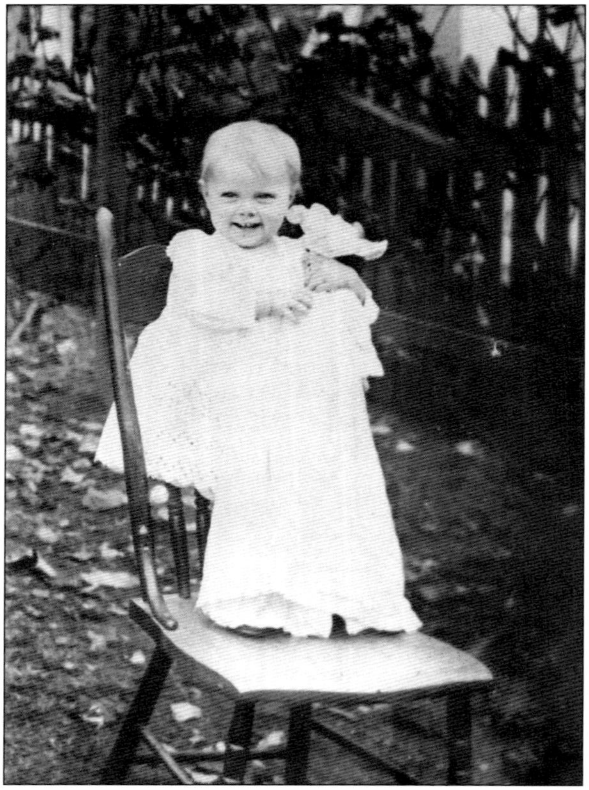

A local child poses for the photographer around 1920.

Dr. A.C. Topie was one of the local physicians at the turn of the last century. St. Bernard always had a number of resident physicians; of more recent memory were Dr. Joseph Speier and Dr. Frank Cunningham. Dr. Jonathan Singer of Mitchell Avenue is the current head of the St. Bernard Health Department.

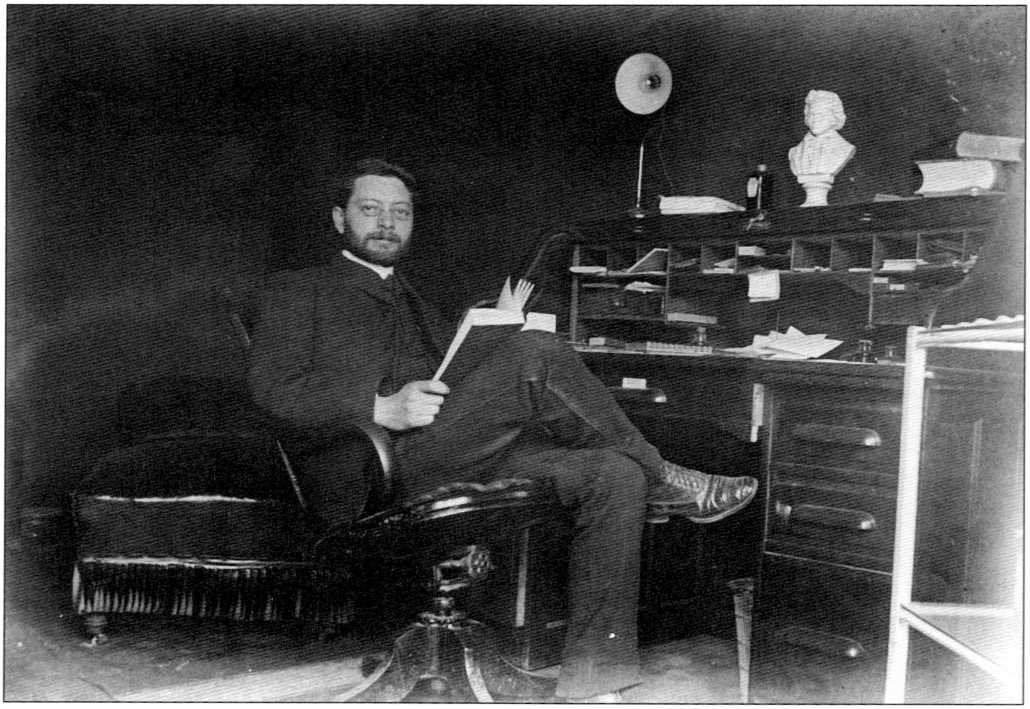

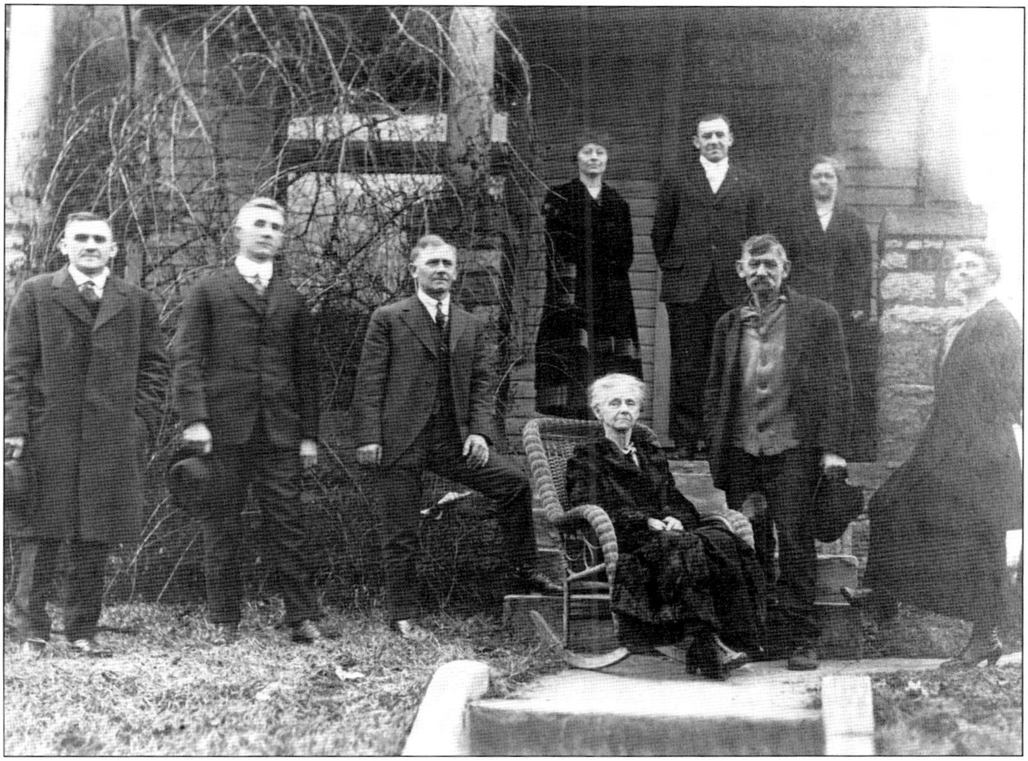

Seen here is the Henn family. Often men would come first from Germany, set up businesses, and then send for the rest of the family. (Courtesy of the Distler and Willenbrink families.)

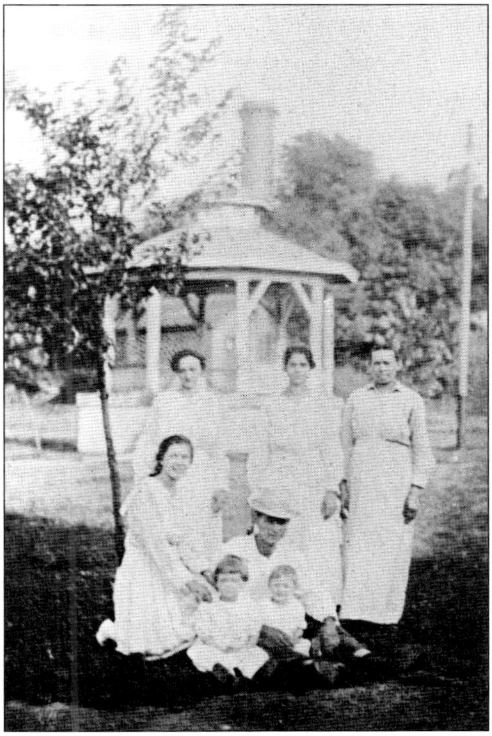

Ladies from the Hennel family are seen here at Vine Street Park. Formerly this was a pasture with backwater from the canal. The area developed as a park, and the fact that it was a natural amphitheater made it an ideal entertainment site. In later years, baseball diamonds were located here, which made games possible for teams of all ages. Among the largest crowds were those that came in August for the German Luau.

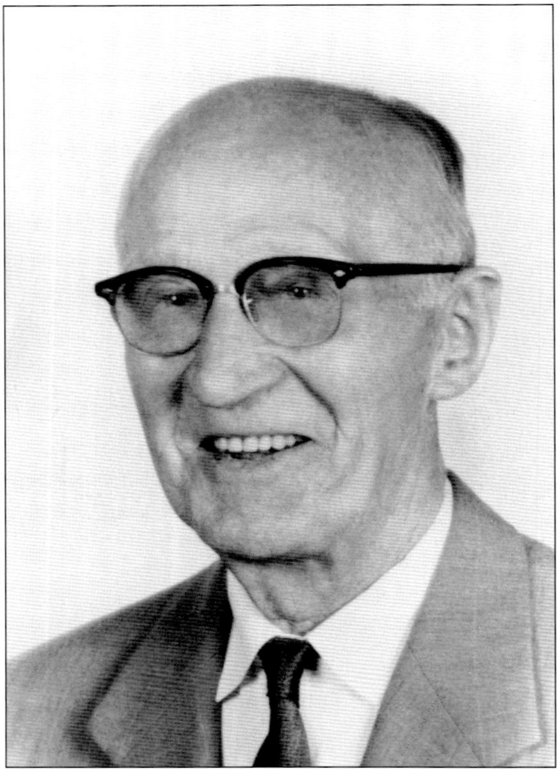

Aloys H. Nurre was one of the first to gradually sell property for new homes in the neighborhood around the Nurre farm. He and his family were strong supporters of the St. Clement Church and school. (Courtesy of Daniel Nurre.)

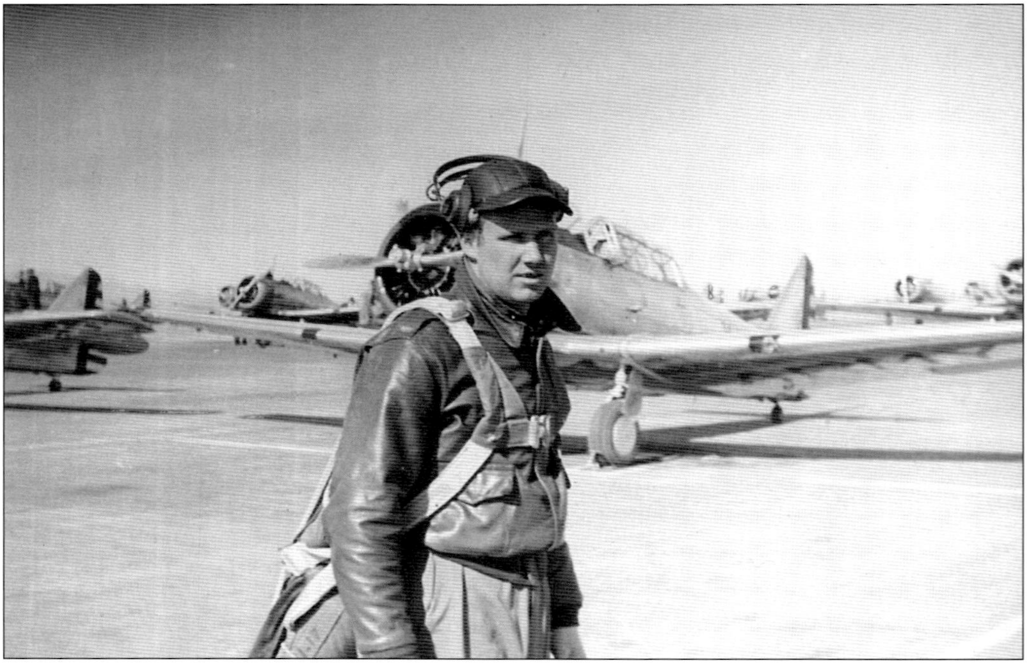

Alvin H. Nurre, a World War II Army Air Force pilot, flew 50 missions in the African, Sicilian, and Italian mainland campaigns. (Courtesy of Daniel Nurre.)

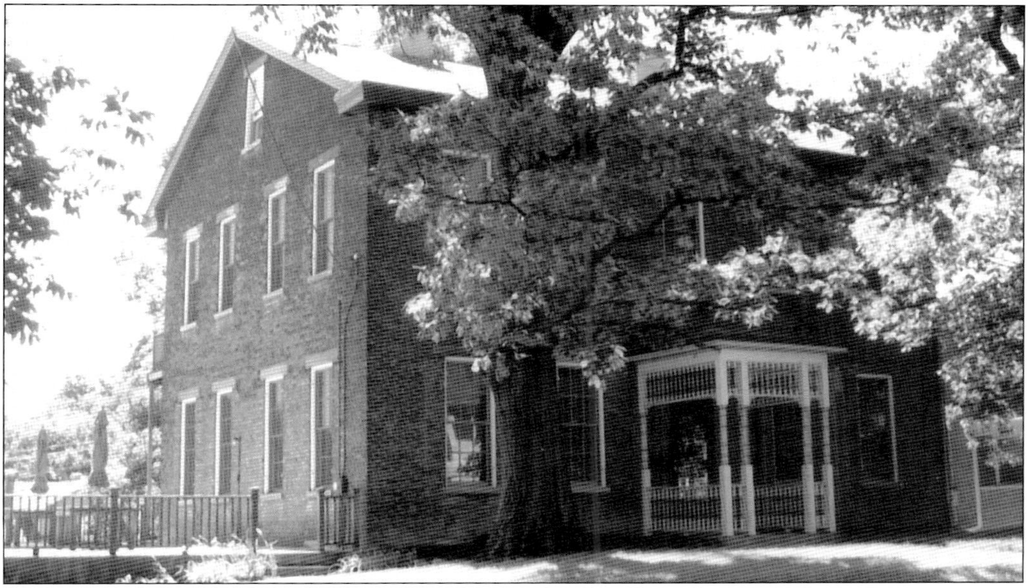

The Nurre homestead remained in the family through the generations for 123 years and is in the National Register of Historic Places. During Corpus Christi processions, worshipers would stop here, where an altar had been constructed for Benediction, before moving on to two or more altar locations. (Courtesy of Daniel Nurre.)

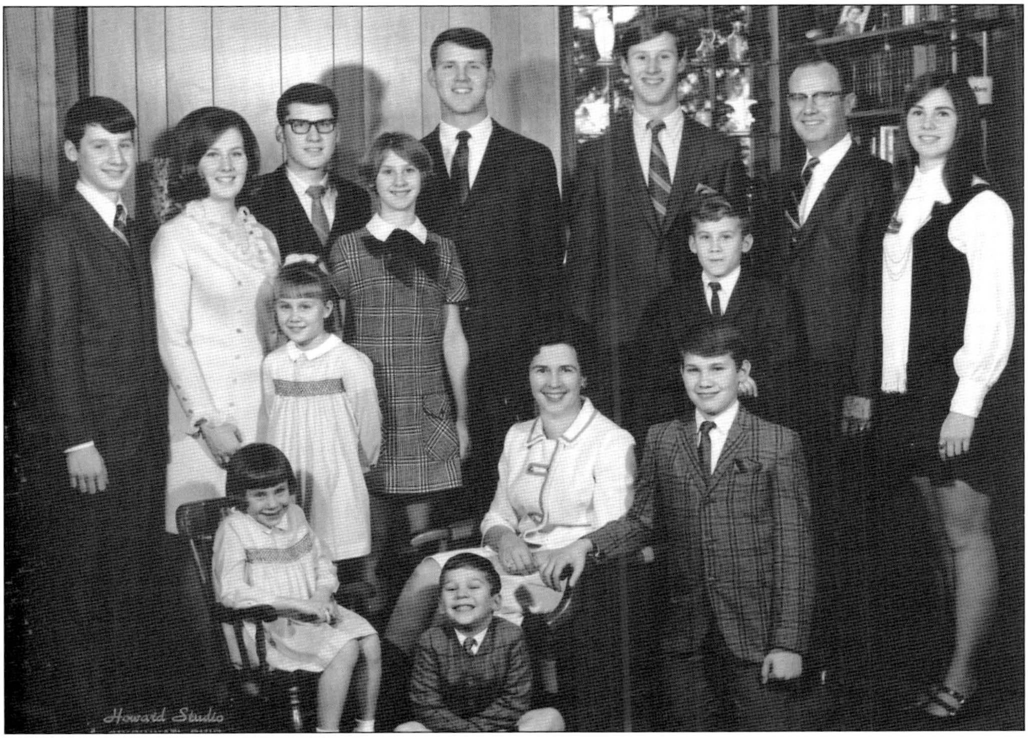

The next generations of the Nurre family included Alvin (second row, second from the right) and his wife, Mary (seated in the center), with their 12 children. (Courtesy of Daniel Nurre.)

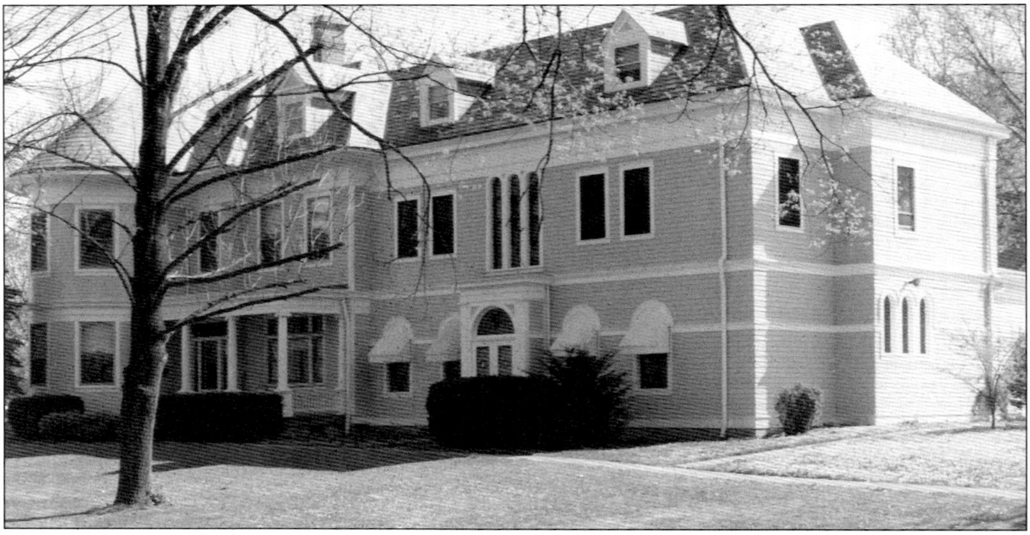

The Wess homestead became Our Lady of the Angels Convent and was located at the intersection of Bertus, Delmar, and Orchard Streets. (Courtesy of Don Wess.)

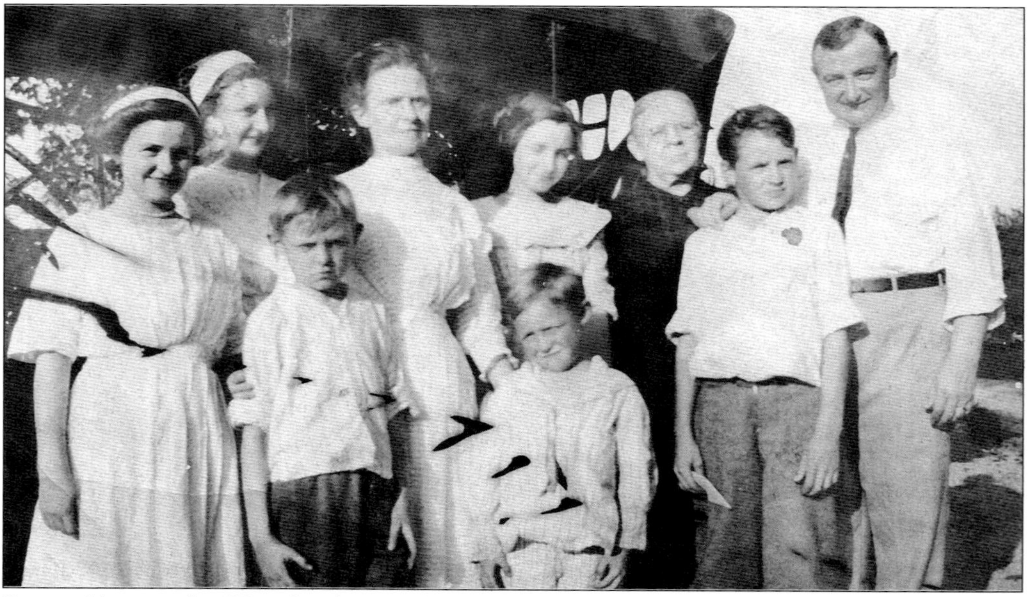

Pictured here is the Wess family. Members include, from left to right, (first row) Marie (Wess) Schrand and Charles, George, and Bernard Wess; (second row) Laura (Wess) Funch, Mary (Schroeder) Wess, Sr. Theresa Marie (Gertrude) Wess, OFM, Grandmother Schroeder, and B.H. Wess. From 1918 to 1921, B.H. Wess was the mayor of St. Bernard. (Courtesy of Don Wess.)

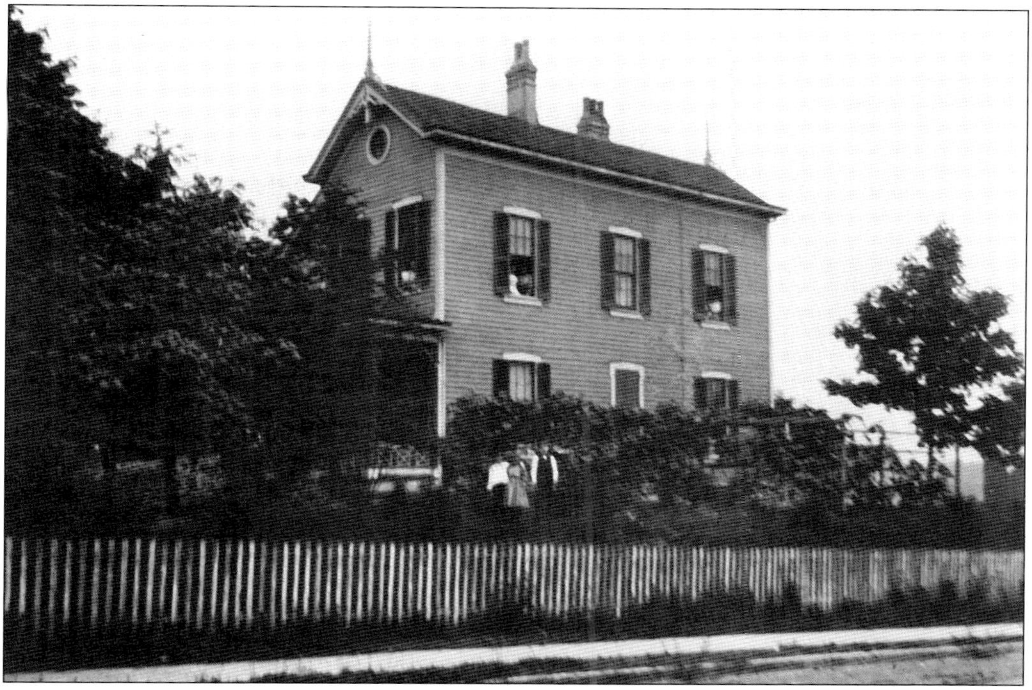

The Broermann homestead was on the corner of Ross and Broerman Avenues. (Courtesy of Nancy Broermann and Kay Heller Phillips.)

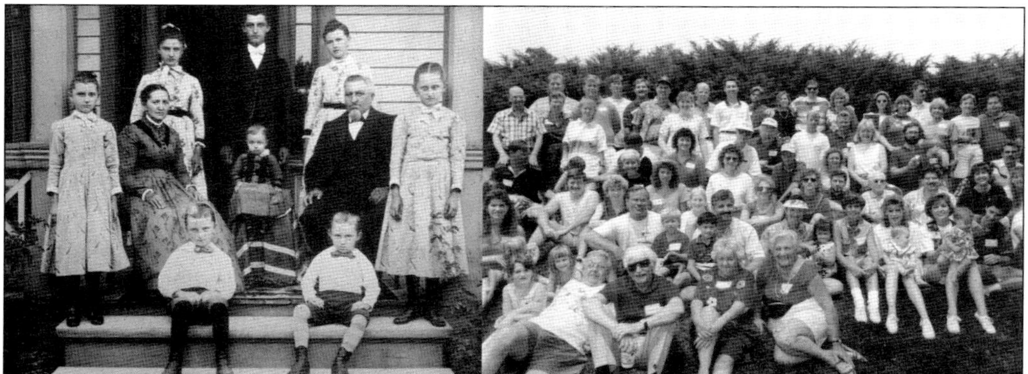

Catharine and Frank Broerman (older couple on porch) are seated with their family. The image on the right of their descendants was taken years later. (Courtesy of Nancy Broermann and Kay Heller Phillips.)

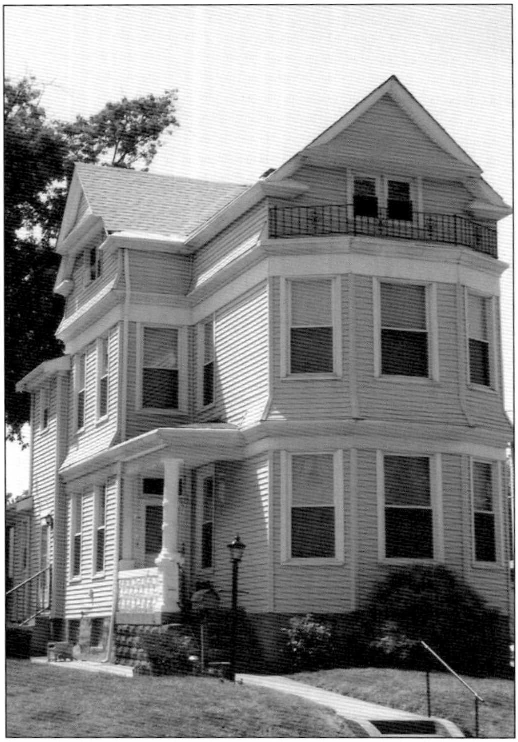

The former Distler home is pictured here as it looks today. (Courtesy of Jan Boylan.)

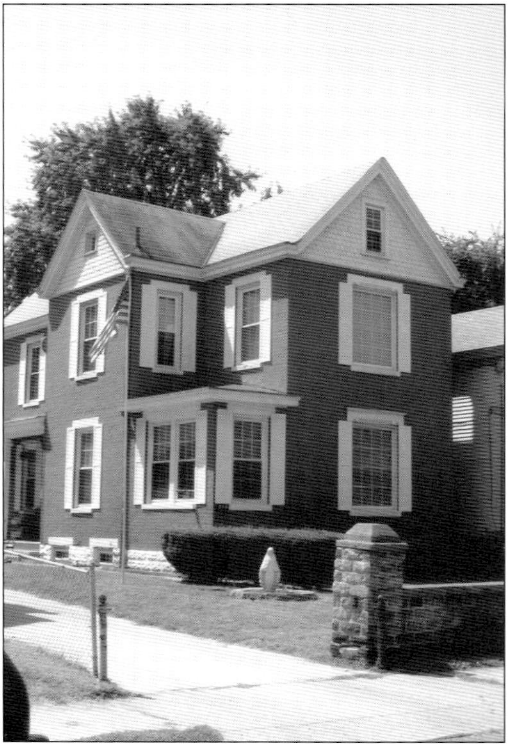

The former Berger home on West Ross Avenue is seen here as it looks today. (Courtesy Jan Boylan.)

Six

Who's Minding the Store?

St. Bernard had its butchers, bakers, and candlestick makers when shops and stores developed along Vine and Spring Grove Avenues. Farm produce and the mills were vital to all. Families who came for baptisms, weddings, and funerals needed refreshments. In St. Bernard, the saloons had the supply. One of the oldest remaining saloons is Meiner's Cafe, founded in 1847, which was across from St. Clement Church. In the mid-1800s, there were hotels located near Ross Lake, the Trotting Park, Ward's Café at Beech Street, and Listermann's on Spring Grove Avenue. Jefferson Hall was located adjacent to St. John Cemetery on Vine Street. Serving those who pass from this life are Kistner Monuments, Wilfred Baxter Burial Vault, and Crematory on Ross Avenue. In the past, Imwalle and Boehmer Funeral Homes on Vine Street served the public for funerals or livery service as required. St. John and St. Mary Cemeteries are the final resting places for some who were born, lived, and died here—they never left. Local stores were located on Mitchell, Greenlee, Ross, and Delmar Avenues. Ranz and Kattus sold meat and staples on Vine Street, and bakeries, including Garmann's and Priscilla's, are a fond memory. Klostermann Bakery still provides goods in quantity to today's supermarkets.

With urban renewal from 1960 to 1970, long-known names and storefronts changed. Originally, the post office in the railroad station moved to Krehe's Feed Store. Then, a new post office in St. Bernard Square was constructed. There were always barbershops, beauty salons, and meat markets. Schmidlin's Hardware and Mackzum's Harness Shop closed, as Joe Schmidlin and Red Mackzum retired. Mackzum's Saloon remains. Hennel's grocery, F&F (Fugikawa's) Fruit Market, and Steinkolk, Carson's, and King's Pharmacies were important. Shoe stores and men's shops, including VandenEyndens and Evens, as well as Stark Dry Goods with clothes for the family, were basic mainstays. Mrs. Boehm and Mrs. Broxterman(n), well-known midwives from earliest years, have passed from memory, and Dr. A.C. Topie, Dr. Joseph Speier, and Dr. Frank Cunningham and dentists Dr. Fred Krause, Dr. Paul Stickley, and Dr. Schilling are still recalled. Independent and chain restaurants serve where Erm's & Vern's and others did in the past. Local banks and savings and loans helped thrifty residents grow their investments. Prohibition put a crimp in the saloon business, but good meals, like "jack" salmon at Meiners on Fridays, were a real family treat.

Hinnenkamp Dairy was the last one based in St. Bernard. The milkman's home delivery was familiar, but it was replaced by today's cash and carry from nearby grocery chains or dairy bars. Dairy Queen has kept those craving ice cream happy for over 25 years. Each neighborhood had its own delicatessen, grocery, or saloon. Perhaps the day will come when the convenience of walking to get the daily bread will return. Dial-a-Ride can get people there if walking is not their thing.

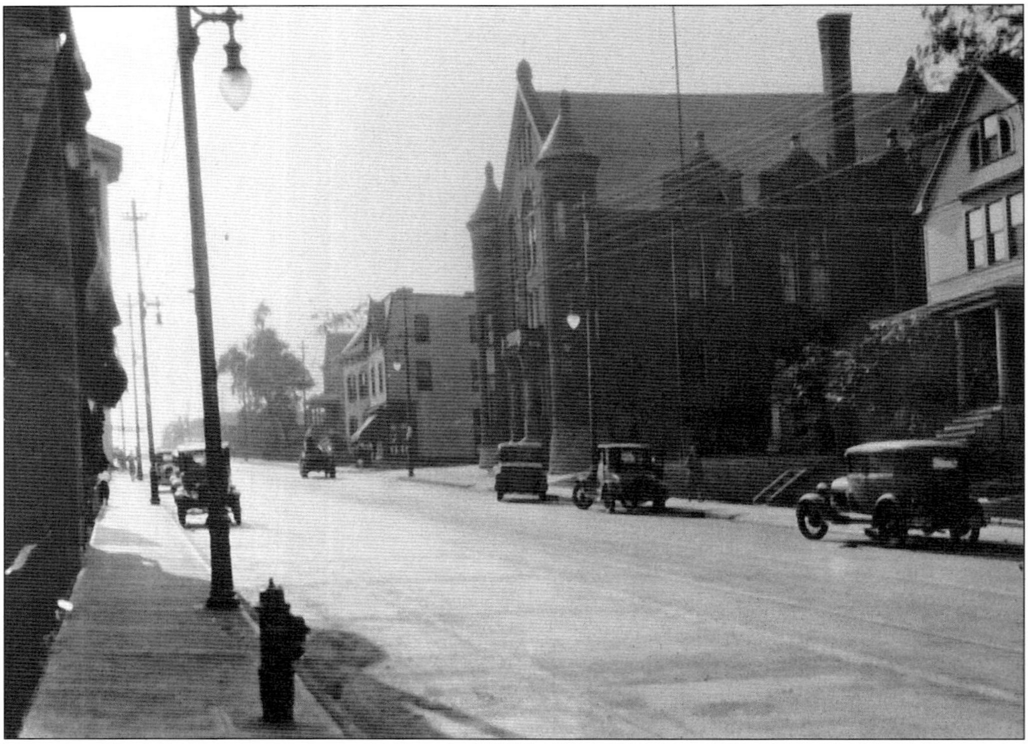

This 1890s view is looking south on Vine Street toward the town hall before the streets were paved.

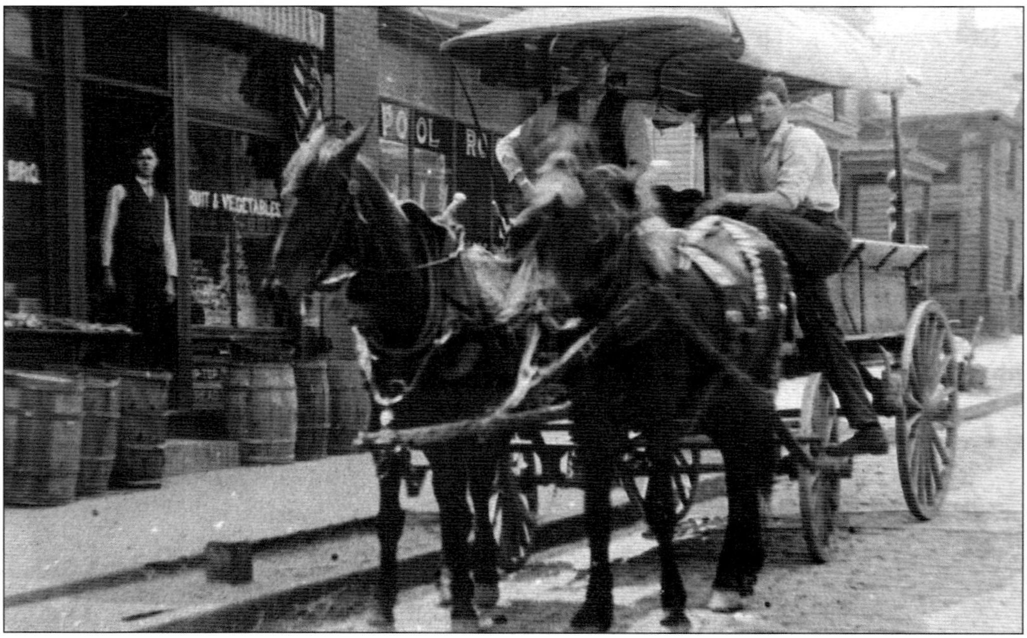

Hennel's Grocery was located in the heart of St. Bernard on Vine Street, close to the home farm and ready sales. Pictured here is Frank in the doorway, and John and Bill are on the wagon.

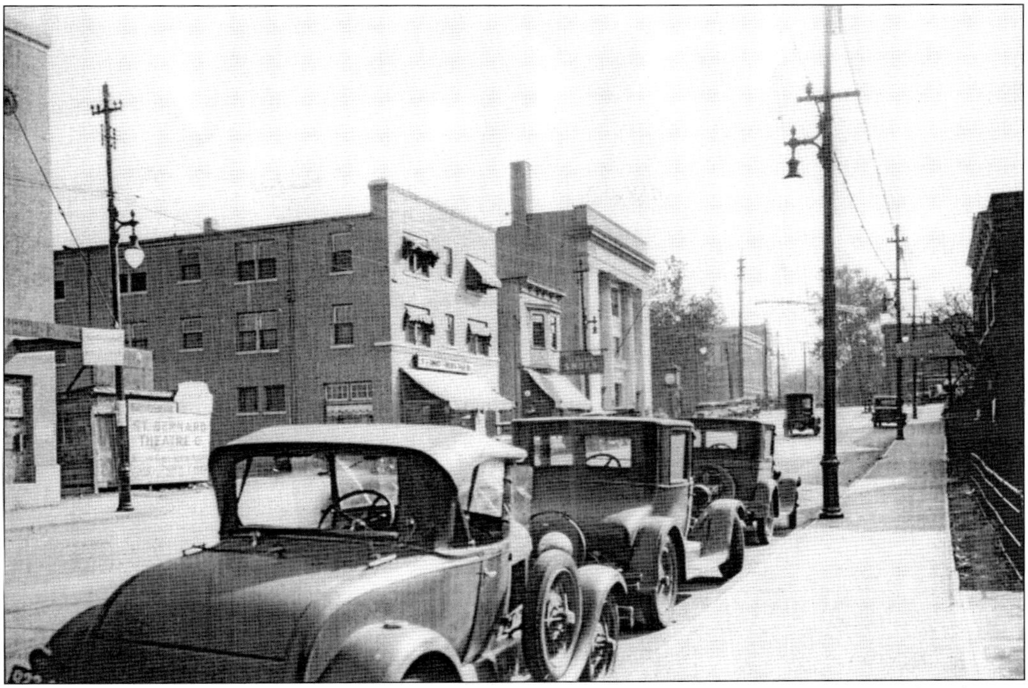

This photograph on Vine Street was taken when the automobile showed promise of replacing the horse and carriage.

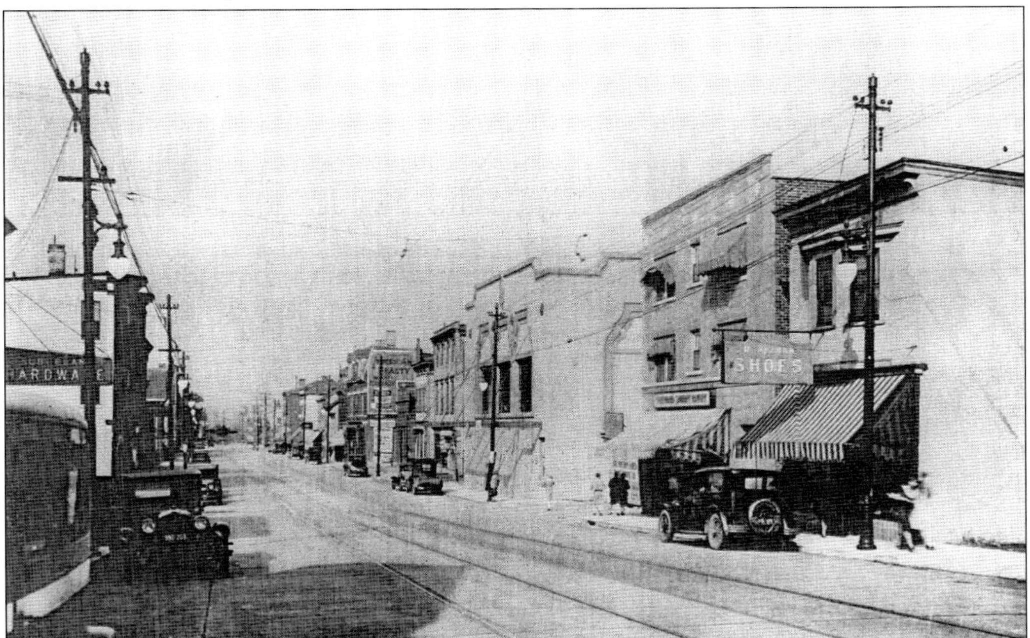

Here is a view of Vine Street looking toward Ross Avenue. The roads were still primitive at the time, but telephone lines had been installed, and the community was coming into the modern age.

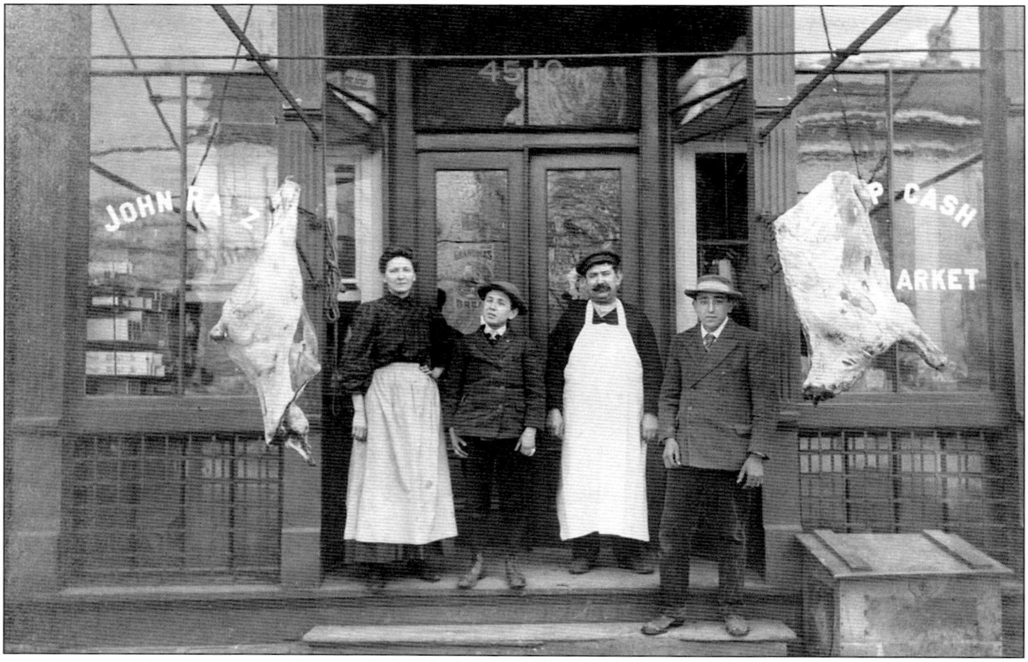

John Ranz (third from left) stands with his family in front of his store on Vine Street with merchandise readily seen by the customer.

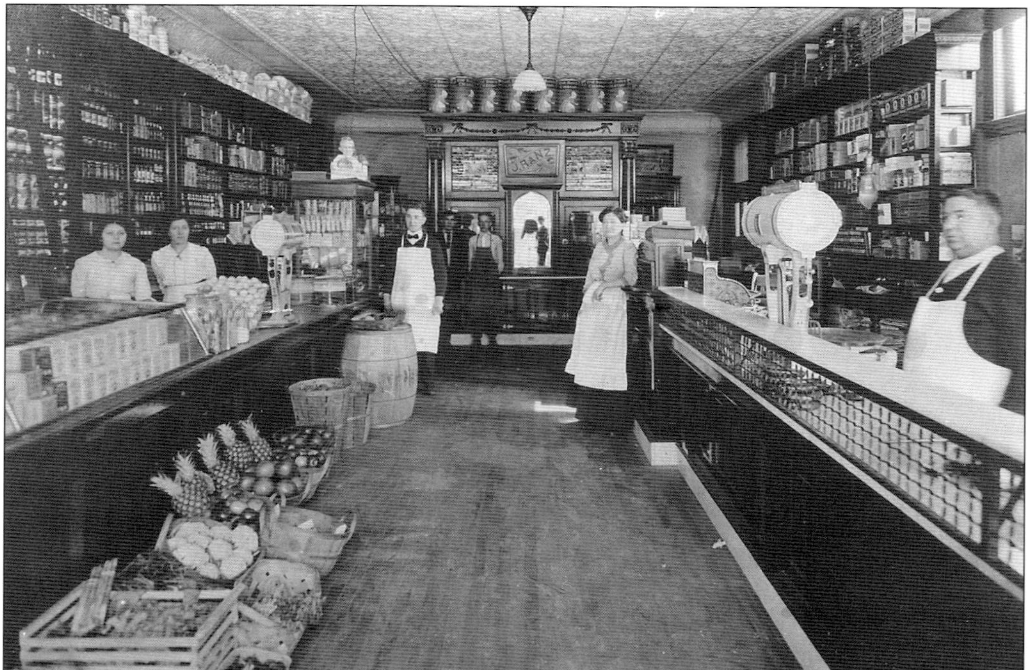

This photograph is of the interior of the John Ranz Store, showing the assortment of products, including pineapples for his clientele. Note the tin ceiling and the mirror at the back of the store with a reflection of the photographer taking this picture.

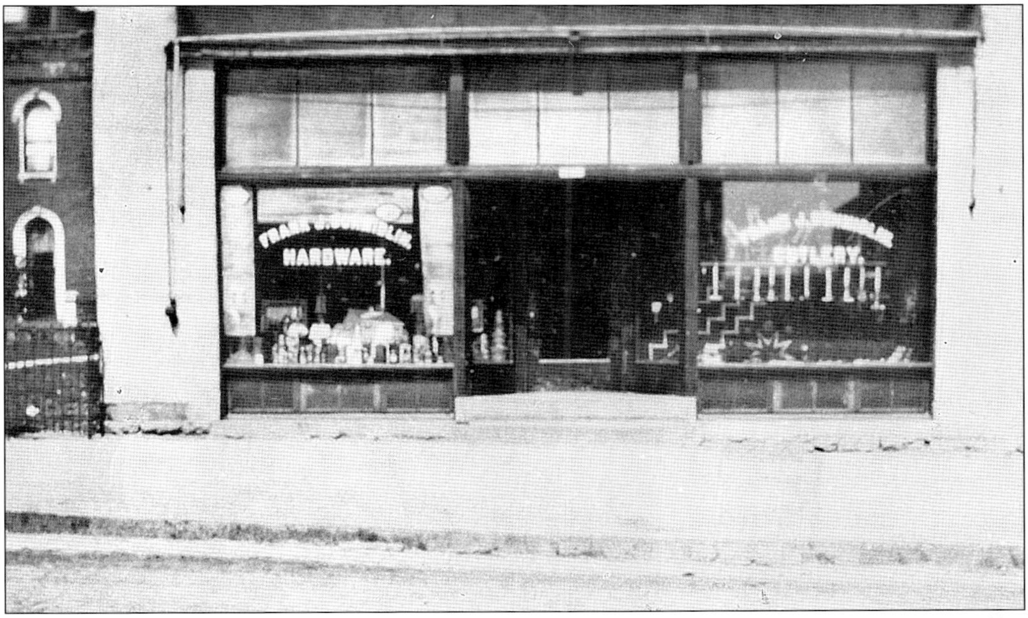

Everything from tacks, tools, parts, and vital household supplies were available at Schmidlin Hardware. Shown here is the store, located across from Church Street on Vine Street.

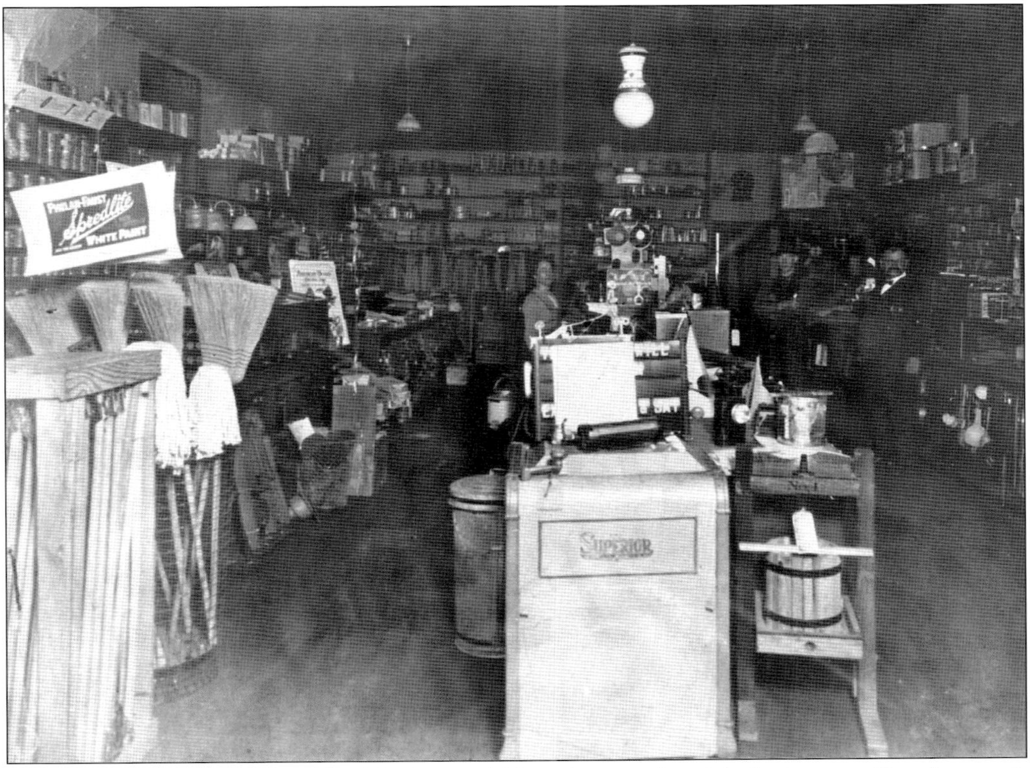

Here is the interior of Schmidlin Hardware. Although it was lit with the latest ceiling fixture, it is not very bright; however, the store seems abundantly stocked.

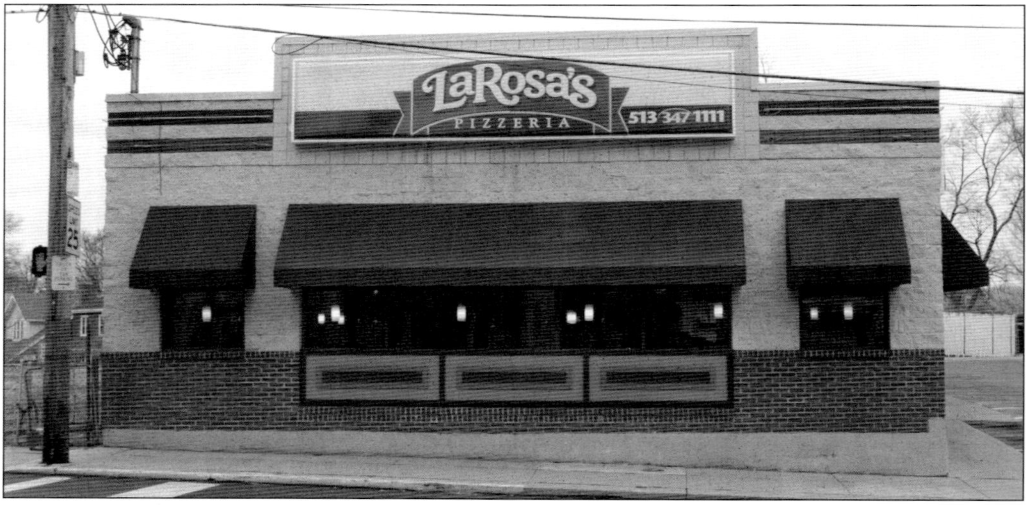

LaRosa's Pizzeria replaced Schmidlin and is in the same building today. With numerous renovations, Scot Inderhees and his family operate this franchise. Roger Bacon graduate Buddy LaRosa founded the chain. (Courtesy of Carrie Inderhees.)

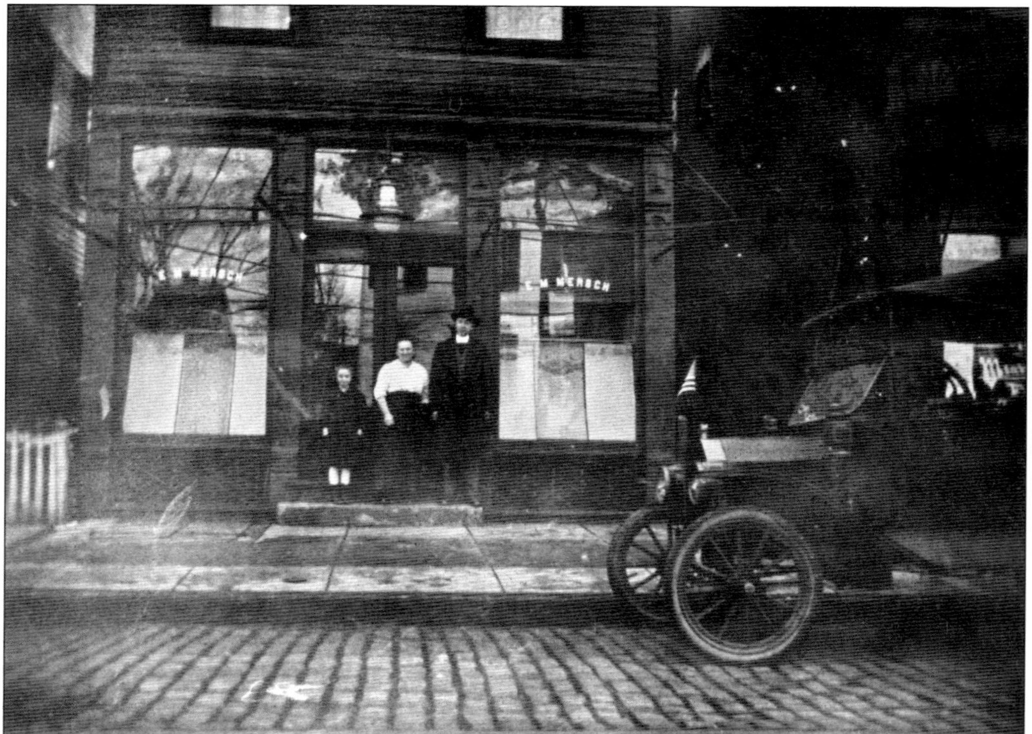

The Mersch Wallpaper Store was located near Lawrence Street next to the present-day Wesbanco office. People usually did their own decorating, and this store was in the neighborhood.

Hamrick's Tailoring was a necessary business since there were no department stores to buy ready-made clothes at the time.

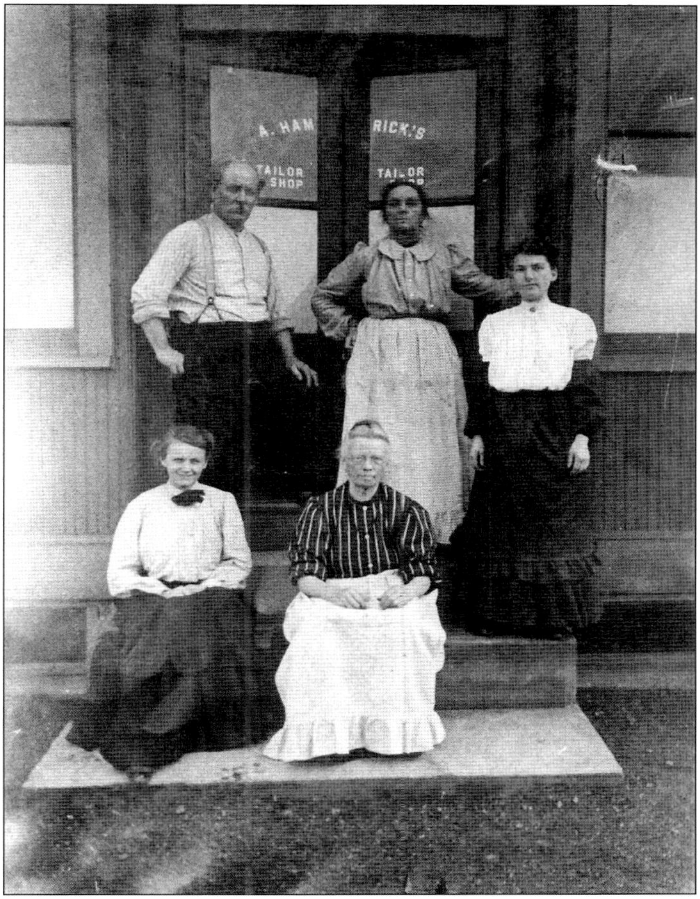

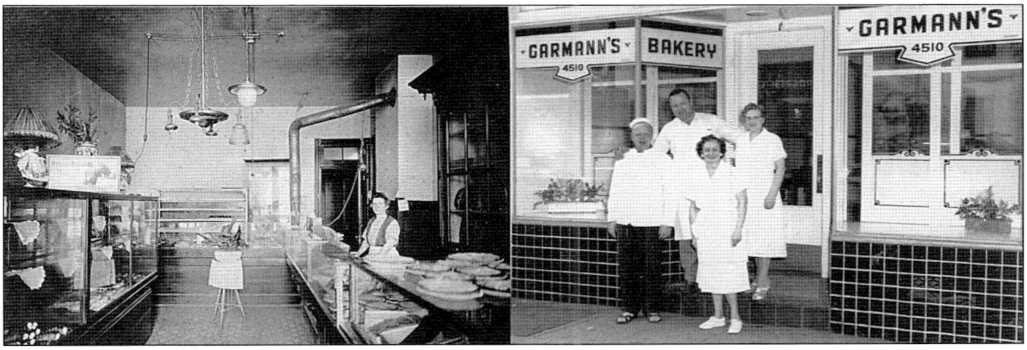

In this composite, on the left is a c. 1900 bakery located on Vine Street. Later, Priscilla Bakery was on Vine and McClelland Avenue. Garmann's Bakery, on the right, had its shop near Bertus Street on Vine Street and was especially popular in the 1950s and 1960s, when its peanut rolls kept young and old customers happy. (Courtesy of Garmann's and Cathy Wilson.)

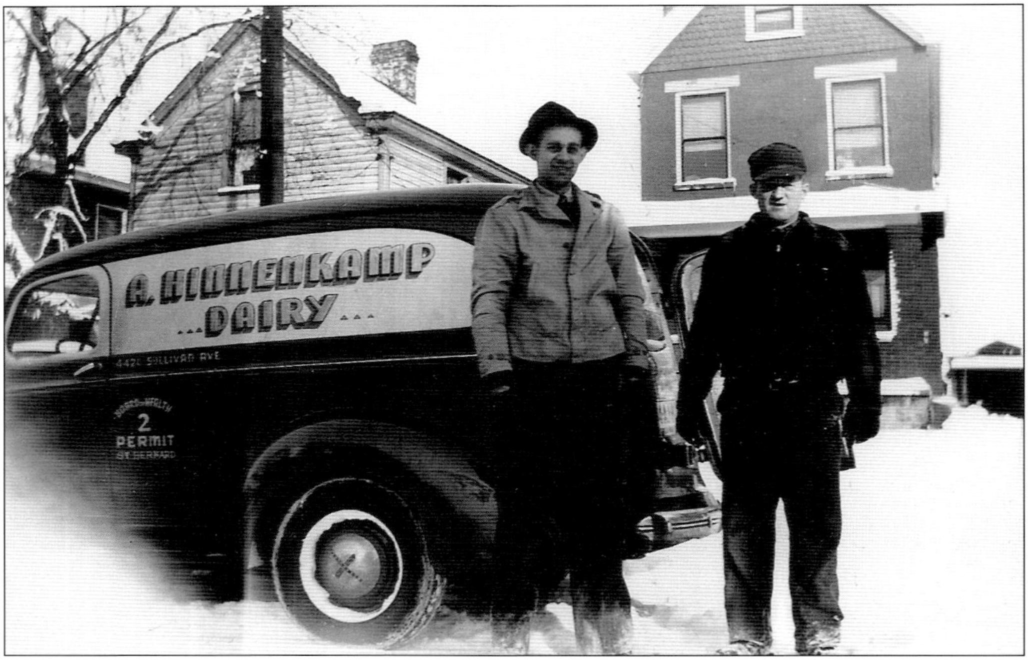

Pictured here are Bill Hinnenkamp (left) and an employee of Hinnenkamp Dairy, located at 4420 Sullivan Avenue. The dairy was founded in 1893 by August Hinnenkamp. Sons Bill and Joe operated the bottling and distribution business, with milk purchased from area farms to provide home delivery to local customers. It was the last St. Bernard company to provide door-to-door dairy-product delivery service within the city. (Courtesy of Mary Lynn Hinnenkamp Mayborg.)

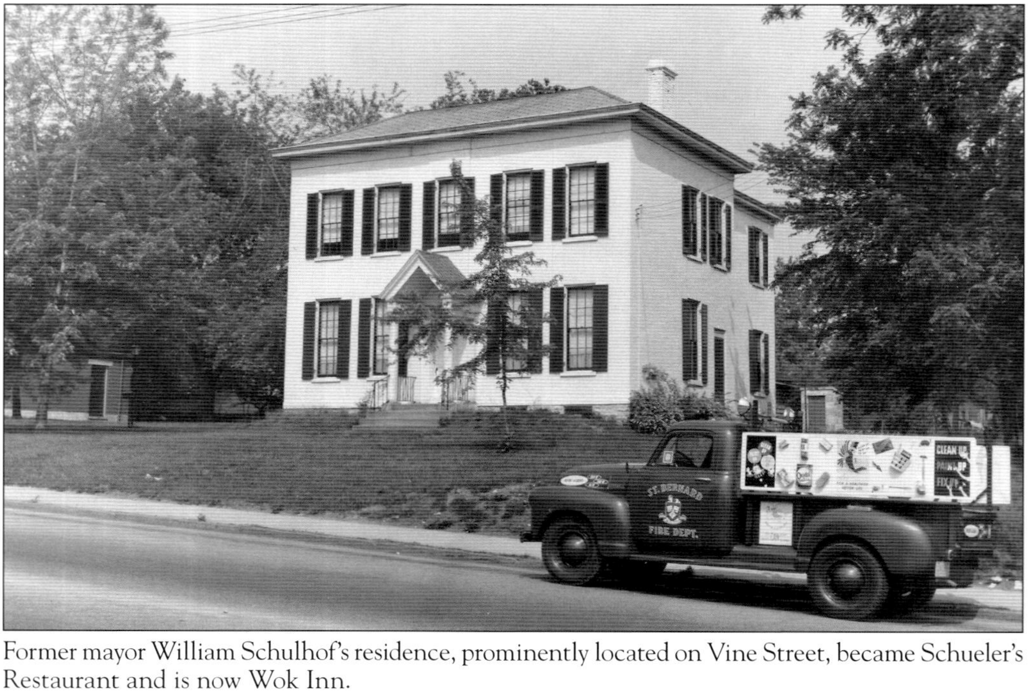

Former mayor William Schulhof's residence, prominently located on Vine Street, became Schueler's Restaurant and is now Wok Inn.

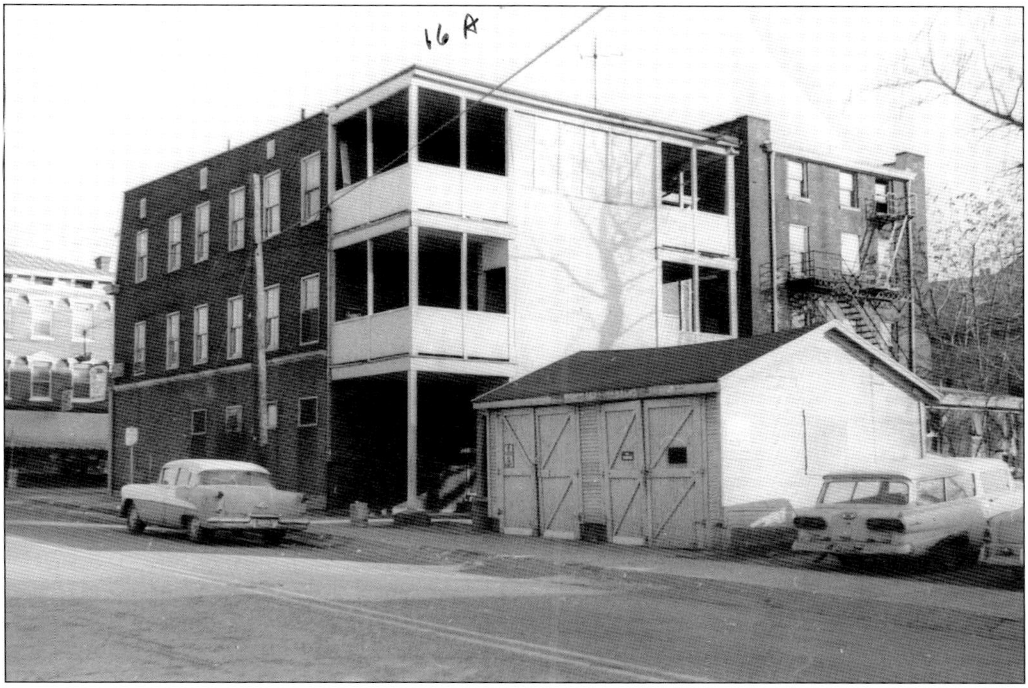

Moon Tavern on Vine Street near Ross Avenue is shown from the back. Tenants who rented the upper floors had porches. This property was removed for urban renewal.

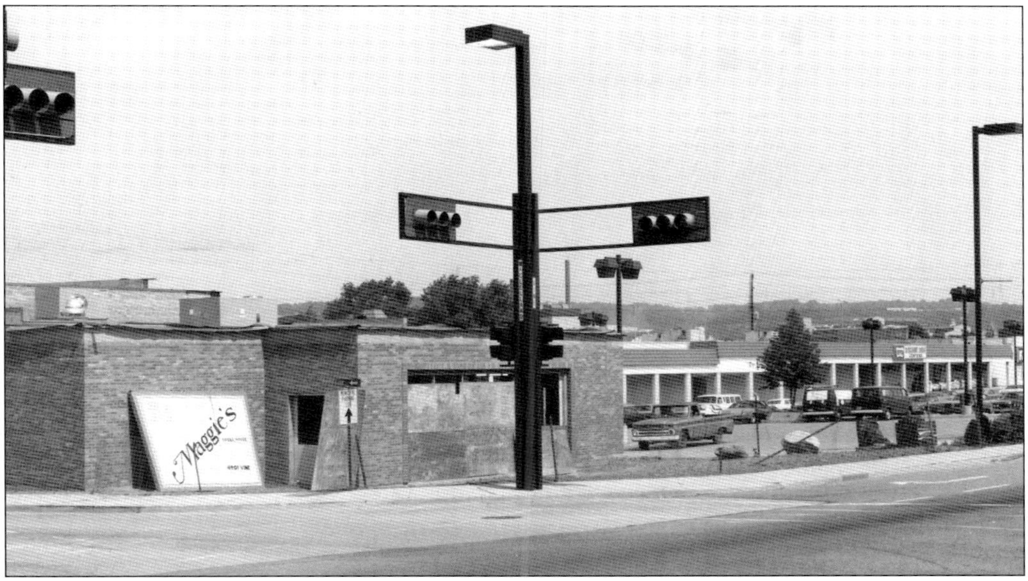

The Schildmeyer family, who had been part of many Vine Street enterprises since the earliest days of St. Bernard, developed the corner of Bank and Vine Streets as Maggie's Opera House. There were three eating places in one facility, a daytime restaurant, a sports bar, and a theatre supper club site where headline Las Vegas entertainers performed. Today, First Safety Bank, Skyline Chili, and Wesley's Sports Bar are found here. Behind these spots is a business office building, and across from that is Lost Corner Pub and Subway sandwich shop. (Courtesy of Howard Goldberg.)

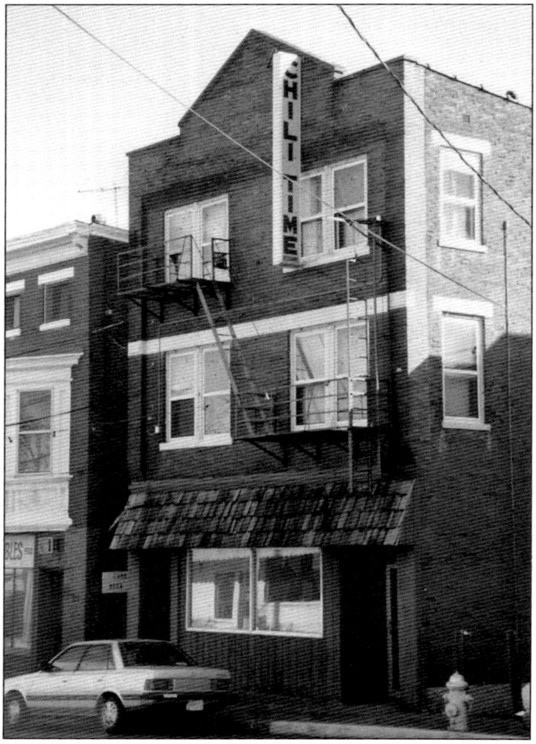

In 1943, Harry and Pete Vidas founded the first Chili Time's Restaurant on the east side of Vine Street. Other restaurants were opened in Bond Hill in 1965 and Roselawn in 1970. (Courtesy of Chris Vidas.)

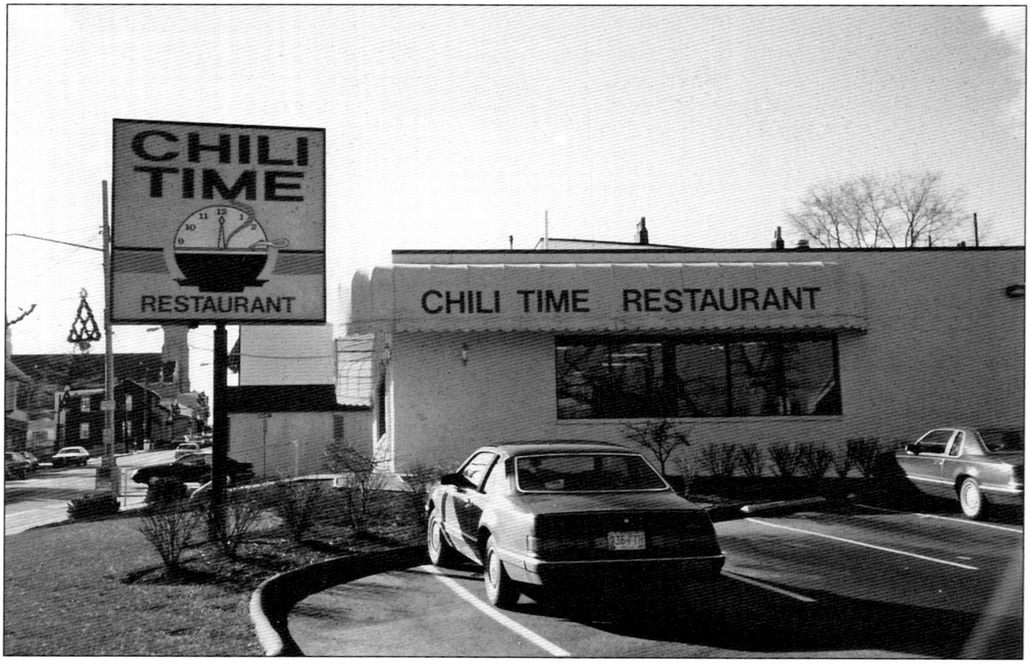

Across the street, today's Chili Time Restaurant opened in April 1986, with Chris Vidas as the head manager. This restaurant is one that generations of families visit when they come back to St. Bernard. (Courtesy of Chris Vidas.)

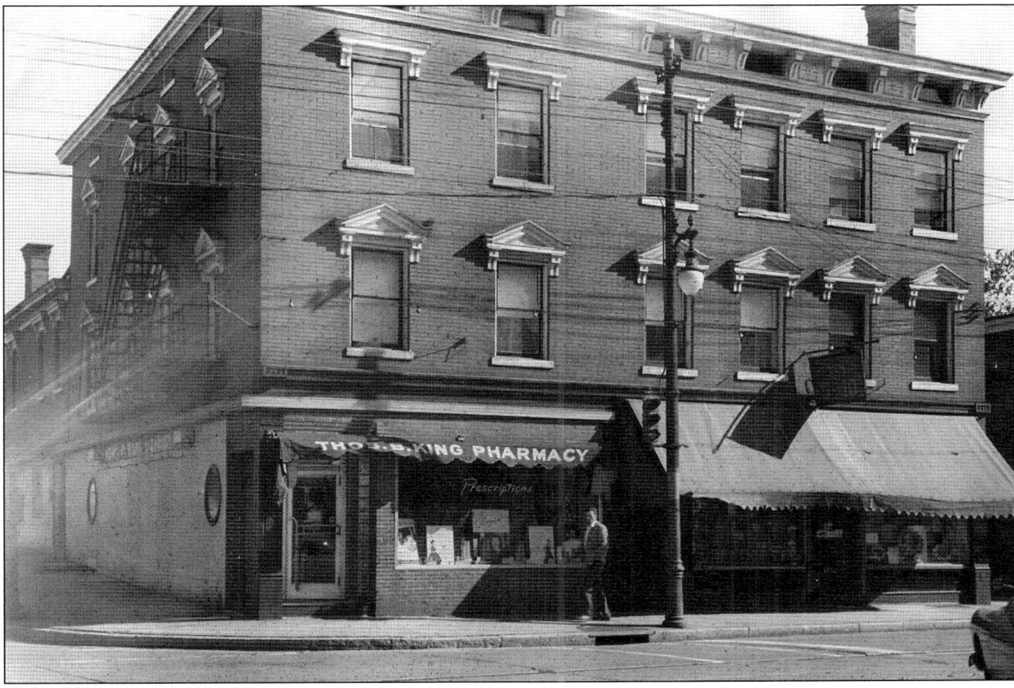

Seen here are King's Pharmacy, Vi and Nate's, and Stark's Dry Goods, with Dr. Joseph Speier and Dr. Stickley upstairs, before construction of the shopping center. (Courtesy of Howard Goldberg.)

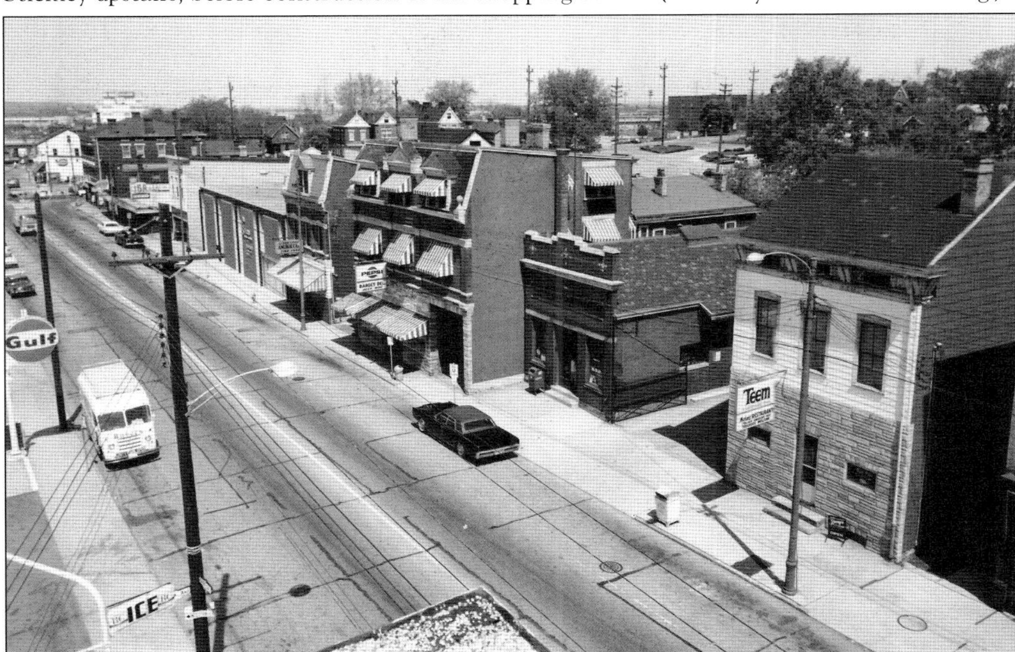

This is Vine Street looking toward the expressway prior to demolition for urban renewal. Seen here are Erm's & Vern's, the post office, the Paddock Club, and Stern's Vending. (Courtesy of Howard Goldberg.)

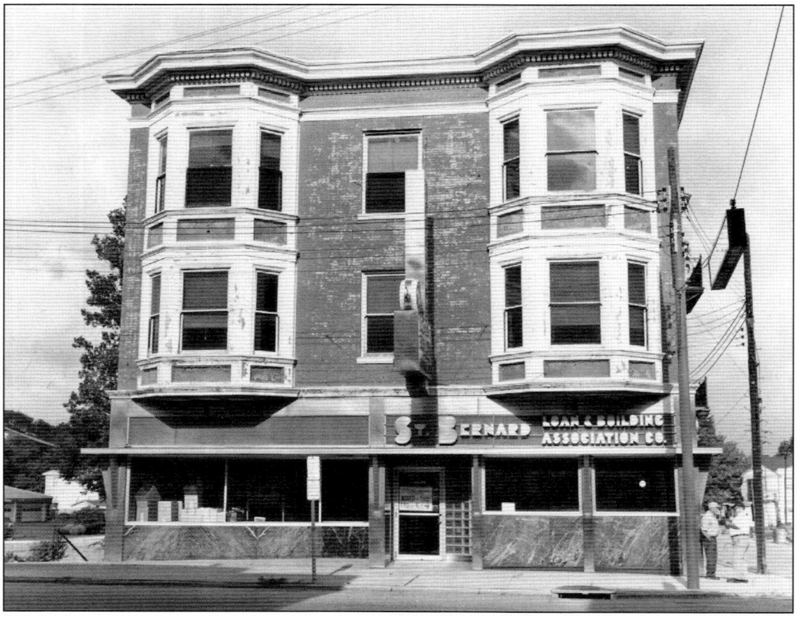

First Federal Savings and Loan was on the corner of Vine and Bank Streets and was removed during urban renewal. Banks and savings institutions have been part of the thrifty St. Bernard that helped residents and workers feel secure. Across the street from this site today is Fifth Third Bank. (Courtesy of Howard Goldberg.)

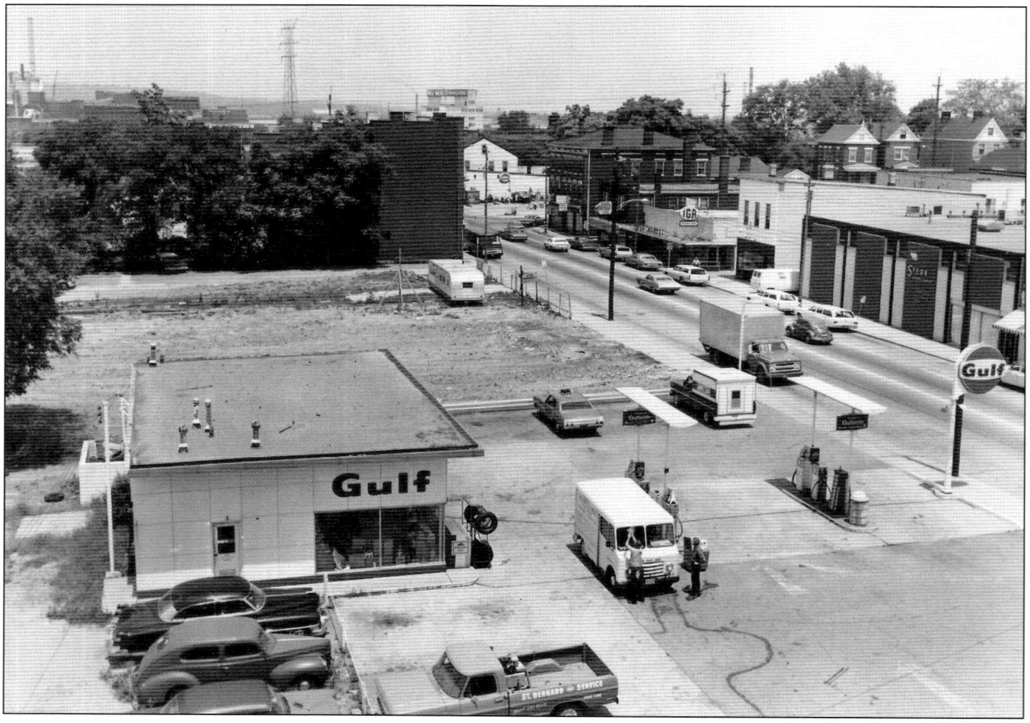

These businesses were removed during urban renewal. In the foreground is Torbeck Gulf. Today, Jerry Day's Auto Service and Greenlee Garage help with auto repairs. In the background are Stern's Vending, Stan's (later Ron Stafford's) IGA, Stark's Vi and Nate's, and King's Pharmacy. This view is looking north on Vine Street toward the NuMaid Margarine plant. (Courtesy of Howard Goldberg.)

Edna Brown Ward and nephew John Ward are outside Ward's Café, located at Beech Street and Railroad Avenue. (Courtesy of Kay Heller Phillips.)

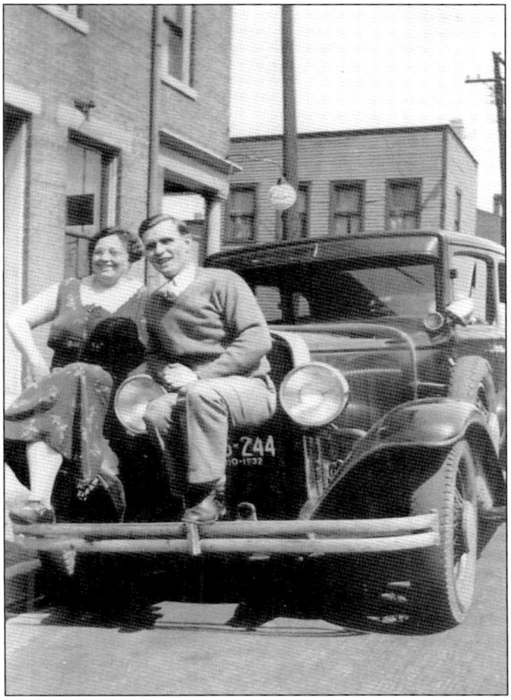

Ward's Café at the corner of Beech Street and Railroad Avenue was also a hotel. Handy for workers in the industrial district, in later years it served as a welding company.

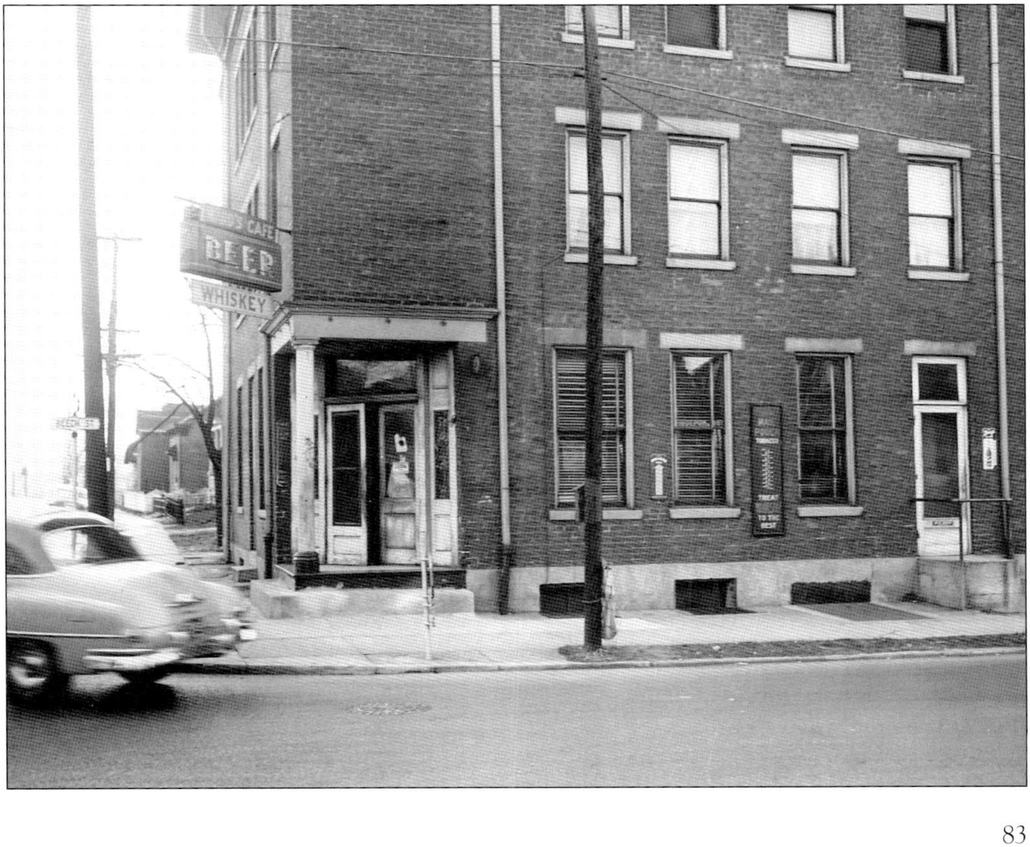

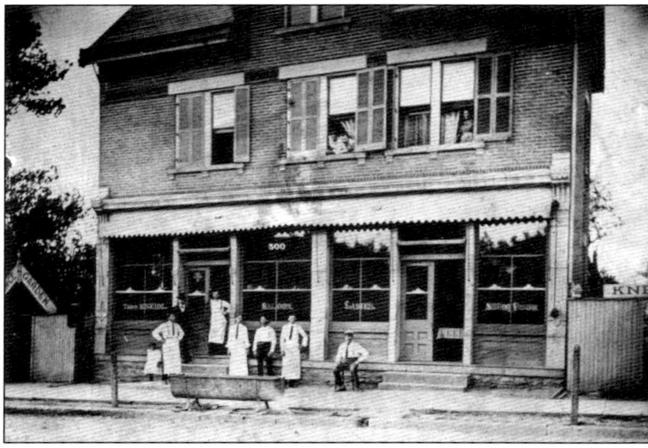

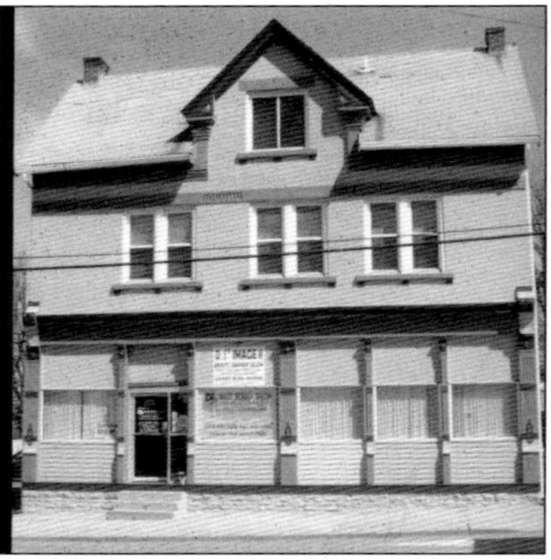

Kneidl Saloon, on the left, was across the street from Keiner's. Mr. Kneidl played the violin and had a summer garden to the rear of the building. Descendant Ron Kneidl is St. Bernard's plumbing inspector. Currently, this is DJs Image II beauty salon, seen on the right. Across the street, Keiner's Cafe and Manthey's Florists have been removed to make way for potential senior housing. On the other corner of Greenlee and Ross Avenues is Scherpie's, a popular delicatessen and caterer, which can be counted on for good food and a great flower sale in the spring. (Courtesy of the St. Bernard archives and Jan Boylan.)

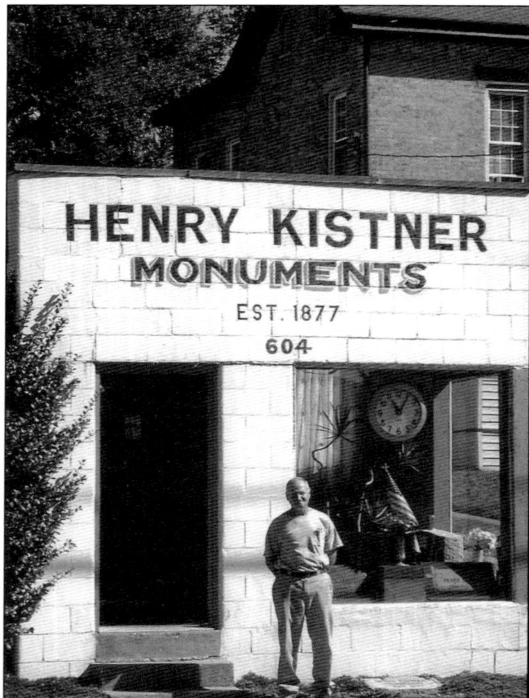

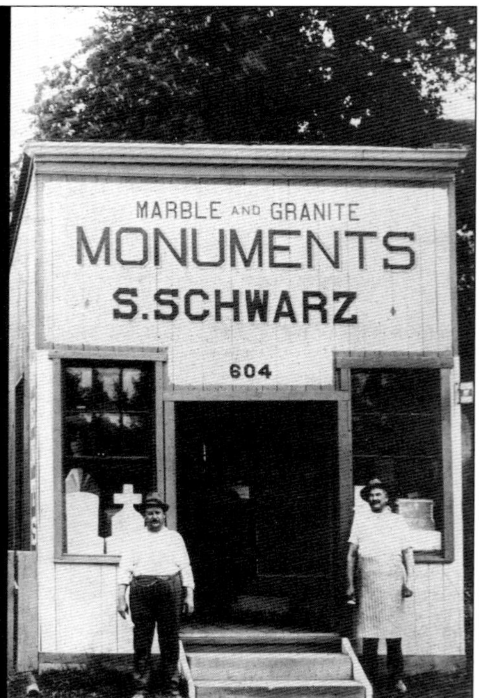

Seen here is Kistner Monuments, formerly known as Schwartz Monuments. Across from St. Mary's Cemetery, it has been a monument shop since 1877. Three generations of the Kistner family have maintained the business since it was purchased from the former owners. (Courtesy of the St. Bernard archives and Jan Boylan.)

Seven

Time for Sports, Fun, and Beer

German and Irish heritage brought appreciation of good spirits. Homemade beer and wine were products of local farmers, and the salary of the canal worker (usually Irish) included 10 cents per day, board, and whisky. Local saloon competition was keen, when 21 beers for $1 and free lunches were known. Sending a son with a pail to bring beer home to dad after a hard day's work was common but of course history now.

From 1825 to 1900, Ross and Chester Lakes were recreation sites for the Cincinnati Gun Club Schutzenfests, American Sailing Canoe Club, White Rat Fishing Club, and numerous hotels. Some hotels even had bowling alleys. Buckeye Trotting Park hosted the eighth annual US Fair in 1860, and for seven days thousands of visitors a day were reported. Fishing, swimming, and ice-skating were part of the canal excitement. Sportsmen and women were here for pleasure and on honeymoons until 1900, when the canal was drained and industry developed.

Baseball and football were enjoyed on school and company teams. St. Bernard boasted a successful men's professional softball team, the Cincinnati Suds, which was based at Ross Park from 1977 to 1982. Local star athletes included Ed Sicking, Moe Burtschy, Tom Kramer, Dave Foley, Tim Foley, and Tony Blum. Musical organizations provided a broad spectrum of entertainment, from drill teams sponsored by the Eagles, Independent Order of Herdsmen, and Daughters of America to local church and school bands and orchestras. The Fun and Beer Club developed as a revolt against Prohibition when folks made their own beer. The R&L (Right & Left) Club was once based at Meiner's Cafe. A model of a right or left hand is placed on the bar, and members are to lift a glass only with the appropriate hand or, if caught using the wrong hand, buy a round of drinks. Eagles and Kiwanis are longtime service associations. The chamber of commerce provided a German Luau at Vine Street Park. Food sales and games of chance provided funds for local service organizations. Proceeds went to pay for the local newspaper *The St. Bernard Bugle*, street flags, and other community benefits.

Holiday activities like Halloween costume contests and Easter egg hunts for the children are still a big draw in St. Bernard. The Fourth of July festival and fireworks at Ross Park is a long tradition. It is sponsored by local officials and has carnival rides, music, and good cooking. Rozzi fireworks displays close the events, and it is enjoyed for miles around. Christmas celebrations at city hall with horse and wagon rides, a model train display, pictures with Santa, hot chocolate, and cookies have been standard fare for years. Memorial Day traditionally honors veterans with local high school bands, politicians, and organizations that take part in a parade to the Soldier's Monument. Awards for God, Flag, and Country student essays are given by the Kiwanis Club.

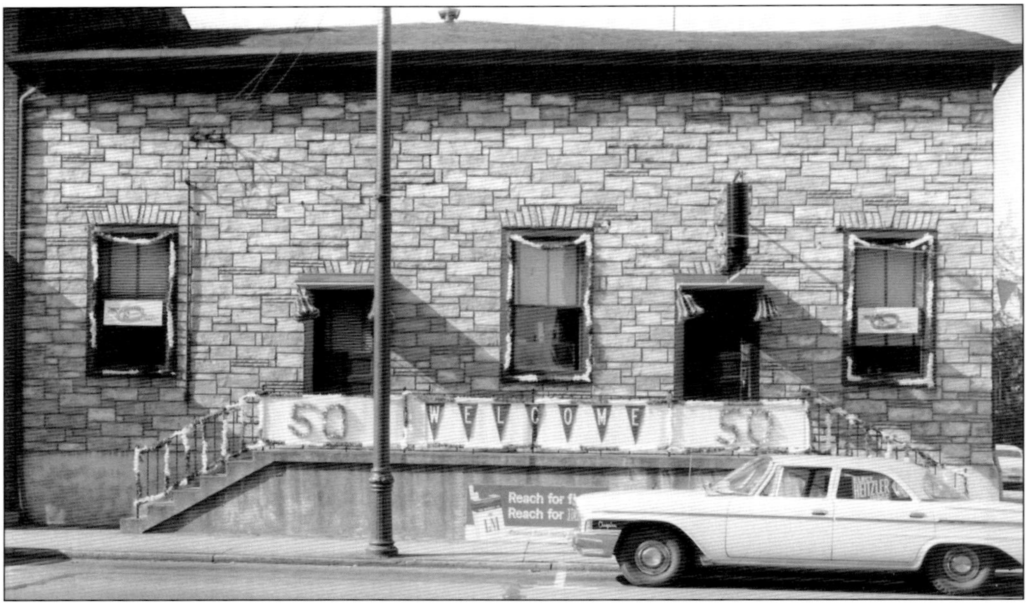

Meiners Café started in 1847 across from present-day St. Clement's Church. At one time, it was a mom-and-pop business with a left-hand entry for groceries that were sold by mom and saloon entry on the right managed by pop. The R&L Club was based here among others. Well-known for "jack" salmon, families enjoyed good cooking and fine beverages frequently at Meiners.

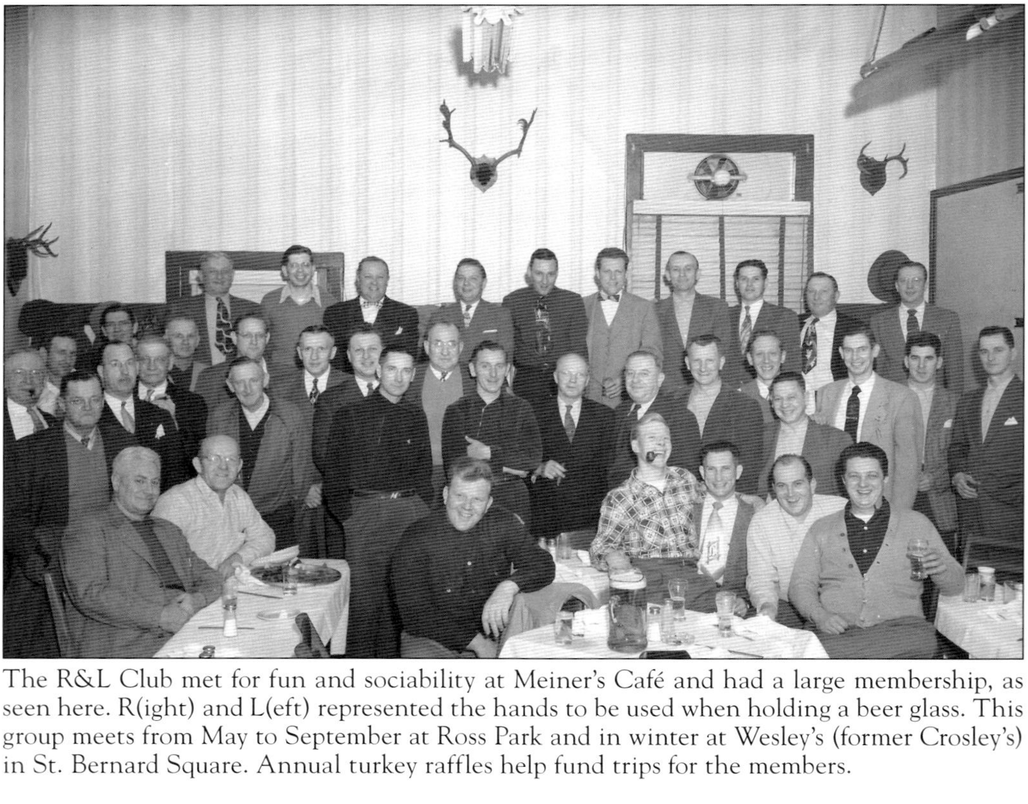

The R&L Club met for fun and sociability at Meiner's Café and had a large membership, as seen here. R(ight) and L(eft) represented the hands to be used when holding a beer glass. This group meets from May to September at Ross Park and in winter at Wesley's (former Crosley's) in St. Bernard Square. Annual turkey raffles help fund trips for the members.

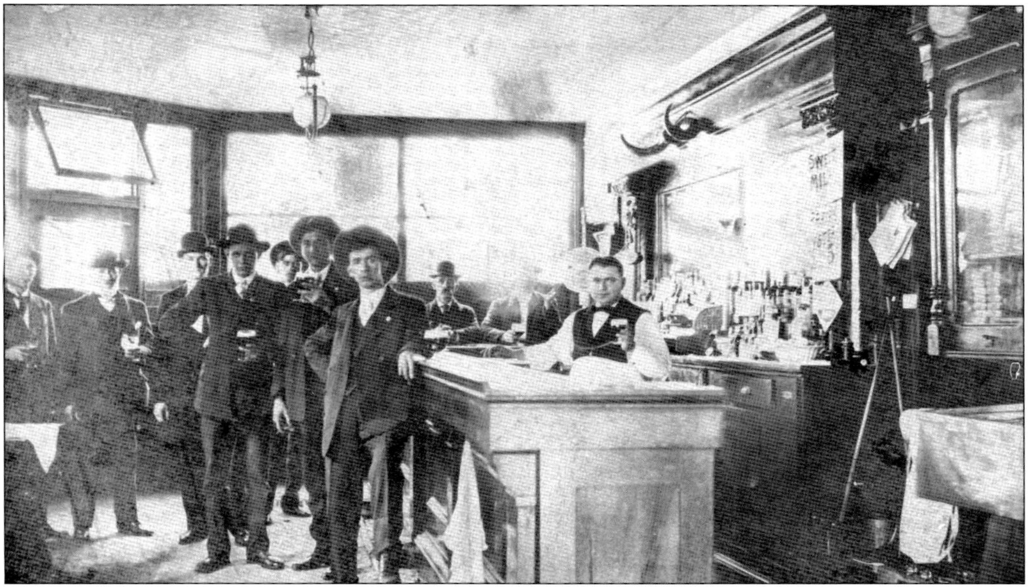

This photograph was taken inside Busam's Saloon, with Charles Busam behind the bar.

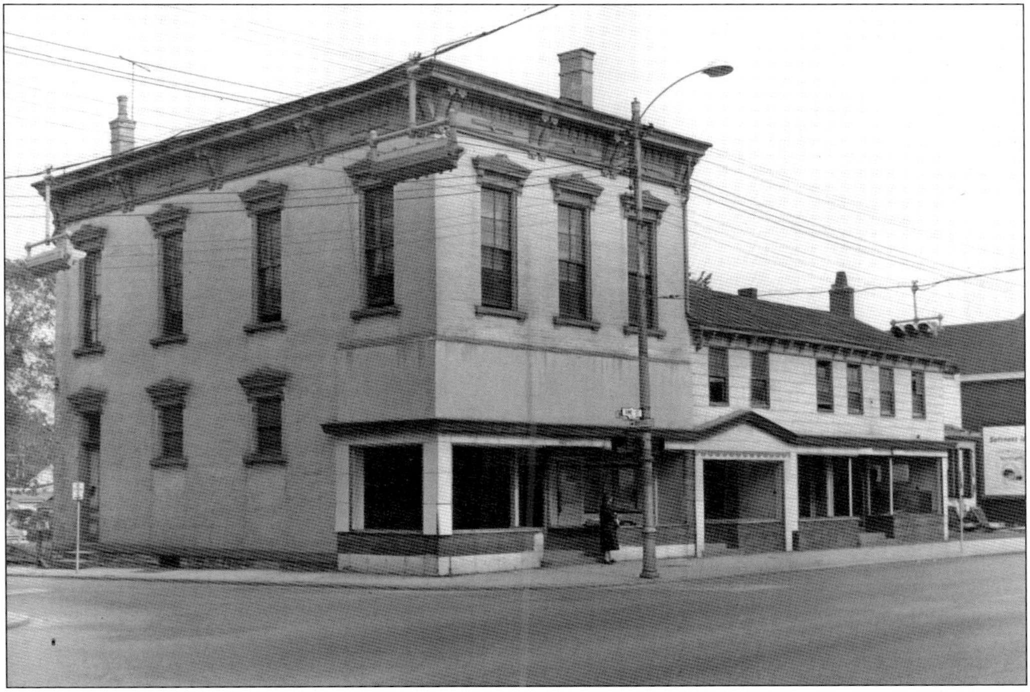

Outside Busam's Saloon, next to the former F&F (Fugikawa) Market, Mrs. Armacost's shop and a laundromat was located here briefly. (Courtesy of Howard Goldberg.)

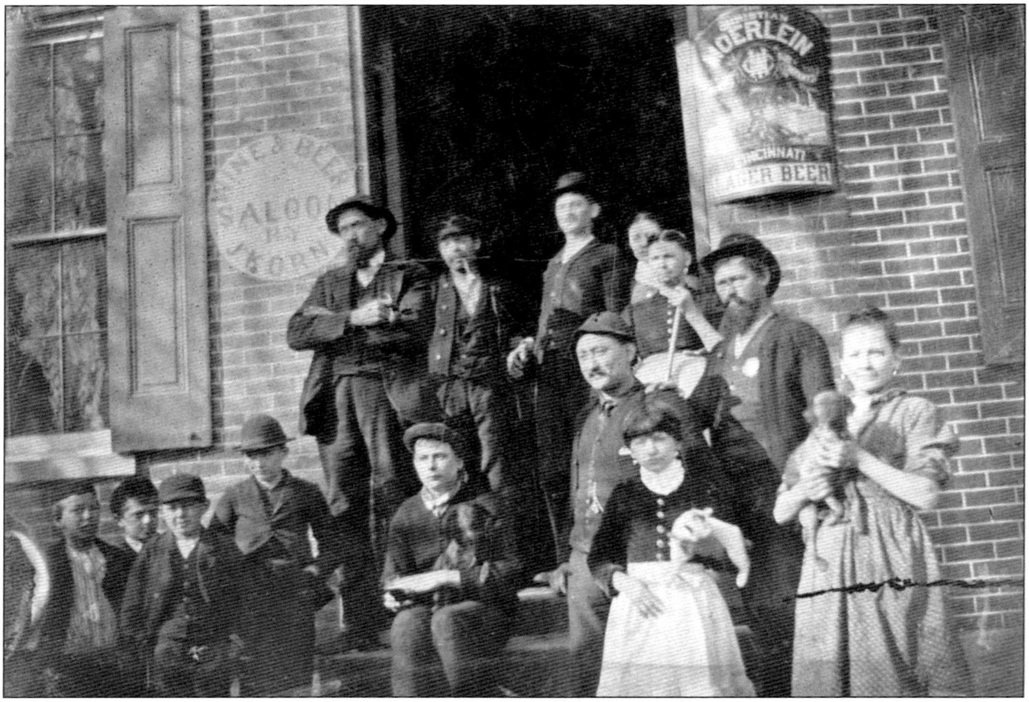

Today, Korn Saloon is now Boomerang's. As in the past, apartments are located above the businesses located at Lawrence and Vine Streets.

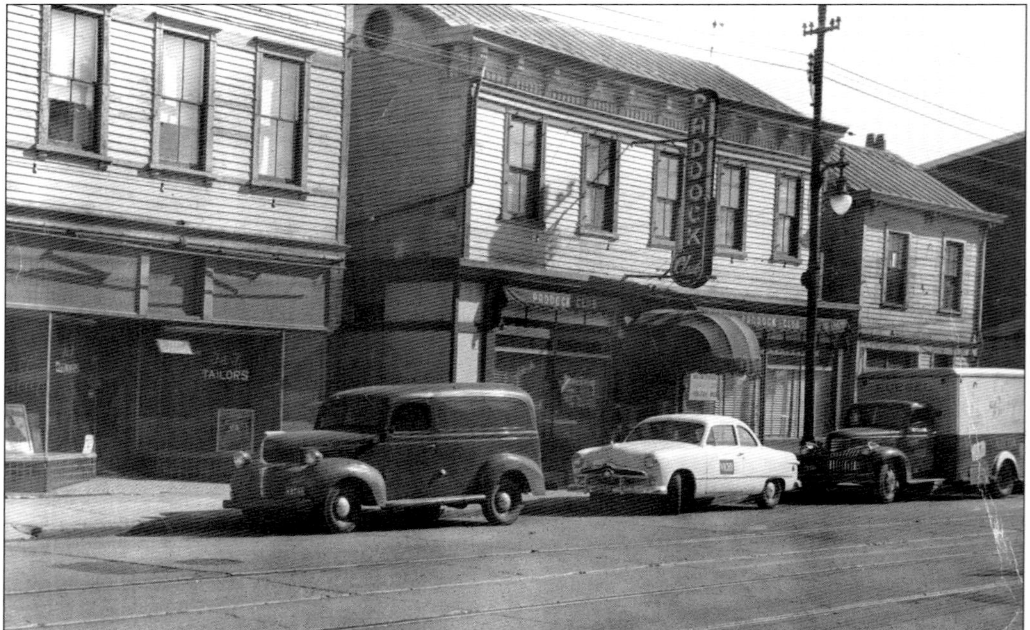

The Paddock Club, with the awning, was a local nightclub on Vine Street. The North Vine Street urban renewal project replaced these businesses with a new shopping mall.

In the 1800s, Ross Lake provided water to the canal and was also the site of the Cincinnati Wooden Sailing Canoe Club with Commodore Judge Nicholas Longworth, Lucien Wulsin, and others. Accessible from downtown Cincinnati, nine miles away by train, many weekends would find serious racing at this 45-acre lake. The clubhouse here boasted a kitchen, an amateur photography lab, and 10 bunks in one room with an outside porch known as "the quarter deck." (Courtesy of the Cincinnati Historical Society, Anne Shepherd.)

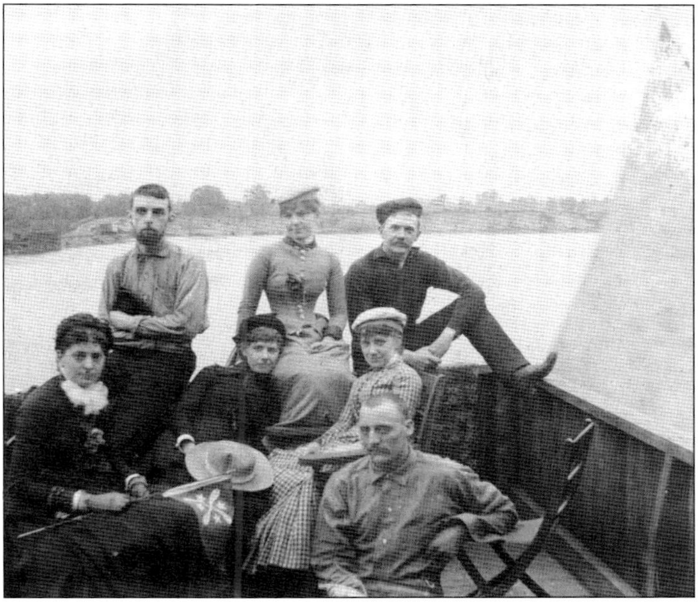

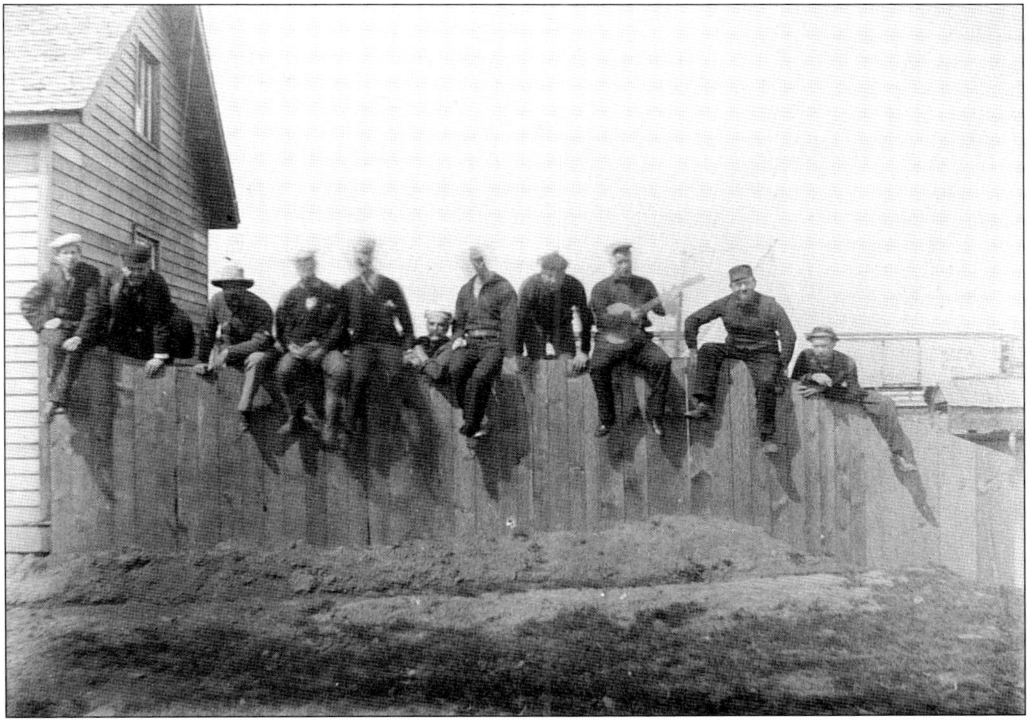

Spectators at the races are seen here. No bleachers were available, so these folks were true hangers-on in an effort to be entertained here. The Schutzenbuckel, an early Cincinnati Gun Club, was also located here, and members of the White Rat Fishing Club enjoyed the thrill of the sport at this location as well. (Courtesy of the Cincinnati Historical Society, Anne Shepherd.)

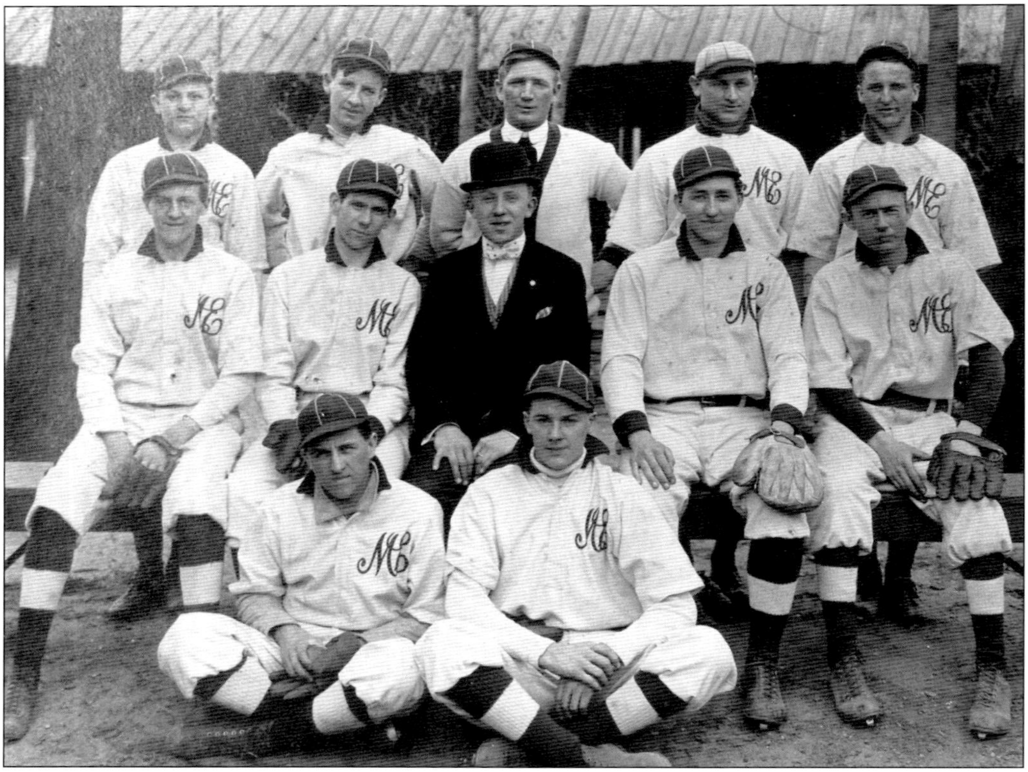

The Meiners Eagles, a local baseball team, was well known in its day. Before the neighborhood developed, a baseball practice diamond was located behind Meiner's Café.

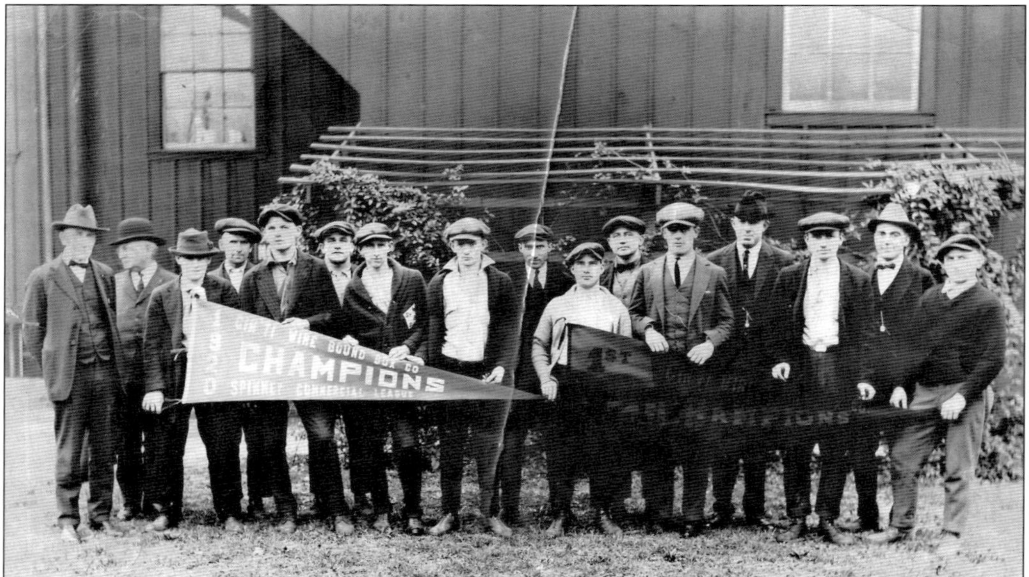

The Wirebound Box Company team was one of the local baseball challengers. Competition was the name of the game, and these were good workers who were proud to be champions.

In 1916, Eddie Sicking was the youngest ballplayer in the National League in major-league baseball at 19 years old. He had a long career between the majors and minors, including a strong run in the Texas League. While in the majors, Sicking played for the Chicago Cubs, New York Giants, Philadelphia Phillies, Cincinnati Reds, and Pittsburgh Pirates organizations. In 1928, he just missed out on the minor-league batting title with a .368 average. Eddie played 37 games for the Cincinnati Reds in 1920. One of his favorite moments in baseball was when his father traveled by train to Indianapolis to watch him steal second and home to win a game. In the minors, Sicking hit above .300 from 1924 through 1931. (Courtesy of James Sicking.)

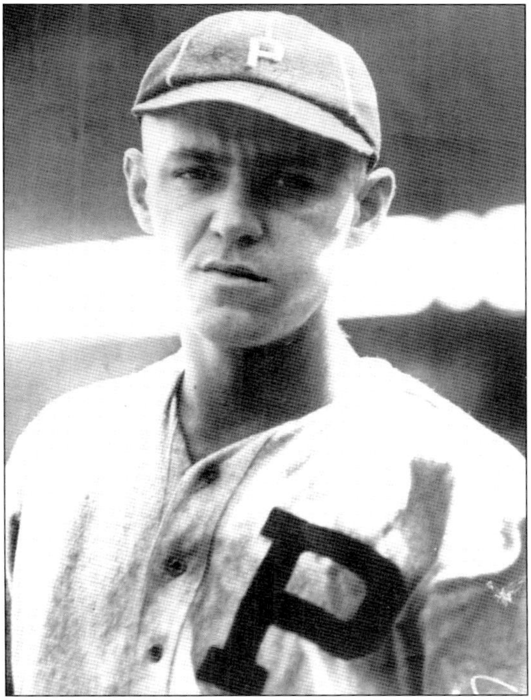

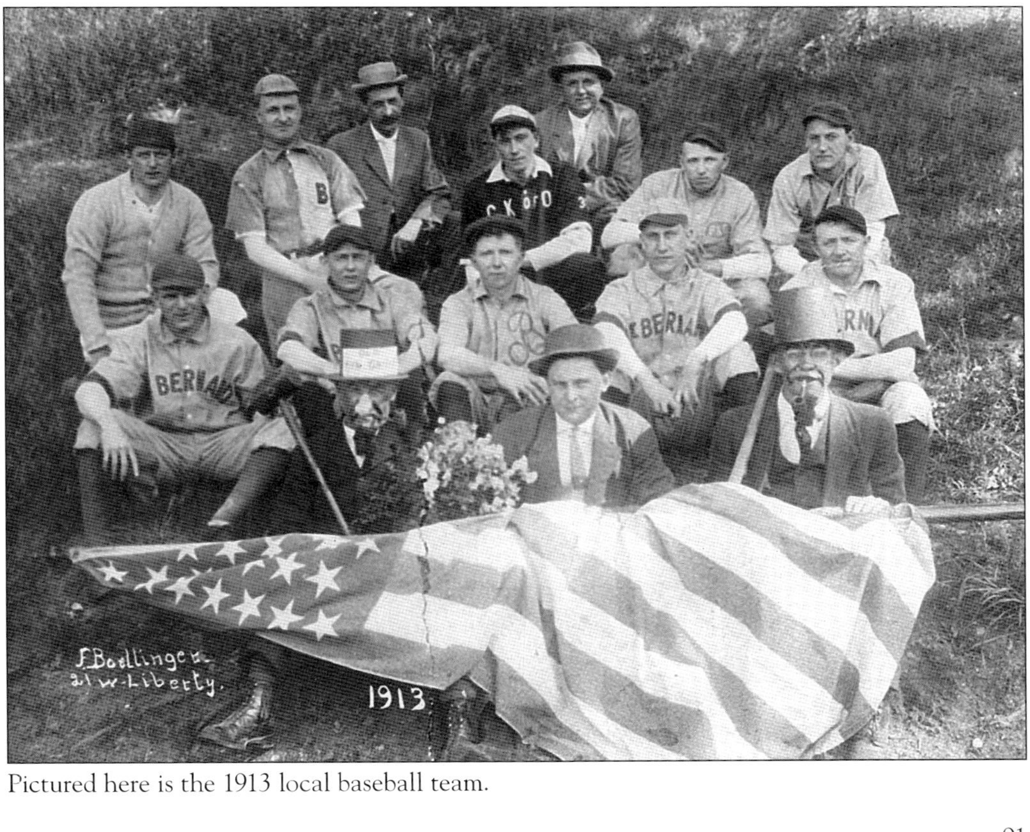

Pictured here is the 1913 local baseball team.

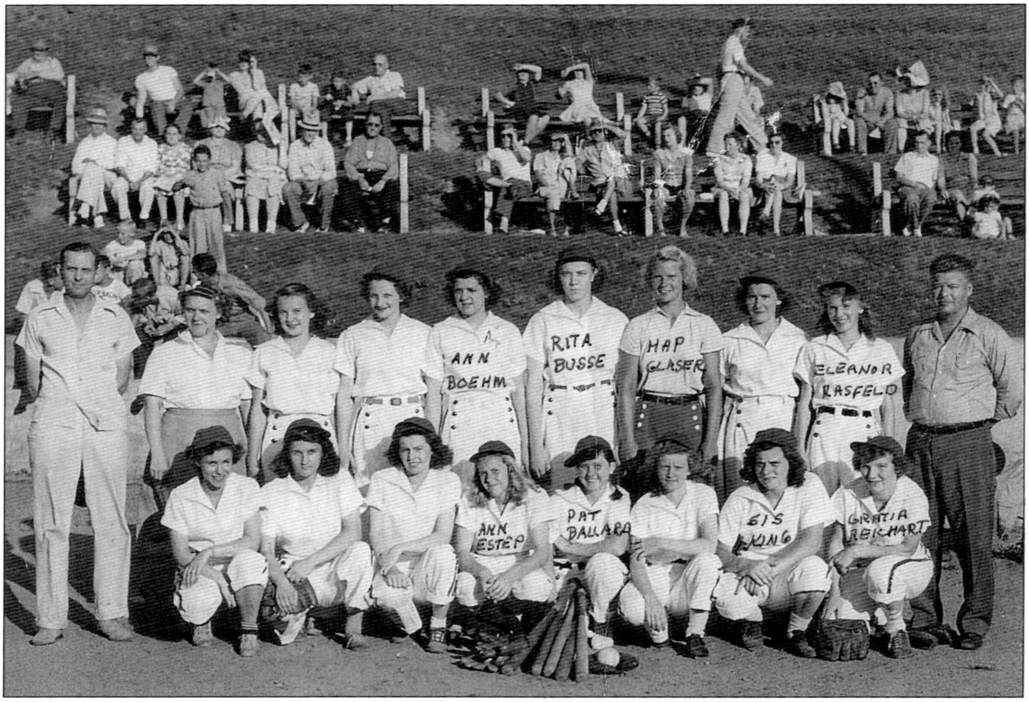

The St. Bernard Merchants, a 1943 woman's fast-pitch softball team based at Vine Street Park, was organized during World War II. It played a highly competitive schedule against such teams as Gruen Watch, Pepsi Cola, and the UC Women's Army Corps (WAC). Some players recalled are Pat Ballard, Ann Boehm, Rita Busse, Ann Estep, Hap Glaser, Sis King, Eleanor Rasfeld, and Gracia Reichardt. Hap went on to play professionally for Mr. Wrigley of Chicago in the All American Girls Professional Baseball League. (Courtesy of Patricia Ballard.)

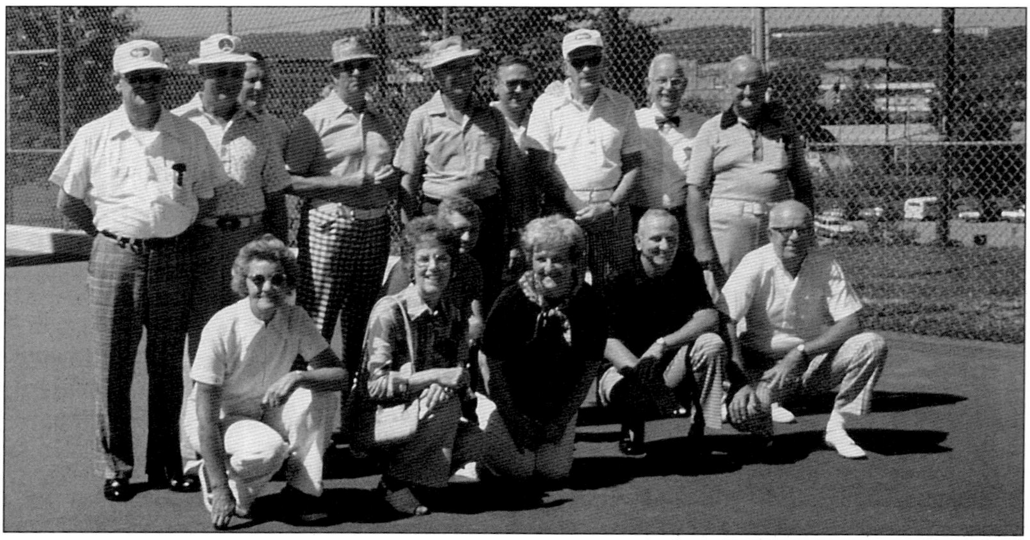

Tennis teams of yesteryear included names like Goldschmidt, Nunlist, Doellman, and Abell among others. The group here is celebrating the completion of new tennis courts above Ross Park in 1973.

Urban Mersch coached the girls' baseball team around 1950. (Courtesy of St. Bernard.)

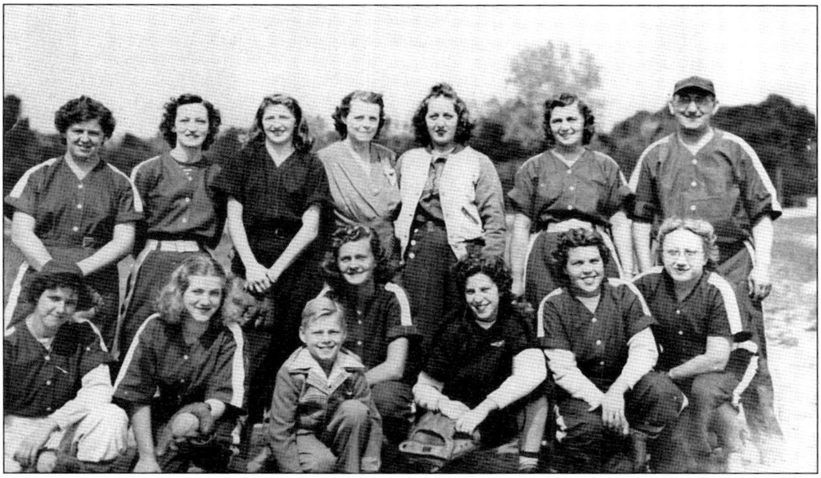

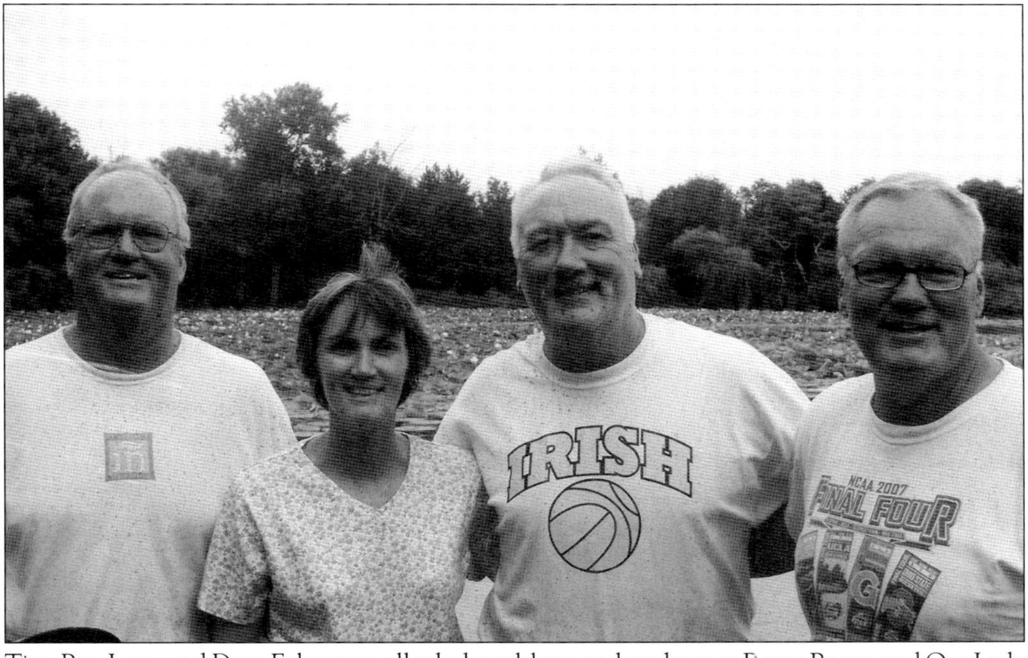

Tim, Peg, Jerry, and Dave Foley were all scholar athletes and students at Roger Bacon and Our Lady of the Angels. Dave, a Roger Bacon 1965 graduate, won a scholarship to Ohio State University and was part of the 1968 Rose Bowl national championship football team. As a 1969 first-round draft pick for the New York Jets, he played three years with Joe Namath before six seasons with the Buffalo Bills as part of what fans dubbed the "Electric Company," paving the way for O.J. Simpson to surpass the 2,000-yard barrier. Jerry, a Roger Bacon 1970 graduate, excelled in basketball and was named to the All-City, All-State, and All-American teams. He played one year at Ohio State and three years at Xavier University. Tim, a 1976 Roger Bacon graduate, won a football scholarship to University of Notre Dame, was on the 1977 national championship team, and was named All-American in 1981. He was drafted by and played for the Baltimore Colts. Peg, a 1977 Our Lady of the Angels graduate, received All-Girls' Greater Cincinnati League honors in both volleyball and basketball, was elected to the *Cincinnati Post* All-Star team, and was one of the first women to receive a full basketball scholarship to University of Cincinnati. (Courtesy of Traci Foley.)

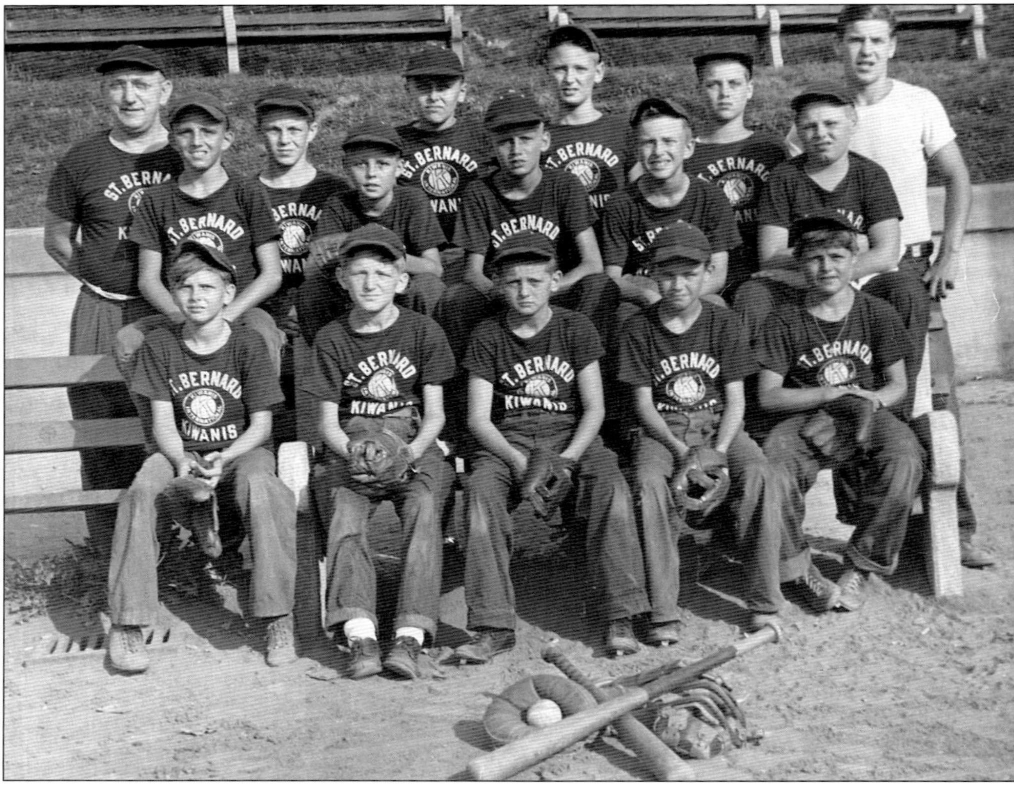

Many St. Bernard boys had their start in local athletics playing baseball for teams sponsored by the local Kiwanis Club. The recreation department and volunteers also have coached softball, baseball, and early boys' and girls' tee ball. Practices in neighborhood parks and games in the larger Vine Street and Ross Parks have provided excellent summer sport for all ages.

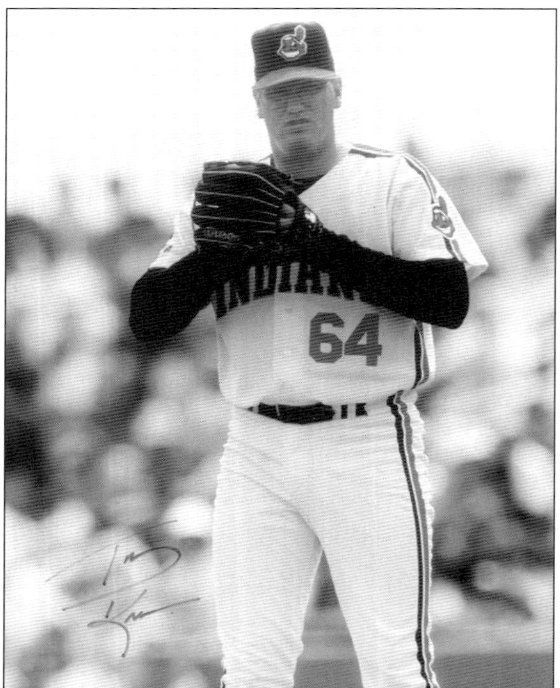

Tom Kramer, born in St. Bernard on January 9, 1968, was drafted in 1987 and played for the major-league Cleveland Indians from 1991 to 1993, along with a number of minor-league ball clubs. He retired after 12 years in professional baseball at the conclusion of the 1998 season. Tom's playing career highlight may be the one-hitter he pitched against the Texas Rangers on May 24, 1993. A home run off the bat of Julio Franco prevented it from being a perfect game. (Courtesy of Mike Niesen.)

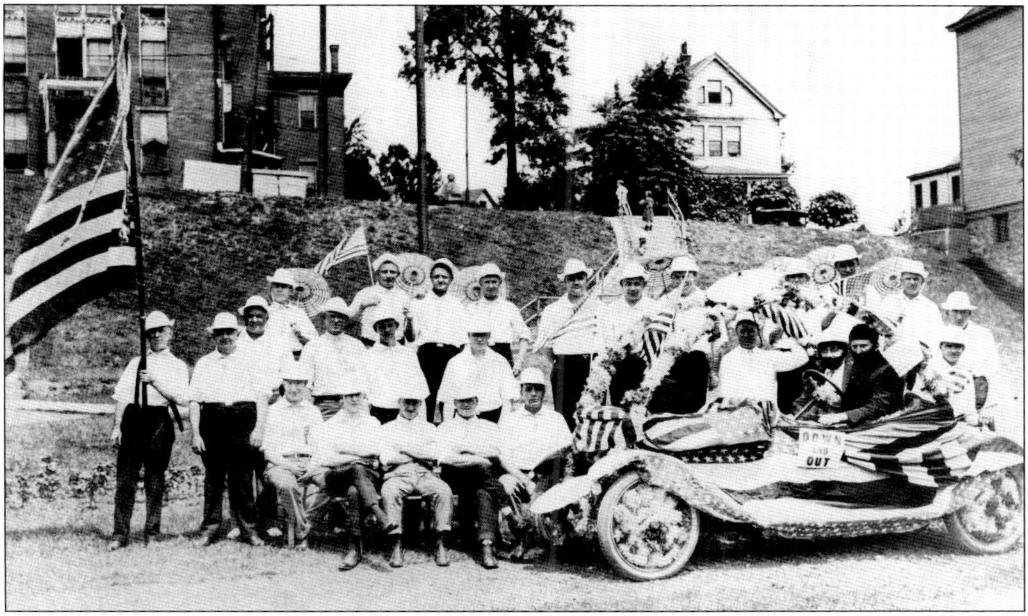

Seen here is the Down and Out Club parade car. Club members met here after a parade for a photograph at Vine Street Park.

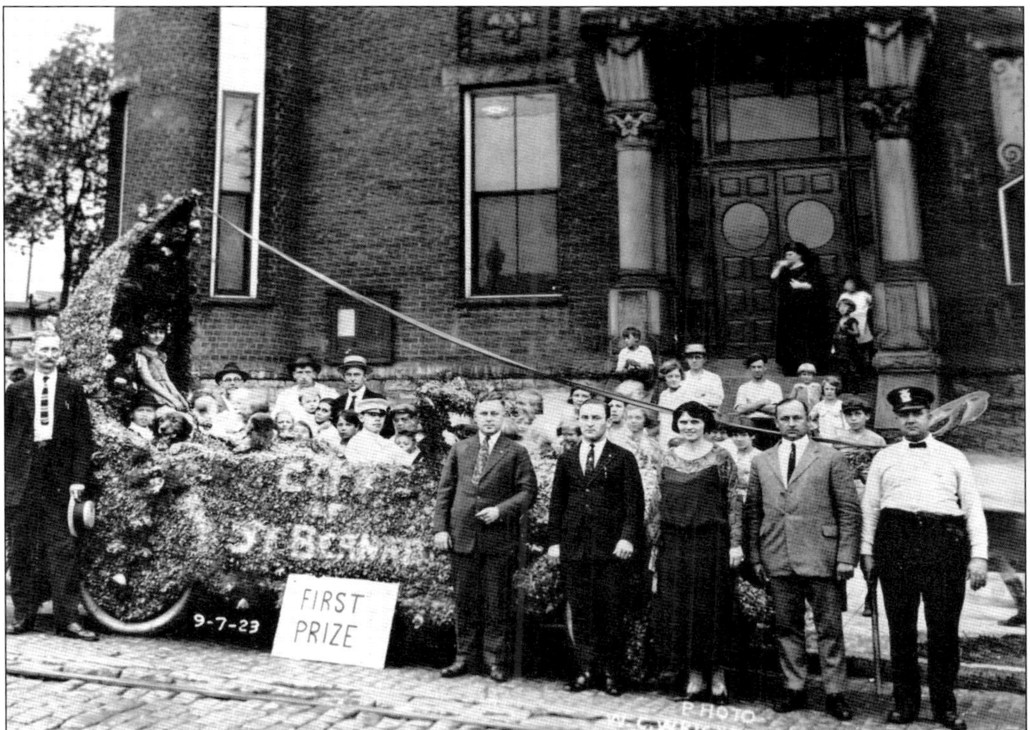

In front of the old town hall, winners of the float parade are here with Mayor Peter Young (left) and police chief Burkhardt (right).

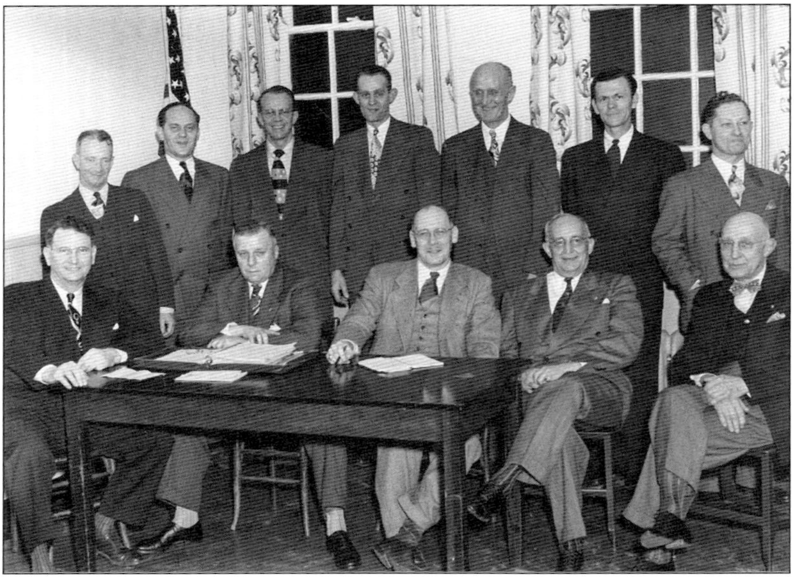

Kiwanis members assist with public-service projects, including support of local Knothole baseball teams and other civic endeavors.

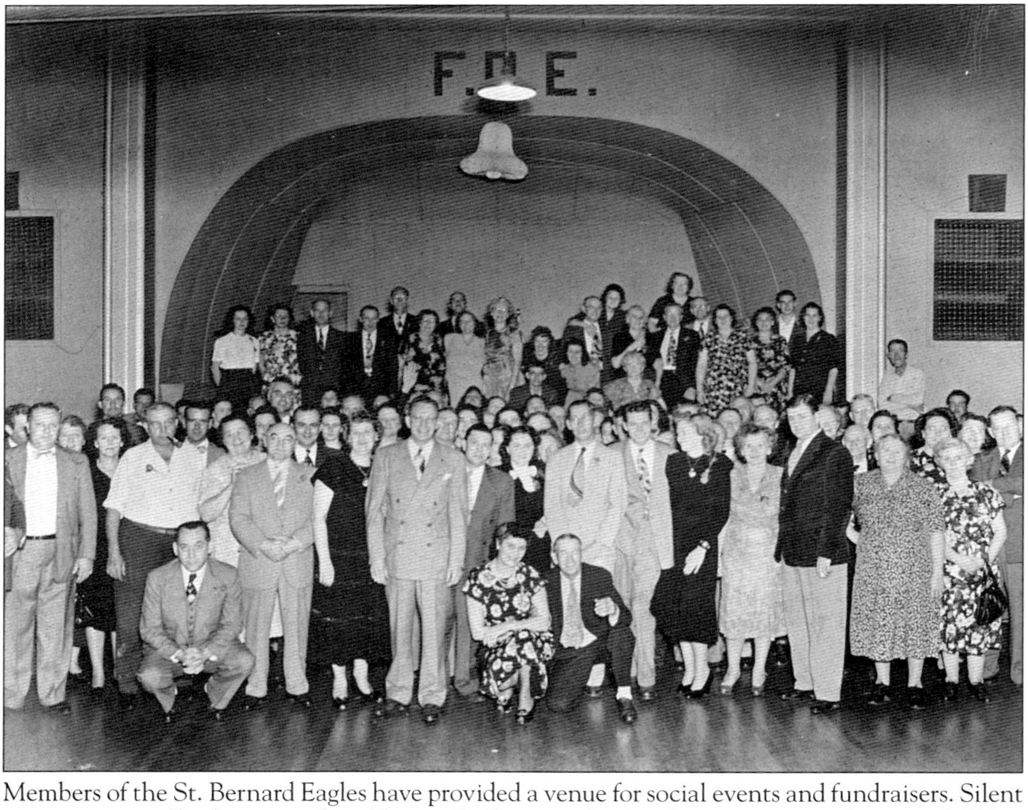

Members of the St. Bernard Eagles have provided a venue for social events and fundraisers. Silent movies, originally shown in the old town hall, were also local entertainment here, with Edna McCann playing the piano in the background. During the 1940s to 1950s, singles dances were held here. Today, Sunday bingo and Friday night fish fries are among the get-togethers that are sponsored. Members have a golf league, and the Ladies' Auxiliary is an active service group.

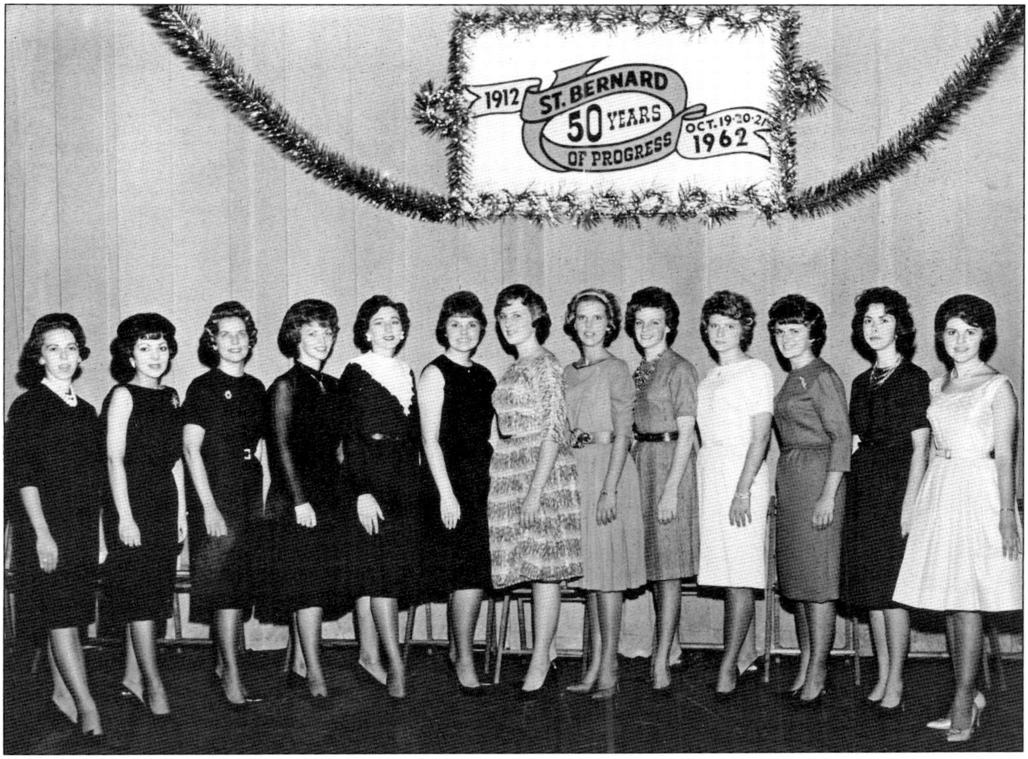

The 50th anniversary of city incorporation meant a beauty pageant in 1962 and a crowning of a queen. The winner that year was Pauline Thompson (fifth from the left).

The German Luau parade, which was celebrated in August, was sponsored by the chamber of commerce. The event culminated in a celebration at Vine Street Park.

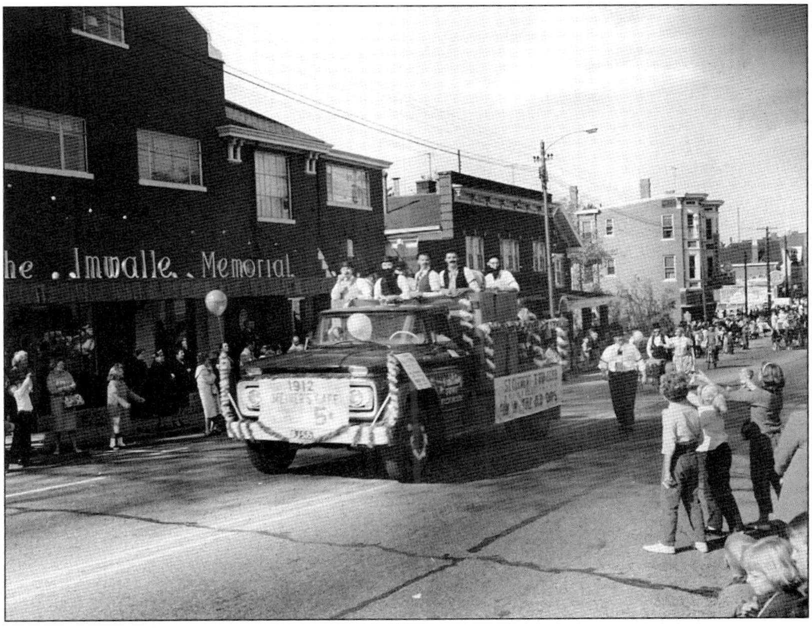

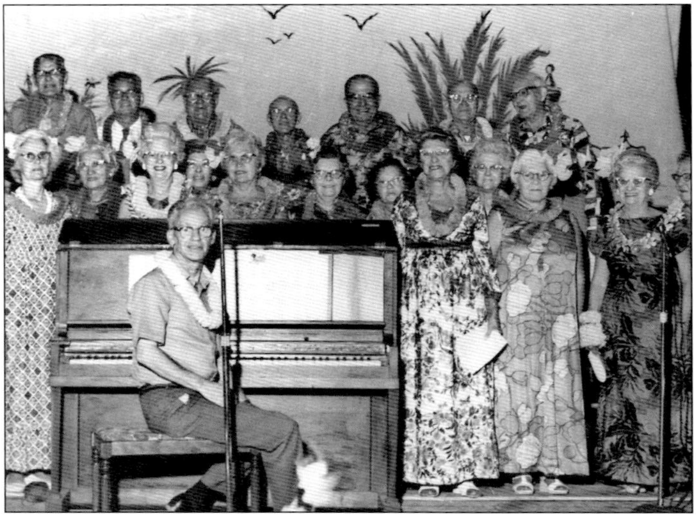

Harry Meyer, the composer of "Our Land St. Bernard," is seen here with his senior-citizens chorus serenading the German Luau crowd.

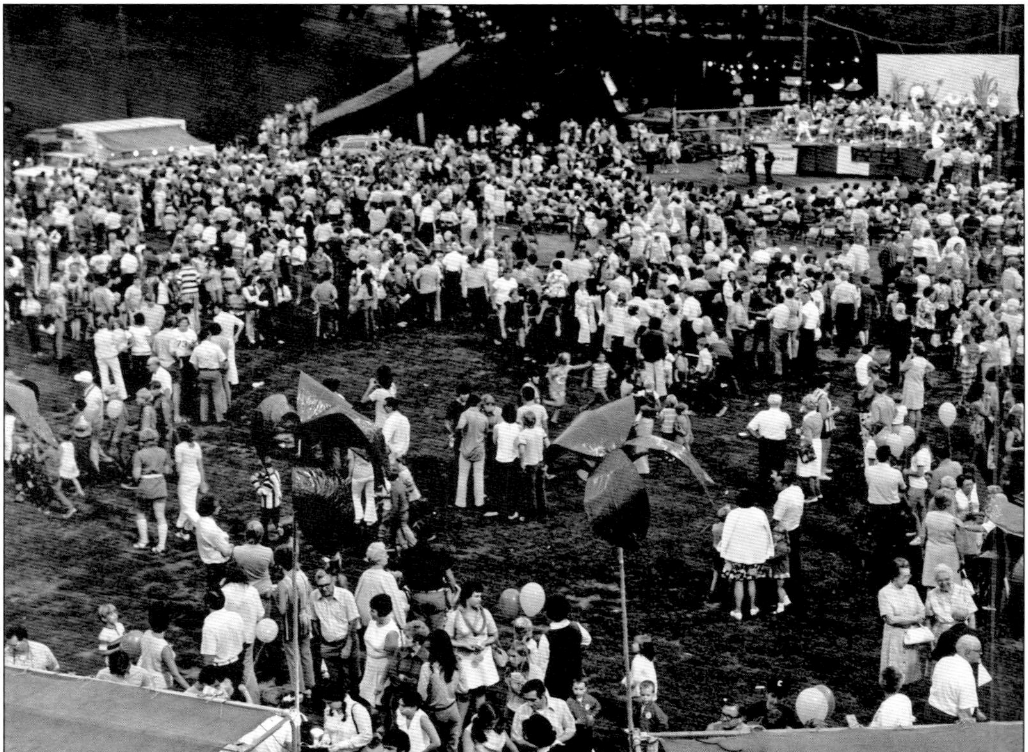

The German Luau was held from 1971 through 1984, celebrating the German heritage of many settlers here in the spirit of Hawaiian hospitality, fun, and food. An annual favorite was the tug-of-war between the Common Cause and Idle Hour Clubs. Boy Scout Troop 354 roasted a pig for pulled-pork sandwiches. Volunteers served shaved ice, Ft. Laramie Sausage, beer, and sodas. Games of chance, a hula contest, and a band concert completed the evening. A 1985 rating of the Cincinnati suburbs by *Cincinnati Magazine* named the German Luau as the "Best Neighborhood Festival" of the 48 neighborhoods.

Eight

Our Business and Industry

Manufacturing industries found St. Bernard's homegrown workforce of skilled and unskilled workers and easy access to transportation of goods and services ideal. In 1825, the Miami and Erie Canal and building construction required stone, sand, and clay materials to be readily available. In 1869, the Broxterman(n) and Boehm families arrived in St. Bernard from Germany and began a family partnership in the sand, ice-hauling, and stone business. Attemeyer's quarrying company excavated sand at the present-day Roger Bacon High School practice field. Some of this fine-quality sand was shipped to produce Cincinnati's renowned Rookwood pottery. Suer brickyard became Roger Bacon Stadium on Mitchell Avenue. National Starch Works established the first global company on the canal. Michael Werk, who was from France, sold candles and developed Werk soaps. The soaps are reportedly the oldest bar soap in the country. In 1837, he loaned money to James Gamble, who with William Procter began a soap and candle business as the Procter & Gamble Company. Purchased for $1 million, 76 acres of the Ludlow property became their new site when fire destroyed the Central Avenue factory warehouse. Production of Ivory and Lenox bar soaps and candles was expanded with the purchase of the Globe Soap Company, as research, innovative technology, and diversification brought granulated and detergent synthetic soaps Dreft and Tide to the marketplace. Other new products included Crest toothpaste, Duncan Hines cake mixes, and Pampers. In 2003, the J.M. Smucker Company purchased Crisco. Trillium Health Care Products, Inc., purchased and renamed Ivorydale as the St. Bernard Soap Company, continuing production of Ivory and multiple brands of bar soaps. P&G Ivorydale Technical Center and Fabric and Home Care Innovation Center remain in St. Bernard today. The names known for many retail products were born in St. Bernard.

Emery Industries, the manufacturer of high-quality beeswax candles, glycerin products, and fine chemicals, is located along the Mill Creek. Over the years, following a transition to Henkel-Emery, the company was obtained by Cognis, and it has since been purchased by BASF, a German-based, fine-chemicals corporation. PMC Chemicals operates from facilities formerly owned by Thoms River and Sherwin Williams. Along the canal were Ubiko Milling, Agrico Chemical, and later NuMaid Margarine. Supporting businesses, such as the Wirebound Box Company and Ivorydale Lumberyard, are now history. Hummel Industries, a stonemason and contractor in 1850, came to St. Bernard in the 1970s, providing outstanding construction in the Greater Cincinnati area. Rough Brothers began as a hardware supplier for greenhouses in Wooden Shoe Hollow. It is now nationally known for greenhouse construction at colleges and private institutions, as well retail outlets. The Antique Boat Connection refinishes, restores, and sells wooden boats that provide living boat history.

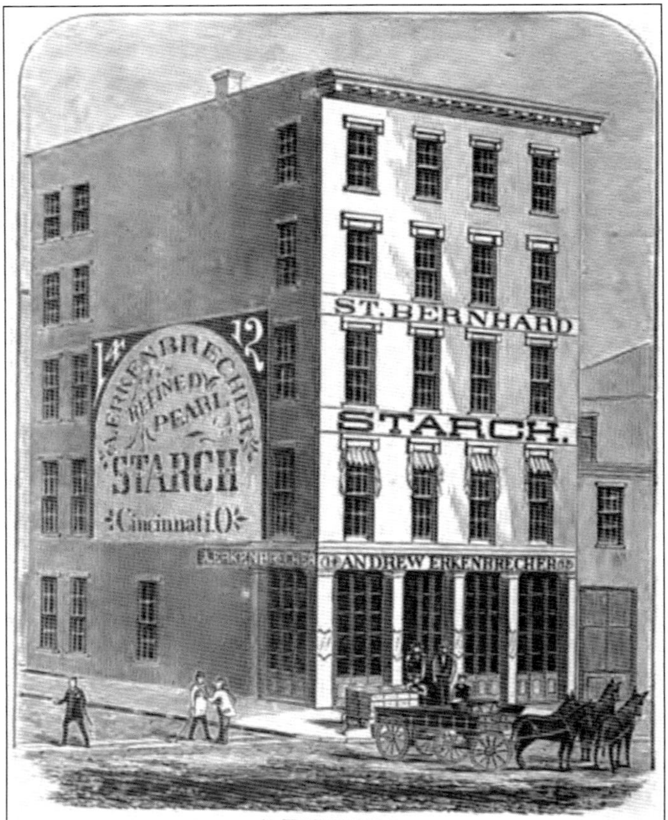

A. ERKENBRECHER.

Seen here is St. Bernard's National Starch Office in Cincinnati for products made in St. Bernard. Company owner Andrew Erchenbrecher was also a founder of the Cincinnati Zoo. (Courtesy of Tom Boehm.)

Early Procter & Gamble had company homes for foremen and their families, which was an early experiment. The homes are the dark buildings to the right of smokestack. (Courtesy of the Procter & Gamble Archives.)

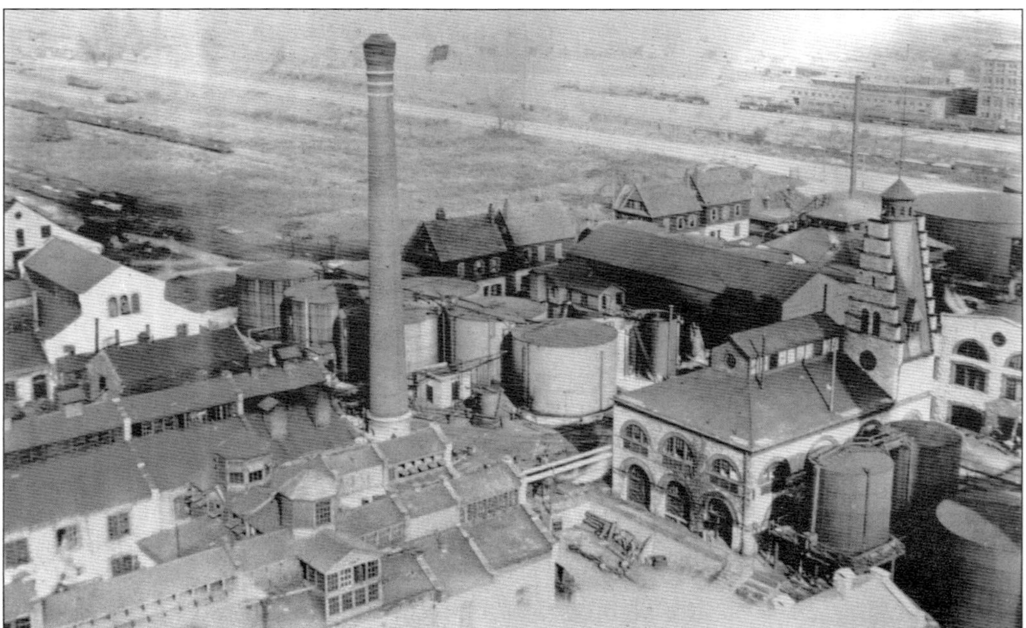

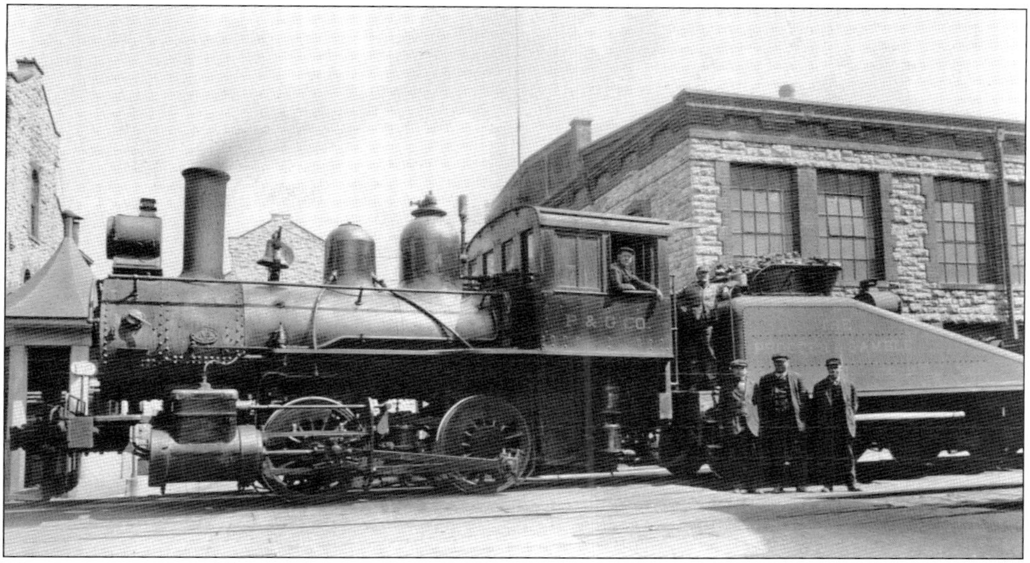

The Procter & Gamble switch engine enabled efficient management of products and raw materials at the Ivorydale factory. (Courtesy of the Procter & Gamble Archives)

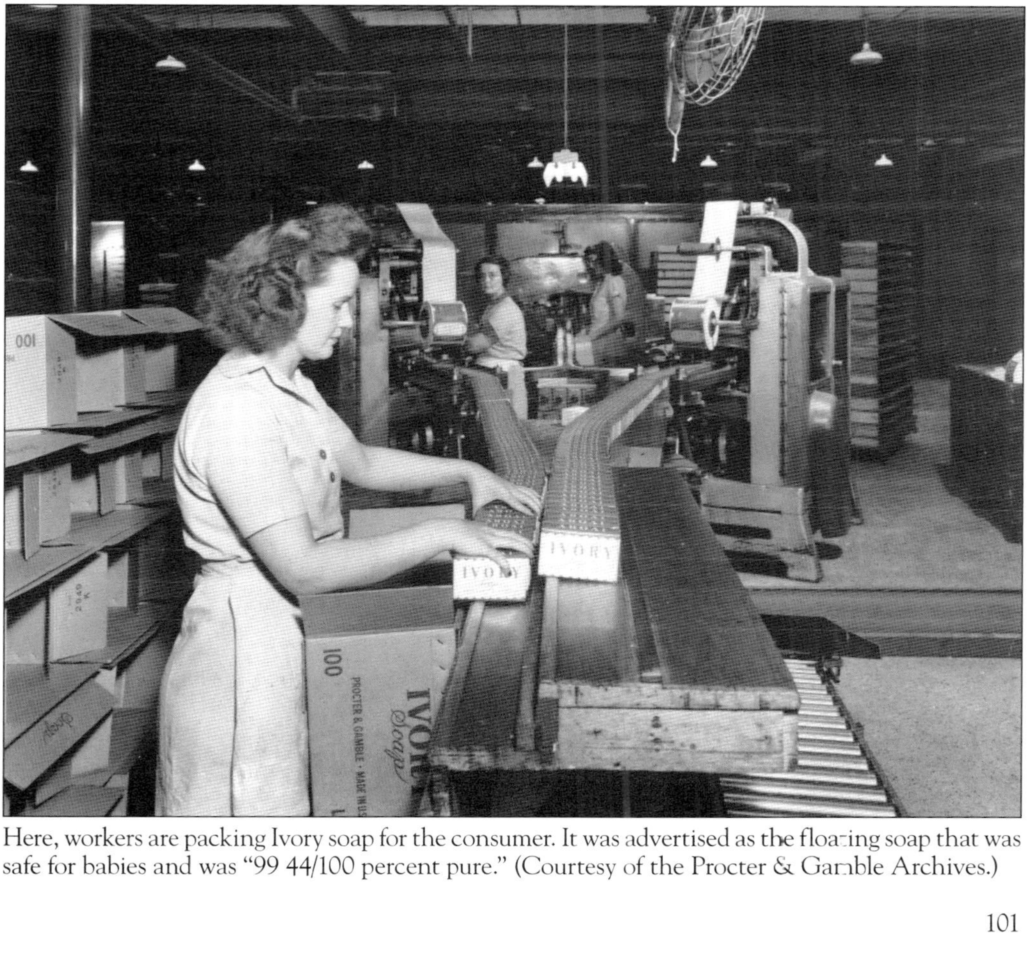

Here, workers are packing Ivory soap for the consumer. It was advertised as the floating soap that was safe for babies and was "99 44/100 percent pure." (Courtesy of the Procter & Gamble Archives.)

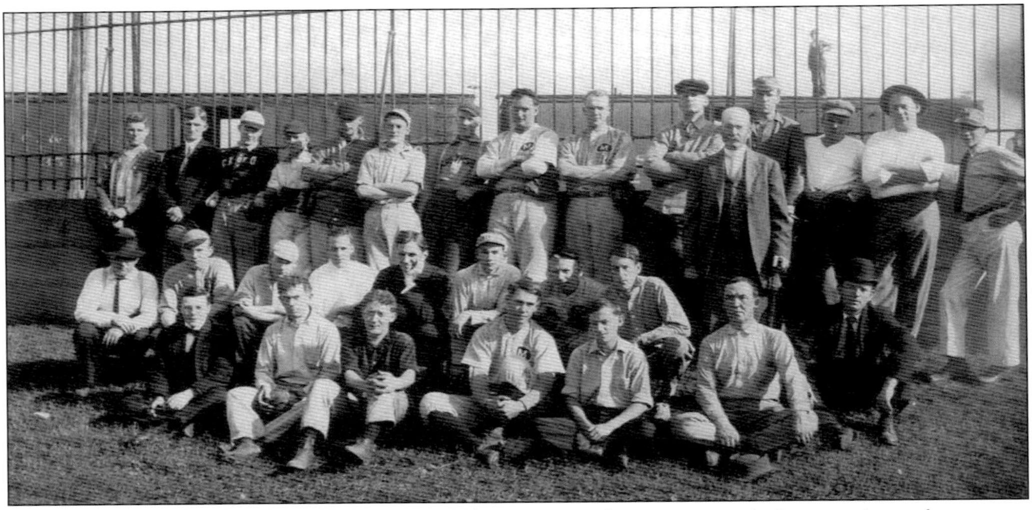

Baseball was one of the company-sponsored sports employees enjoyed. At one time, there were also tennis courts and archery ranges for recreation provided by the company. (Courtesy of the Procter & Gamble Archives.)

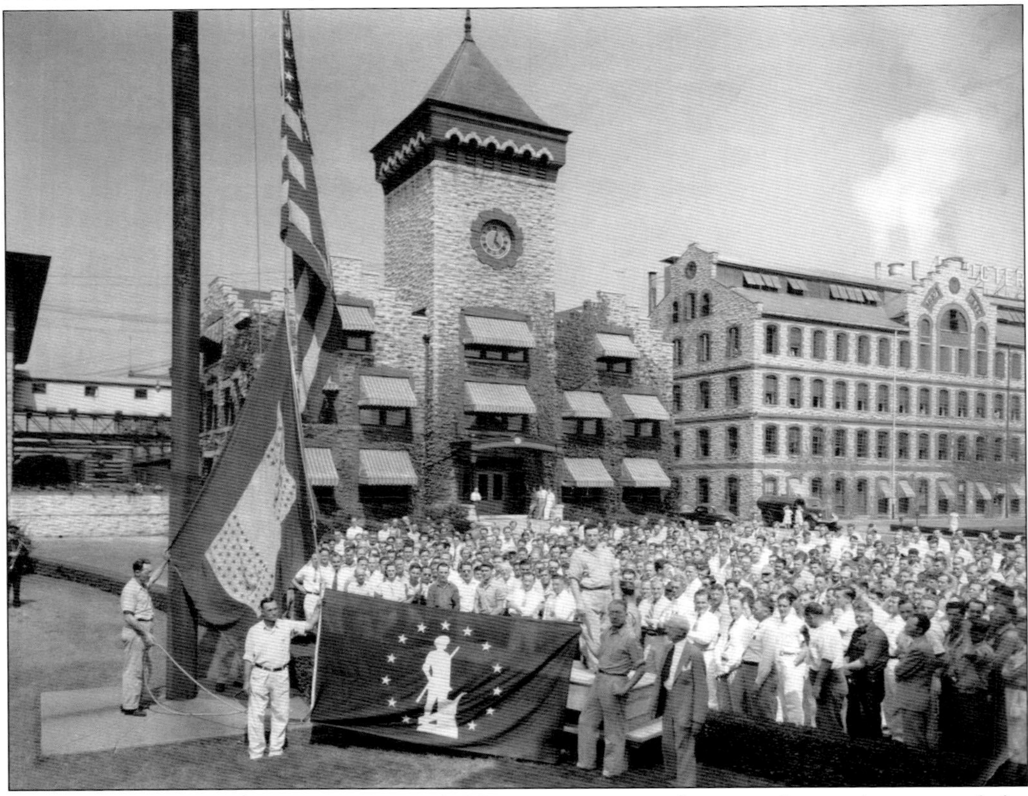

Celebrations for employees were special. Here, at a memorial event, they gather around the flagpole. Note the buildings in the background that formerly had only two stories; two more were added to provide more manufacturing space to meet increased demand. (Courtesy of the Procter & Gamble Archives.)

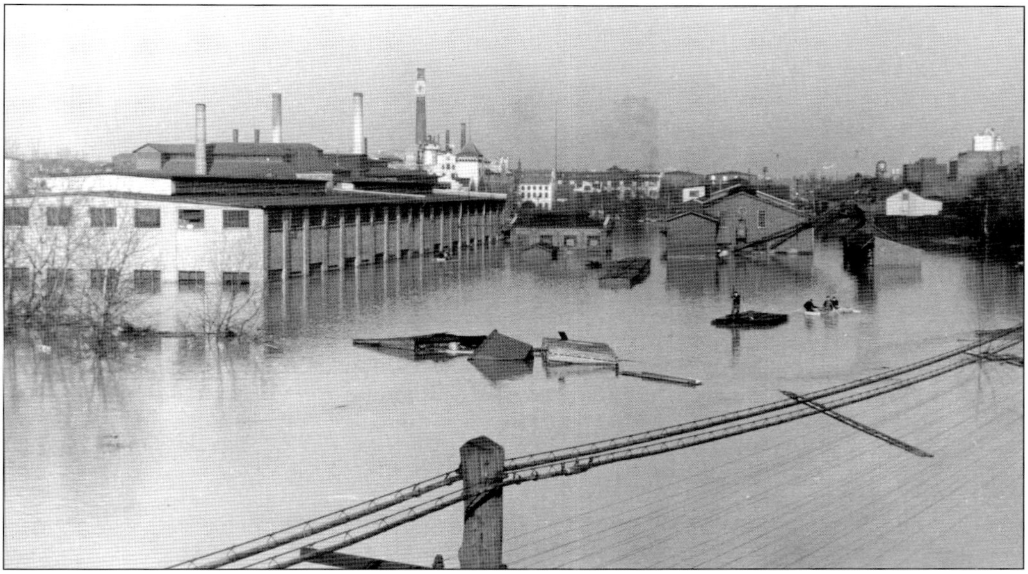

The 1937 flood also affected Procter & Gamble. When heavy rains followed heavy snowmelt, the Ohio River flooded and backed up into Mill Creek and into St. Bernard. Flooding over some buildings and up to the second story of others, Ivory soap was found floating on the second floor of one building. (Courtesy of the Procter & Gamble Archives.)

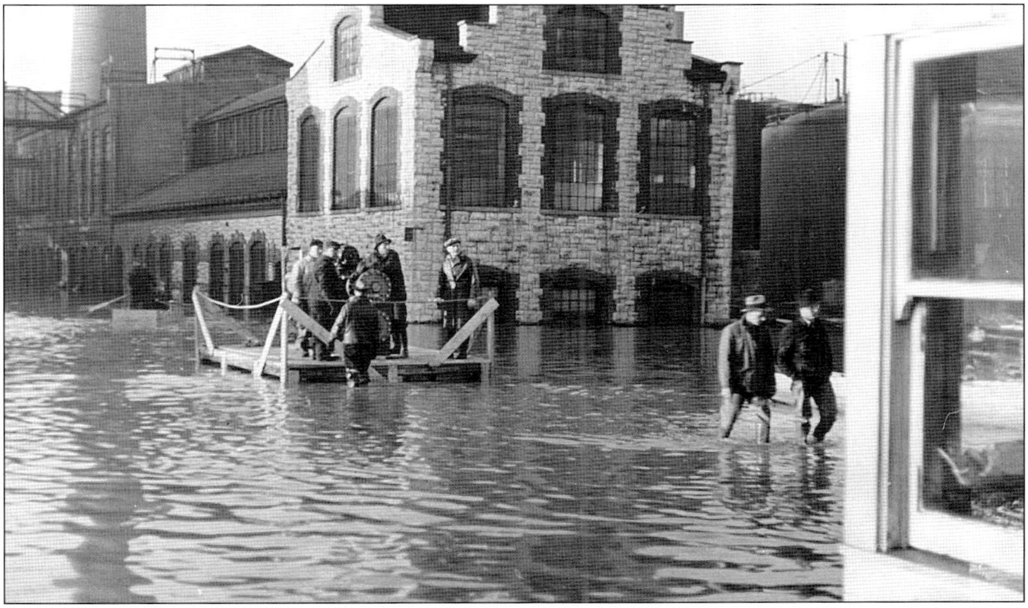

To the rescue! Dedicated employees came to make sure boilers and products survived the flood. (Courtesy of the Procter & Gamble Archives.)

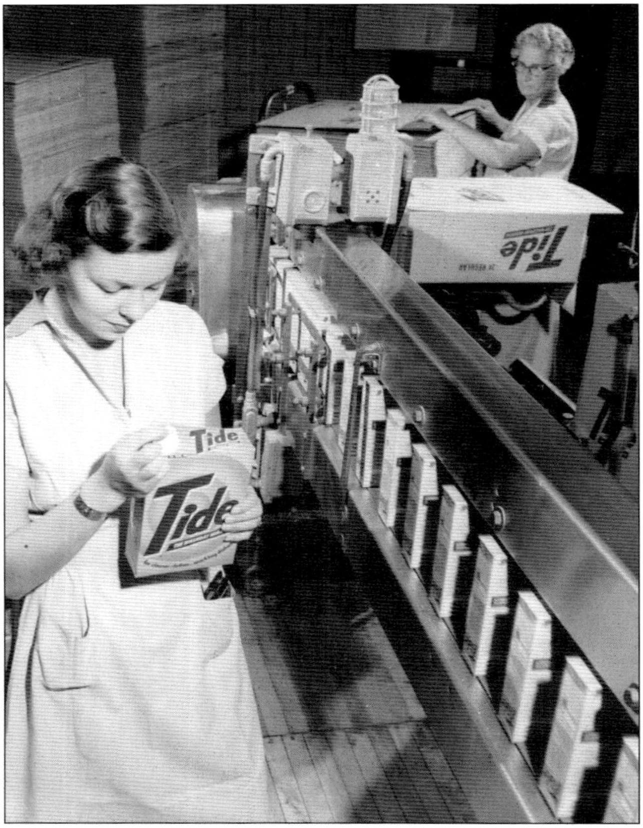

Synthetic detergents became world famous in the early 1930s. Here, the granulated Tide is being packed out in boxes for shipment to the consumer. Dreft and Cheer were also featured brands here. (Courtesy of the Procter & Gamble Archives.)

Procter & Gamble had a reputation for outstanding employee relations, especially in instituting profit sharing, stock options, and other benefits for those whose dedicated hard work and loyalty helped increase quality and improve production. William Cooper Procter, grandson of cofounder William Procter, was a college graduate who started as a laborer and became chairman of the company. This monument was erected by his employees as a lasting tribute of their respect for him and his ideals at the plant site in St. Bernard. (Courtesy of the Procter & Gamble Archives.)

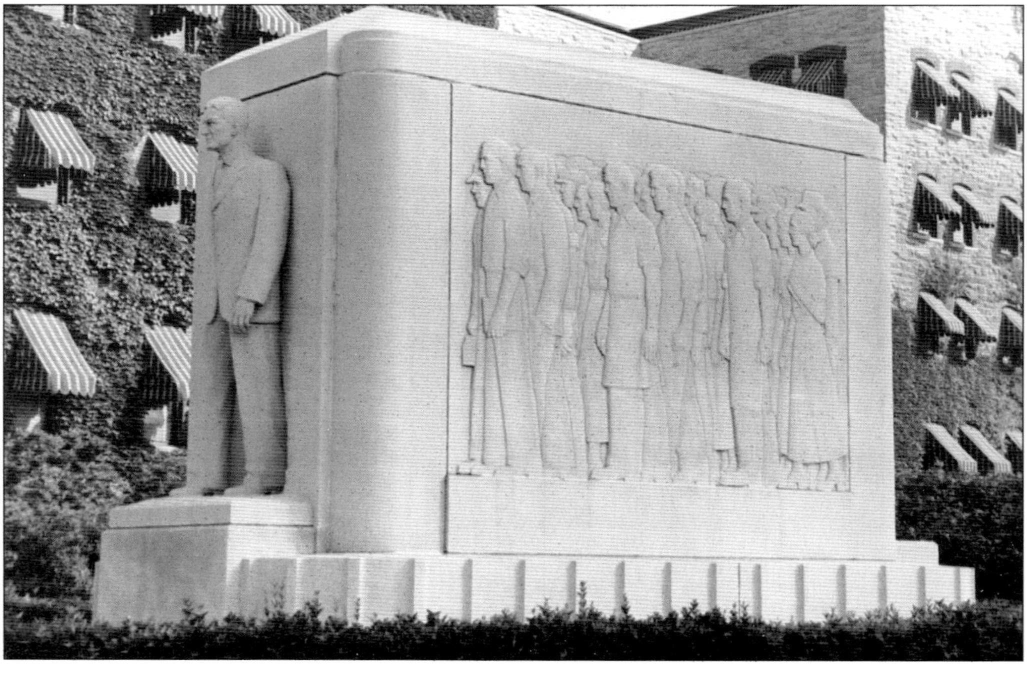

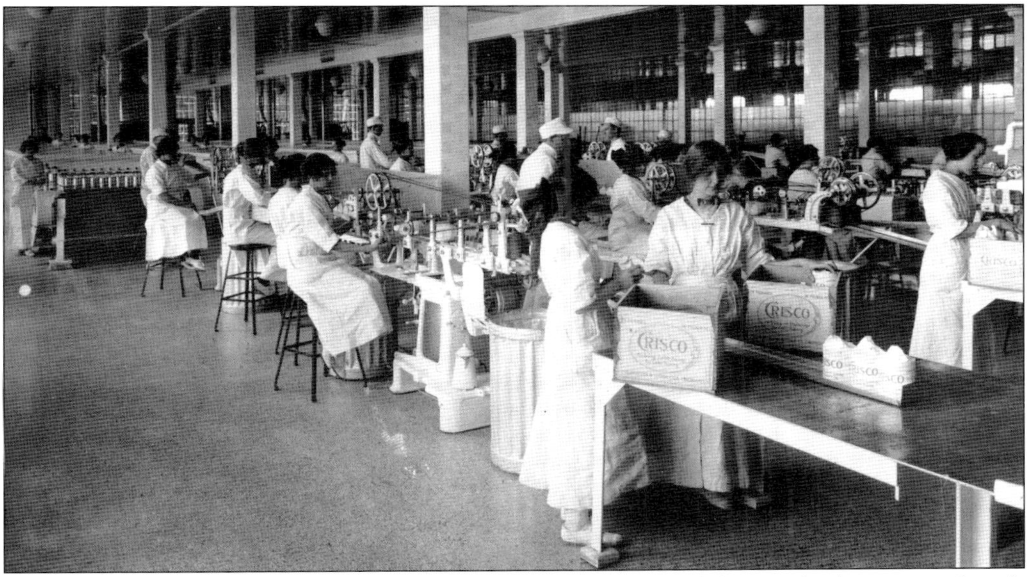

Since its introduction in 1911, the Crisco brand has revolutionized the way food is prepared, with its products remaining as staple ingredients in kitchens across the nation. Crisco shortening was developed during the early 1900s as an economical alternative to animal fats and butter. It was the first solidified shortening product made entirely of vegetable oil and by a process that resulted in it staying in solid form year-round, regardless of the temperature. (Courtesy of the J.M. Smucker Company Corporate Archives.)

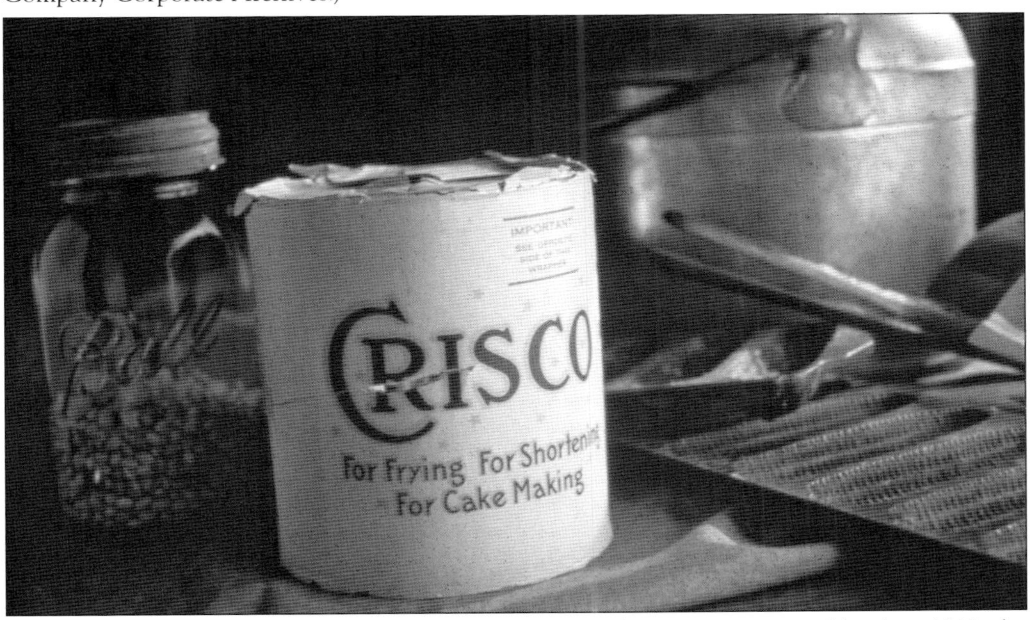

Through its continued marketing efforts—first in print advertisements, a cookbook in 1912, the first home economist tour in 1913, the first radio programming in 1923, and the first television commercial in 1949—the Crisco brand has continued its growth. Crisco manufacturing remains in St. Bernard, and it is the leader for cooking oils and shortening within US commercial operations. (Courtesy of the J.M. Smucker Company Corporate Archives.)

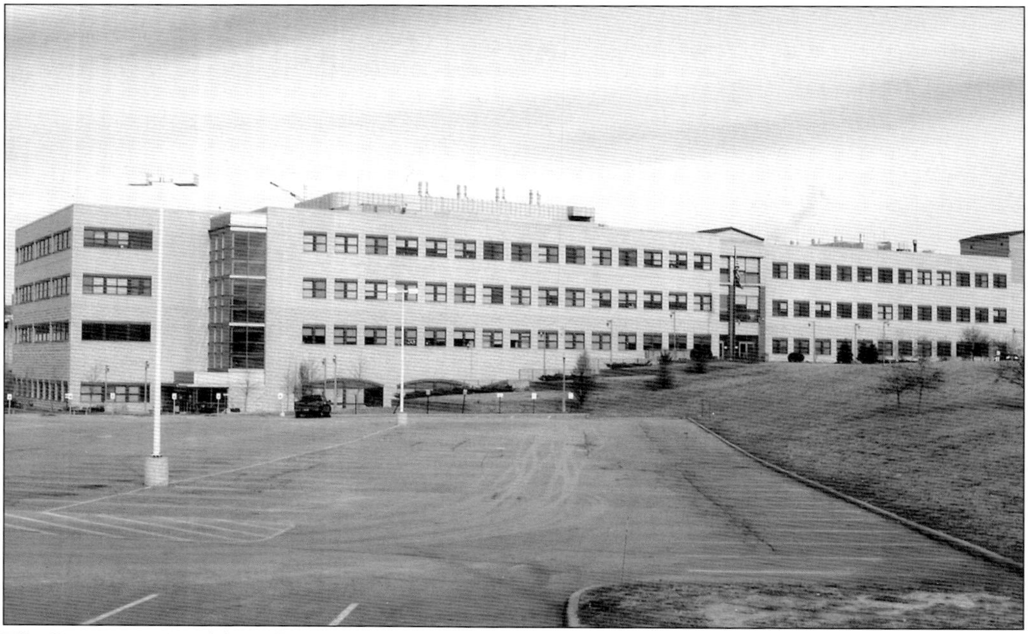

The Procter & Gamble Millennium Building is connected to the research laboratories in the historic building across from Spring Grove Avenue. This is where some new product innovation takes place, testing prior to making a new item available in the marketplace. (Courtesy of Jan Boylan.)

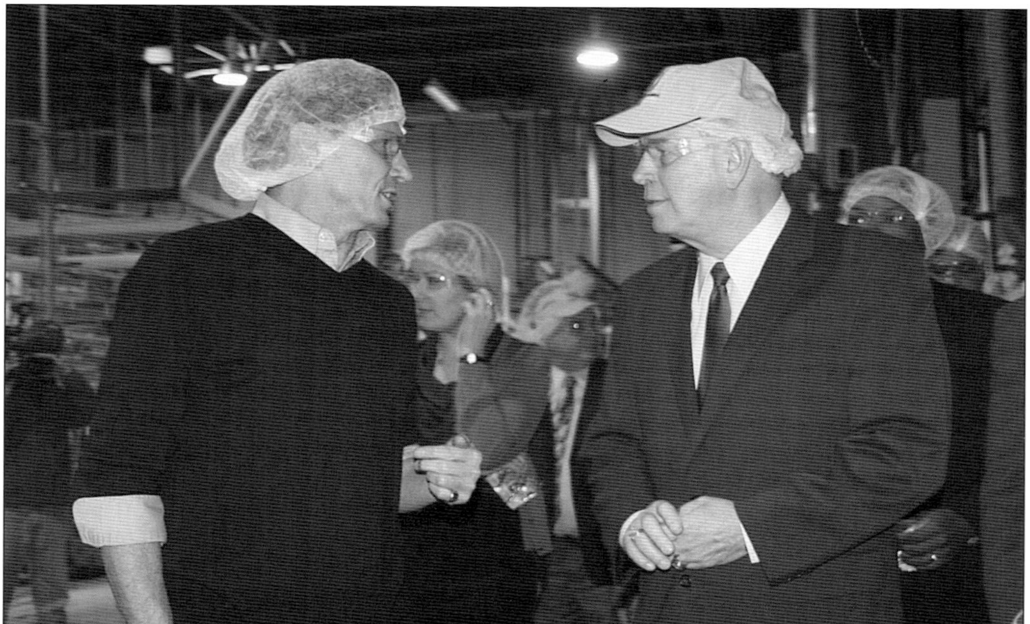

Governor Ted Strickland (right) visits with Tom Wilmanns, vice president of Personal Care and general manager of the St. Bernard Soap Company, in recognition of growth and job creation in 2010. (Courtesy of the St. Bernard Soap Co., Alan Wedgeworth.)

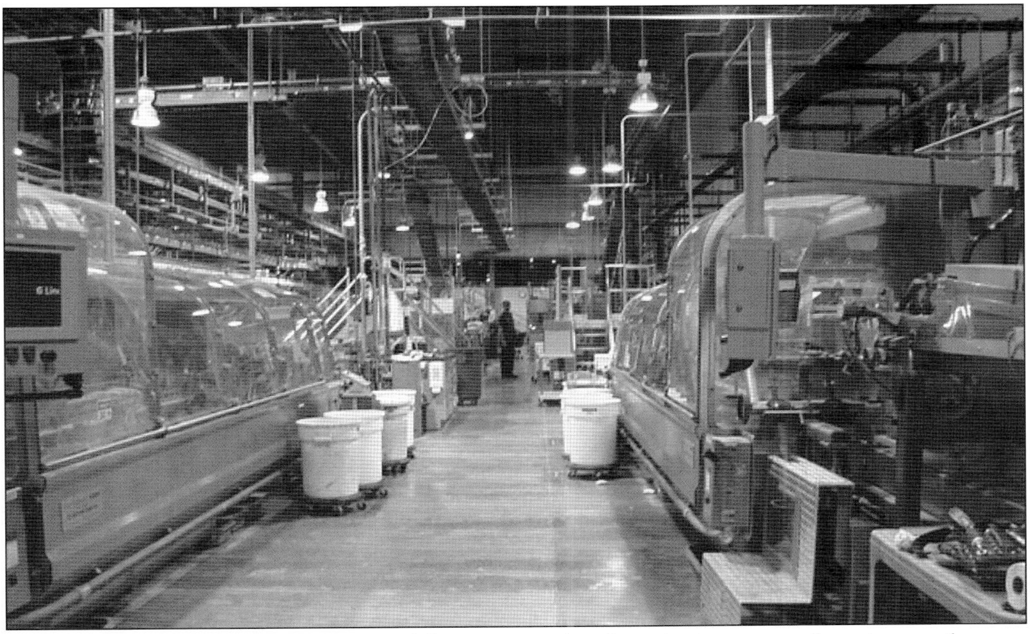

St. Bernard Soap Company has state-of-the art, specialized production areas where it manufactures multiple brands of soaps with differing formulas for competing companies, including Procter & Gamble, Colgate Palmolive, and Unilever. (Courtesy of the St. Bernard Soap Company, Alan Wedgeworth.)

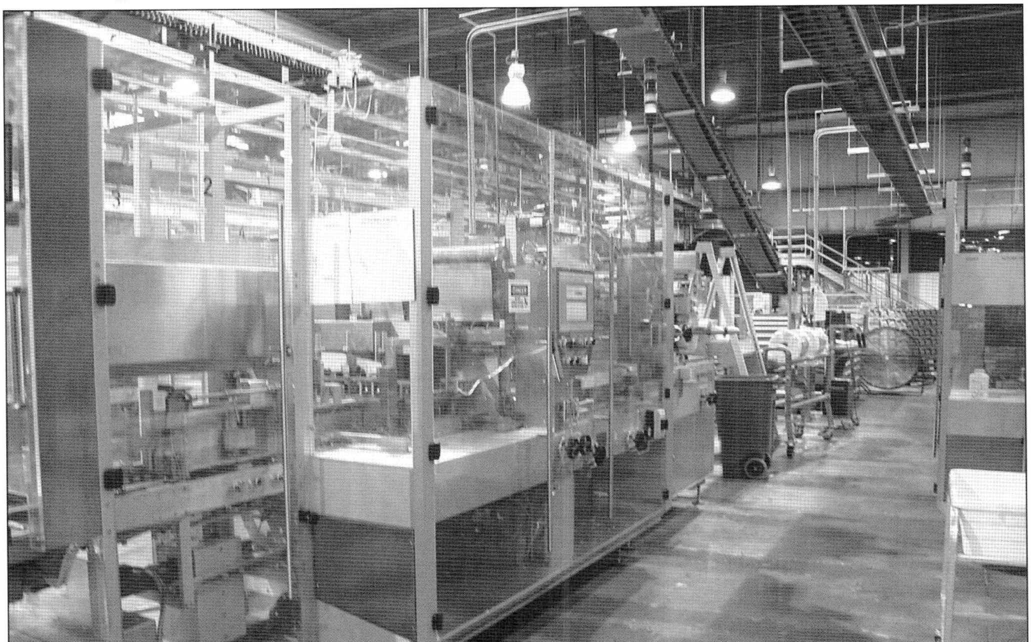

Use of cutting-edge automated production lines that demonstrate efficient and effective output by St. Bernard Soap Company are seen here. (Courtesy of the St. Bernard Soap Company, Alan Wedgeworth.)

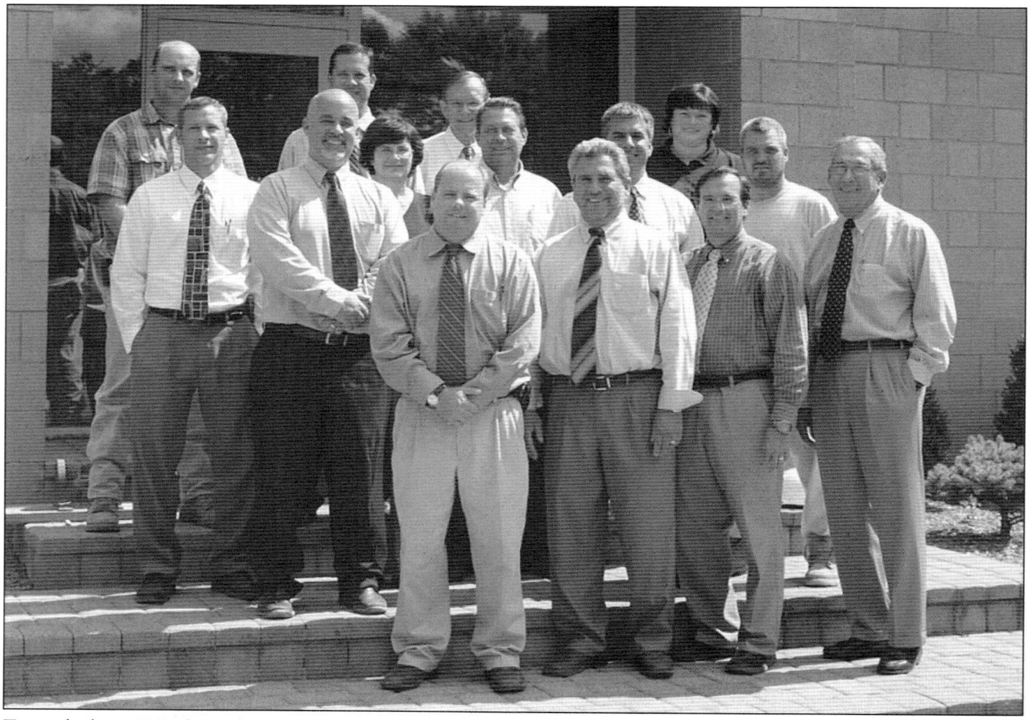

Founded in 1850 by John Hummel in Cincinnati, flooding and other circumstances led Hummel Industries to move to St. Bernard. Members of today's staff are shown here at their office on Oak Street overlooking Interstate 75. Their construction of major stone buildings in the Greater Cincinnati area has stood the test of time. (Courtesy of Hummel Industries, Greg Moratschak.)

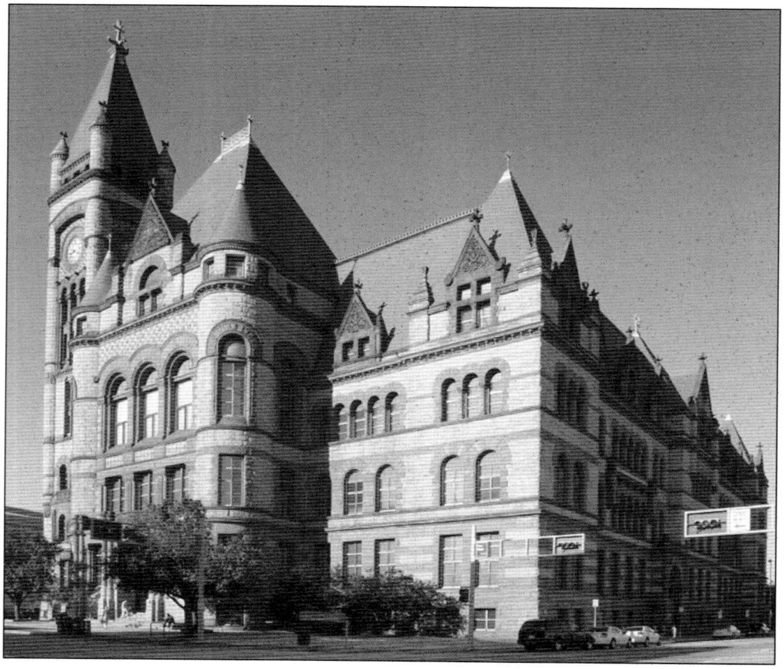

A landmark Hummel project was Cincinnati City Hall. In addition, it has used its skills at St. Peter in Chains Cathedral, the Athenaeum, and Vernon Manor Hotel. (Courtesy of Hummel Industries, Greg Moratschak.)

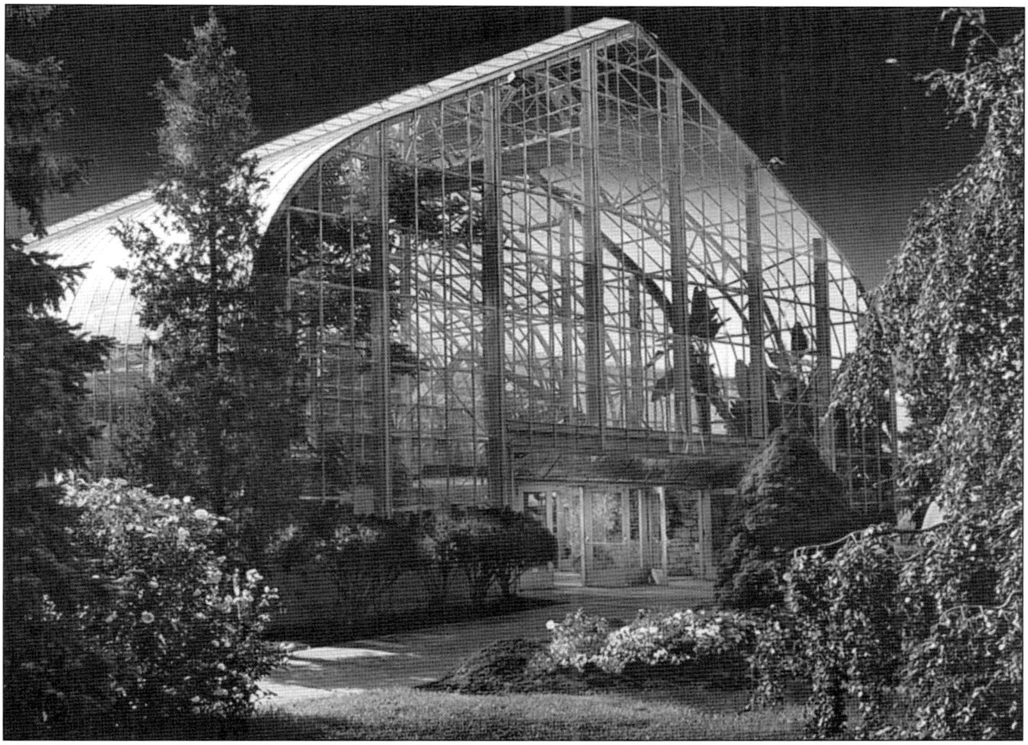

Founded by four brothers, Rough Brothers was sold to Albert Reilly after World War II. Beginning as a hardware shop, they developed garden greenhouses for stores with custom designs for agricultural colleges, individuals, and companies. Krohn Conservatory is one example of their design ingenuity. (Courtesy of Mike Ward, Rough Brothers.)

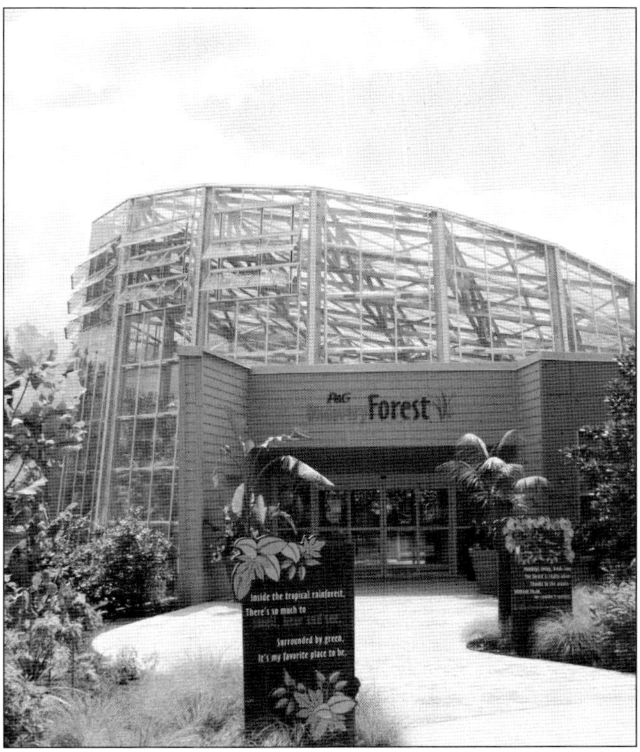

Rough Brothers construction of the Schott Educational Center at the Cincinnati Zoo presents an artistic, practical usage for greenhouse materials. (Courtesy of Mike Ward, Rough Brothers.)

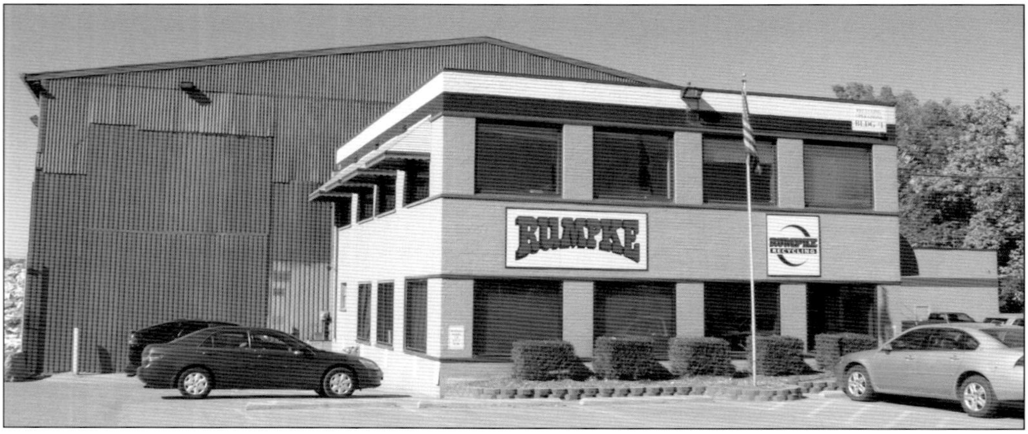

Here are the offices of Rumpke Recycling Center in St. Bernard. With consciousness of environmental concerns, this company is important to the community, as well as to the region. (Courtesy of Rumpke Recycling Center.)

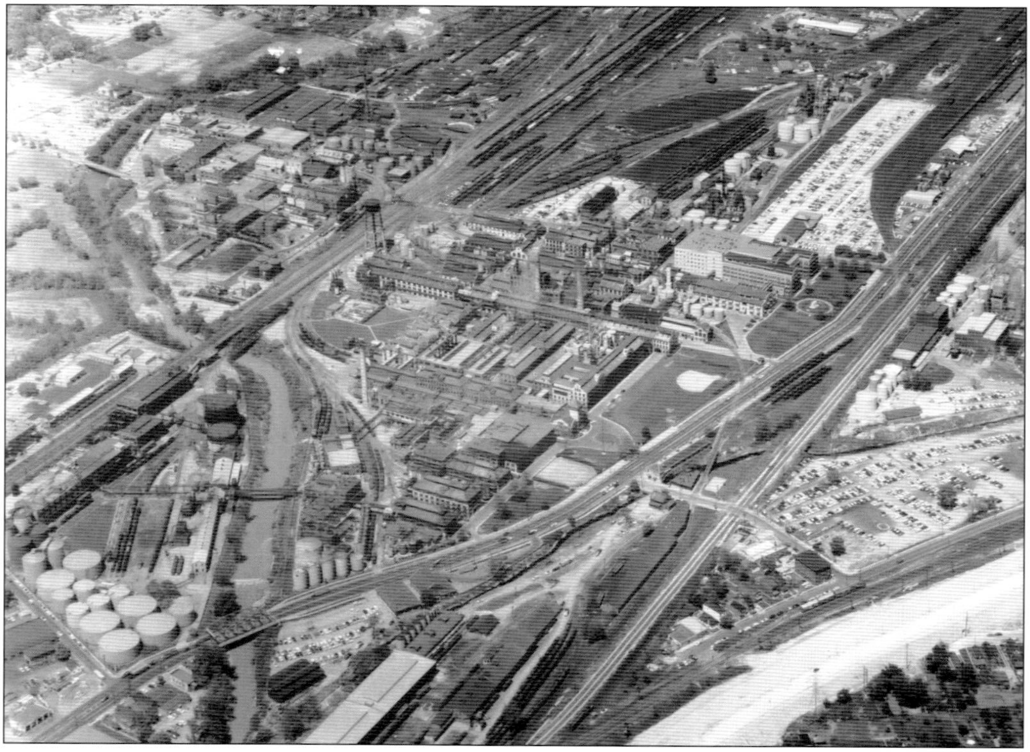
Primarily in the Procter & Gamble area, this c. 1948 overview of the industry shows the value of transportation by road and rail. (Courtesy of the Procter & Gamble Archives.)

Nine

Government of the People, by the People, for the People

Millcreek Township legislators, including John Ludlow, helped establish early government. The influx of German settlers took leadership roles to meet growing community needs. A rising population brought village incorporation in 1878 and the beginnings of new safety, service, and maintenance departments. Competing volunteer hose reel houses provided fire protection, and lampposts were constructed and a lamplighter was hired. In 1895, St. Bernard's water works and light plant assured that local needs were met without dependence on Cincinnati. In 1912, city incorporation brought St. Bernard, Ludlow Grove, and Ivorydale areas together to create the borders. With paid police and fire departments, elected officials worked to construct the community and opportunities. City leaders made a point of working with businesses, industries, and residents to make the face of St. Bernard attractive, as well as a prime location for viable investment. Legislation was created to permit closure of the light plant when Interstate 75 bisected the community; city buildings had to be moved that changed the city's footprint.

In 1985, *Cincinnati Magazine* rated St. Bernard no. 3 of Cincinnati's suburbs, as well as the "most underrated suburb, and third best of 48 communities for city services." This was made possible by a great location, including a strong local tax base overseen by the tax department. The police and fire departments mix of training, accreditation, and long-term service provide excellent response in an emergency. Specialized courses, coupled with team training by local corporate fire personnel necessary in a city with so many chemical plants, have provided a key to safety in the workplace. Nearby communities benefit from the city's mutual aid agreements, and a neighborhood watch brings individuals together to learn about community safety.

The service department takes pride in keeping the city manicured with parks and streets cleared of snow, ice, leaves, dirt, and debris. Twice-a-week garbage collection and recycling keep the city green. The paving of streets and the maintenance of sewers and sidewalks with upgrades to infrastructure meet local logistics needs. The superior health, recreation, and development departments set St. Bernard apart from other municipalities. Dial-a-Ride and medical transport has been key to elderly and youth segments of the population for years. A municipal swimming pool, ball fields at Vine Street and Ross Parks, tennis courts, and a workout center are available to keep residents fit. Encouraging new business and property maintenance to keep values high are the tasks of the development department. Advantages of the small city remain, even as the local population has diminished. The charter now helps maintain a basic governmental structure to assure that the council and administration can continue to work with residents to meet the immediate needs of today and prepare for the future.

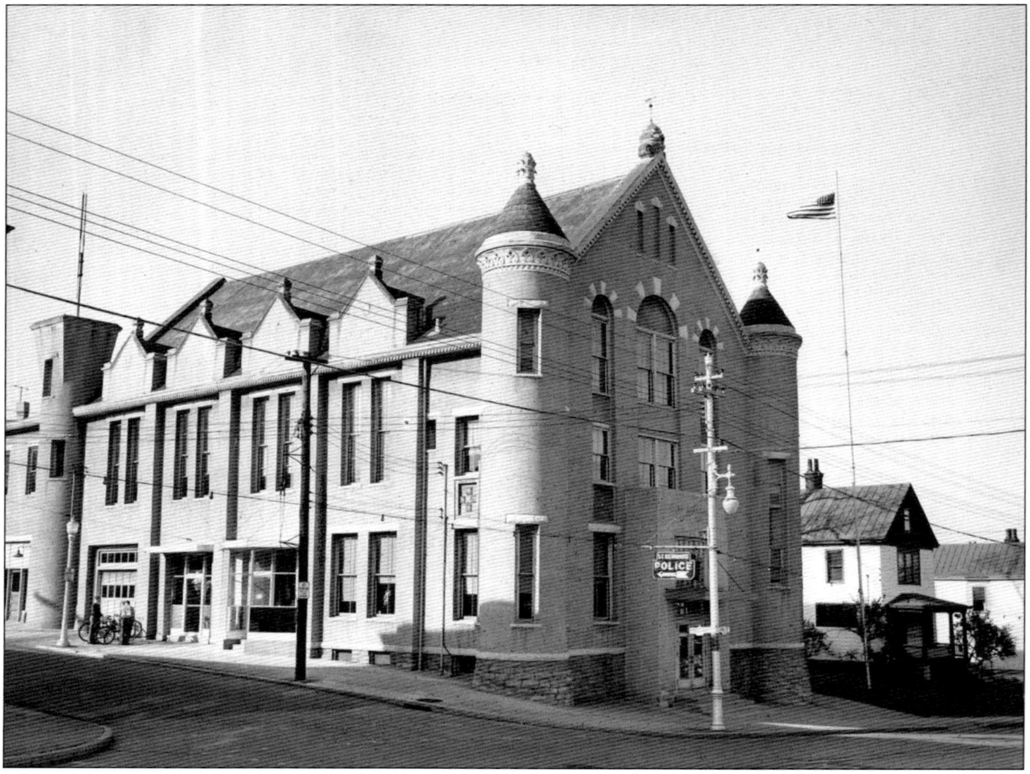

Following incorporation as a village in 1878, government offices were needed. Here, the St. Bernard Town Hall architectural design bears a distinct resemblance to castles on the Rhine—a reflection of local German heritage.

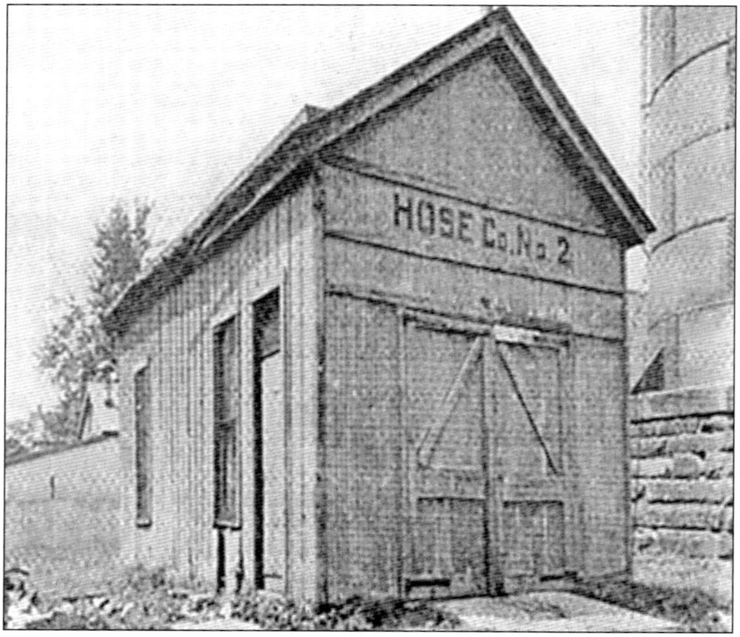

The Nurre Hose Reel house, where early volunteer firefighters kept their equipment, was on Tower Avenue next to the water tower. Two similar buildings on Vine and Oak Streets provided protection until a paid fire department was established in the new town hall.

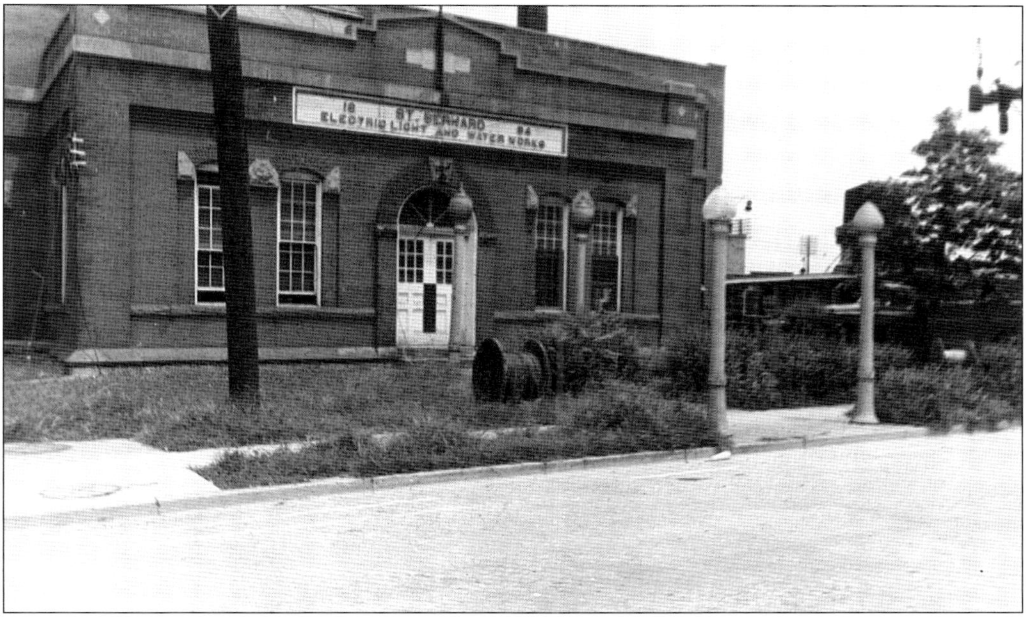

St. Bernard Electric Light Plant and Water Works, dedicated in 1895, was a major boost to the community. It assured independence and provided the opportunity for major improvements. Artesian wells were the water source, and a water tower was constructed where Franklin Park is today. During the 1937 flood, people from neighboring flooded areas came here to get fresh water. In the 1950s, the expressway eliminated part of Oak Street. The cost to move and replace generators was considered too high, therefore, power and water has been contracted from Cincinnati.

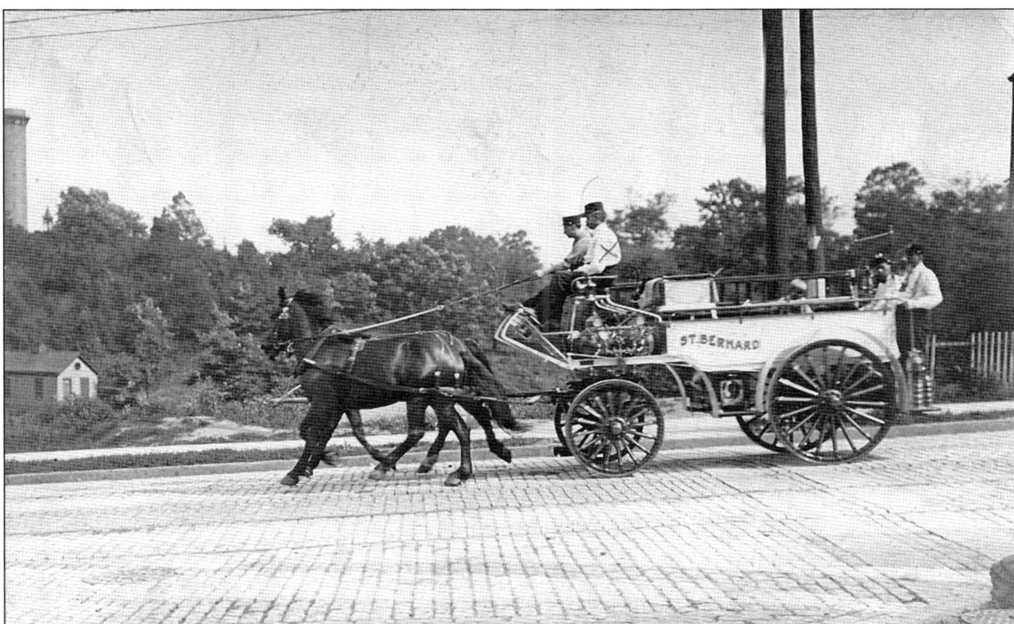

Fire chief Frede and fellow firemen drove the chemical wagon, an early upgrade from the Washington No. 1 Pumper and hose reels used in the past. (Courtesy of Gail Bittner Nurre.)

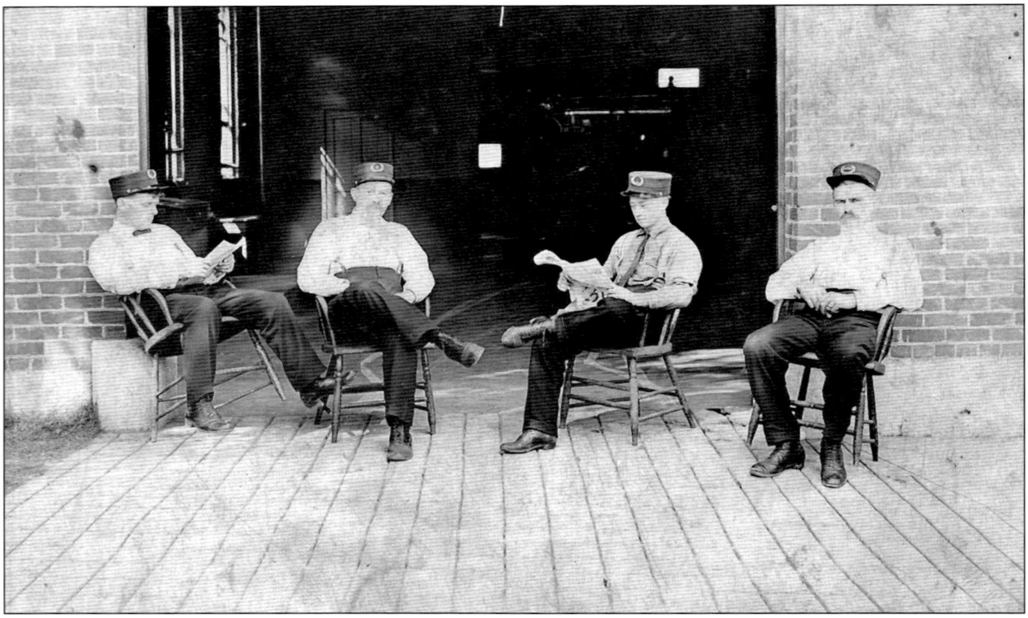

Here are members of the early fire department, including Chief Frede (far right), ready to provide assistance to their fellow residents. The department had quarters at the back of the original town hall. (Courtesy of Gail Bittner Nurre.)

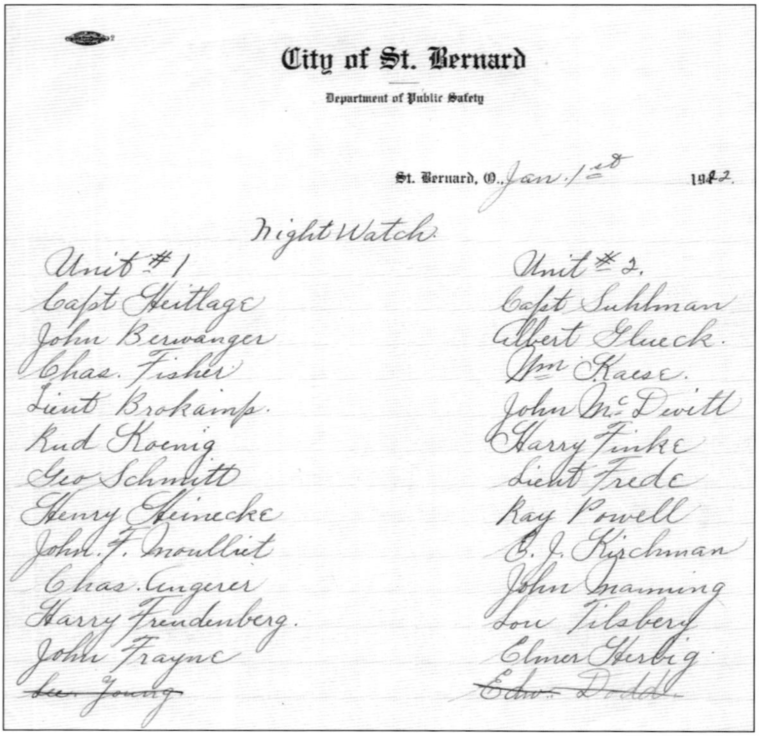

City of St. Bernard

Department of Public Safety

St. Bernard, O., Jan 1st 1912.

Night Watch

Unit #1	Unit #2.
Capt Heitlage	Capt Suhlman
John Berwanger	Albert Glueck.
Chas. Fisher	Wm Kaese.
Lieut Brokamp.	John McDevitt
Rud Koenig	Harry Finke
Geo Schmitt	Lieut Frede
Henry Heinecke	Ray Powell
John F. Moullier	E. J. Kirchman
Chas. Angerer	John Manning
Harry Freudenberg.	Lou Tilsberg
John Frayne	Elmer Herbig
~~Geo. Young~~	~~Edw. Dodd~~

This is the fire department's night-duty roster.

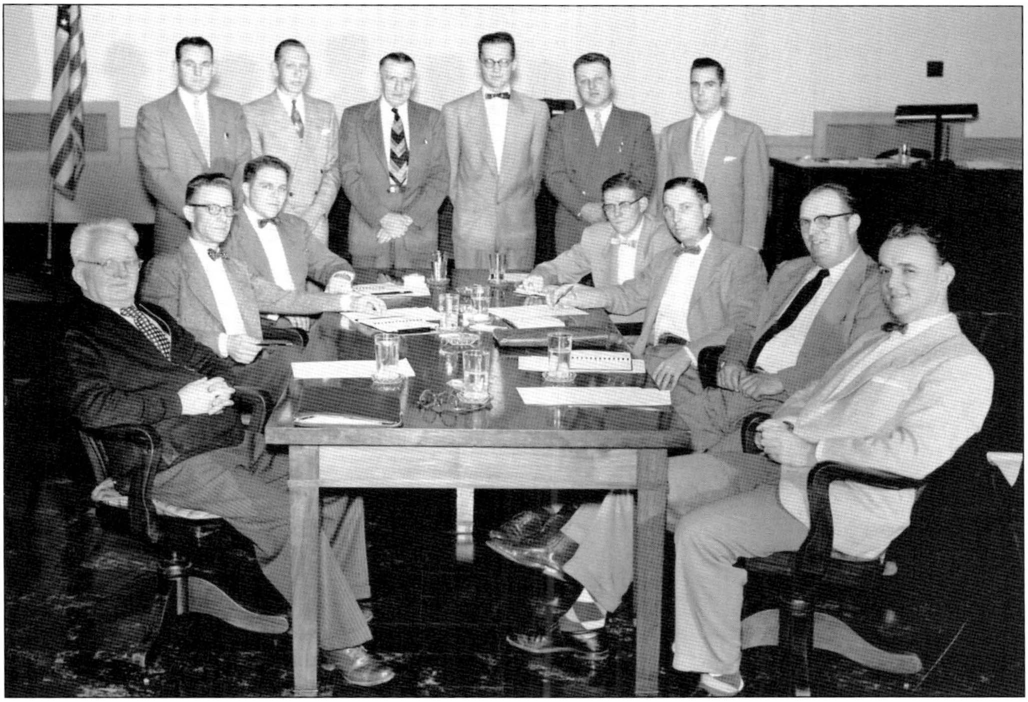

In the 1950s, the city council is seen here with Mayor Frank Pohlkamp (standing in the back row, third from the left) in a meeting at the old town hall council chambers.

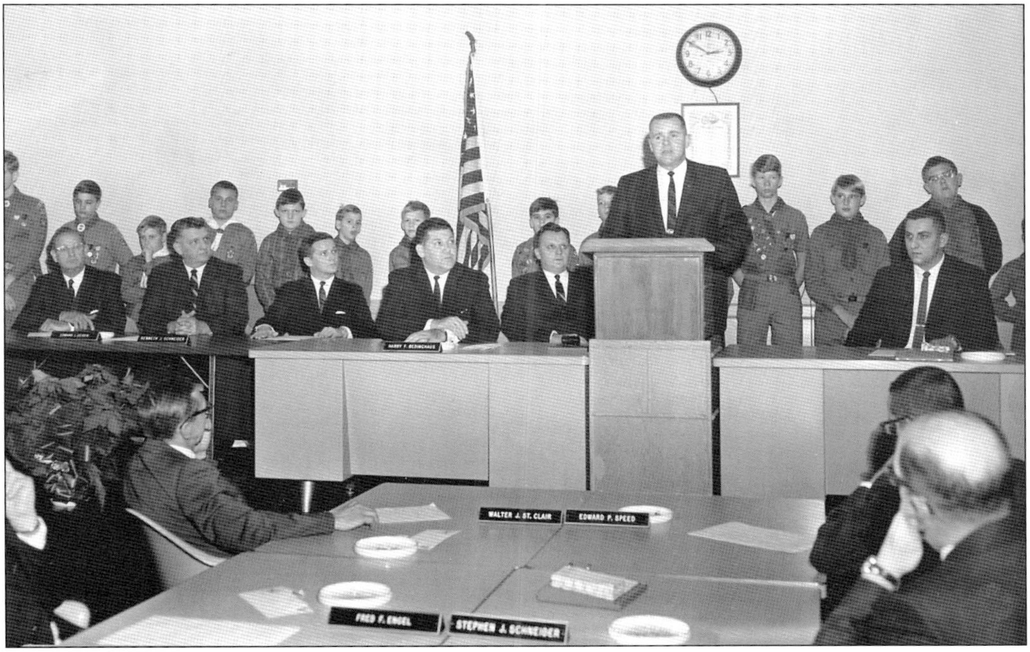

The Boy Scouts and Girl Scouts each have a night to take part in a city council meeting. This meeting was years ago in the old town hall. Scouts help the council and administration give reports as part of gaining their citizenship badge.

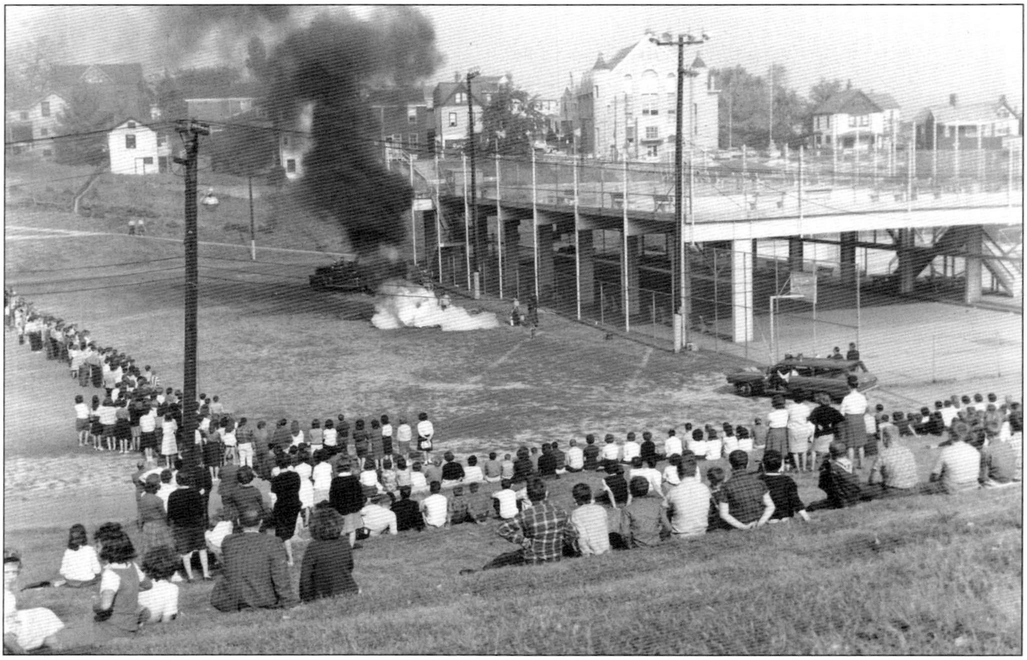

Pictured is a fire-prevention demonstration at Vine Street Park for students of local schools, sponsored by the St. Bernard Fire Department to underscore safety issues. The old town hall is in the background, as is the pavilion, which is a recreation area that used to be flooded in winter for ice-skating.

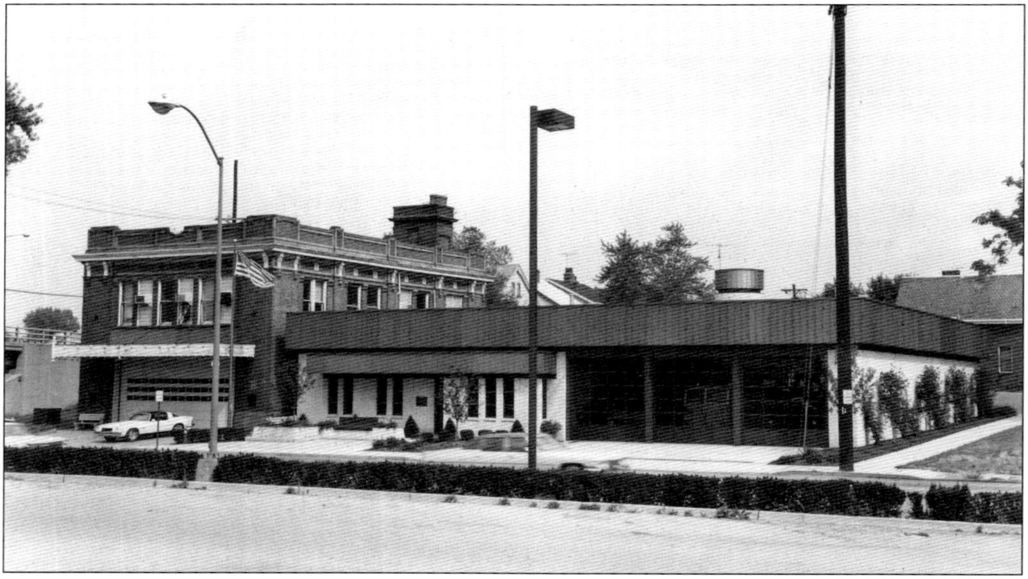

Here are the second and third fire stations. The new station was erected because of construction of Interstate 75, which required space where the former station stands on the left, before demolition. Today, the newer, modern fire station is on the right. This construction required the closing of Clay Street at Vine Street and the opening of Clay Street at Ross Park to allow residents to get to their homes. The first fire station was at the original town hall.

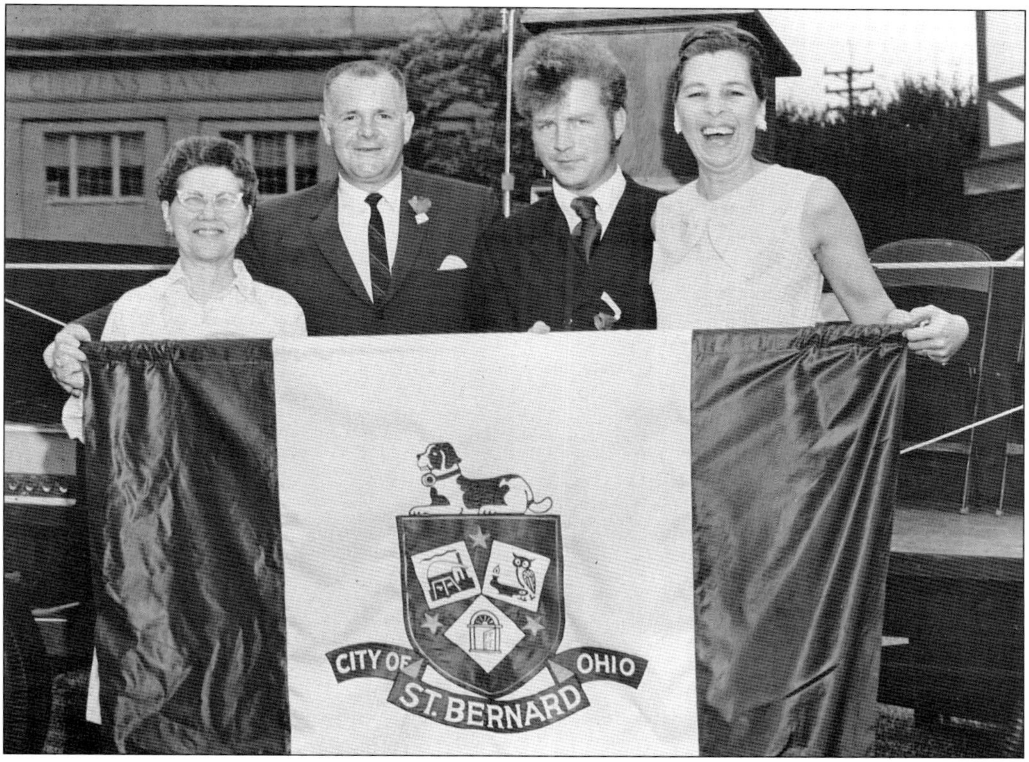

Michael Salt is seen here on leave from the Vietnam War. He requested a St. Bernard flag to fly from his tent overseas. In response, the St. Bernard Woman's Club sponsored a contest for students, and this flag was the result. Pictured here are, from left to right, Alberta Kaestle, the founder of the club; Mayor Charles "Red" Young; Salt; and Carolyn Kuderer. The three central blocks reflect industry, scholarship, and government. St. Bernard was not named for a dog, but for its hilly terrain and an Alpine monk, St. Bernard de Menthon, who was known for his hospitality.

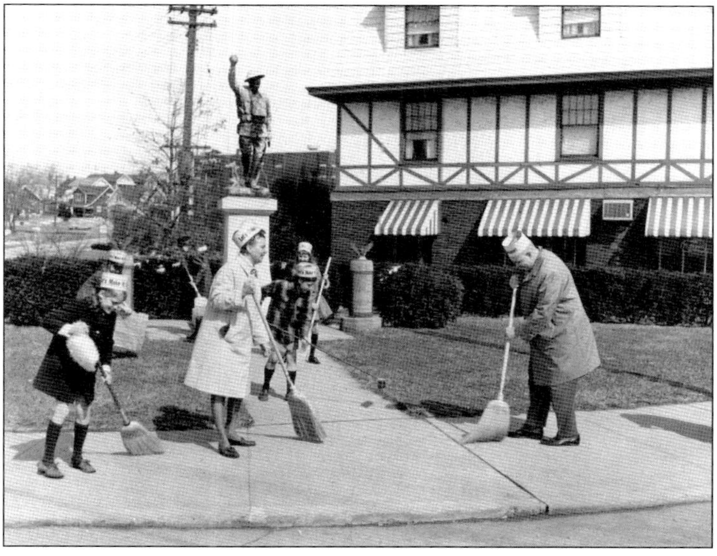

Throughout the years, each administration has encouraged beautification projects—and they have pitched in to help. Here, former mayor Charles Young and his crew work at Washington Avenue and Vine Street. Washington Grill, the former café, is in the background. It was located along the Miami and Erie Canal where the new city hall is today.

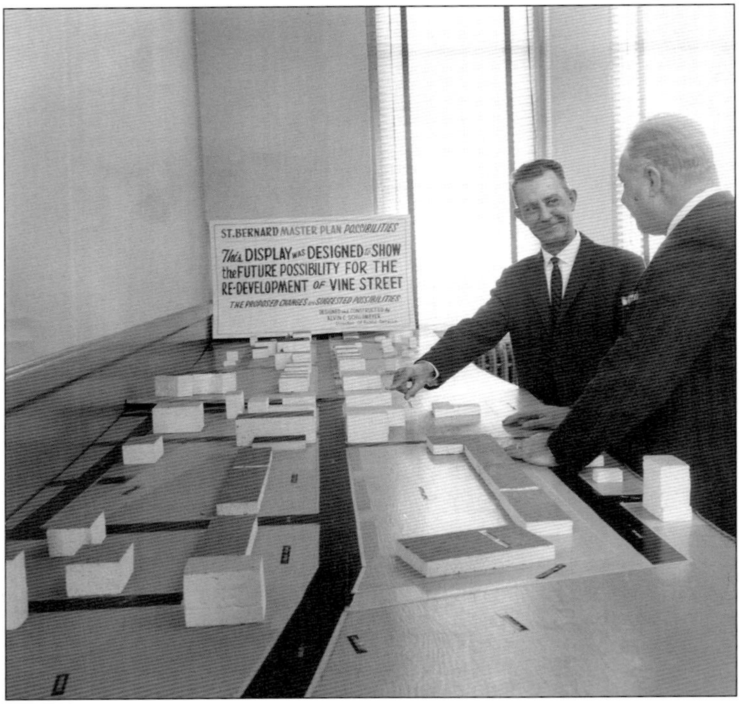

Adrian Kathman (left) and Alvin Schildmeyer show a display of proposed changes with urban renewal. Construction of Interstate 75 bisected the community and brought change to the commercial and residential areas as well. The city purchased properties along the Vine Street corridor to provide new shopping malls.

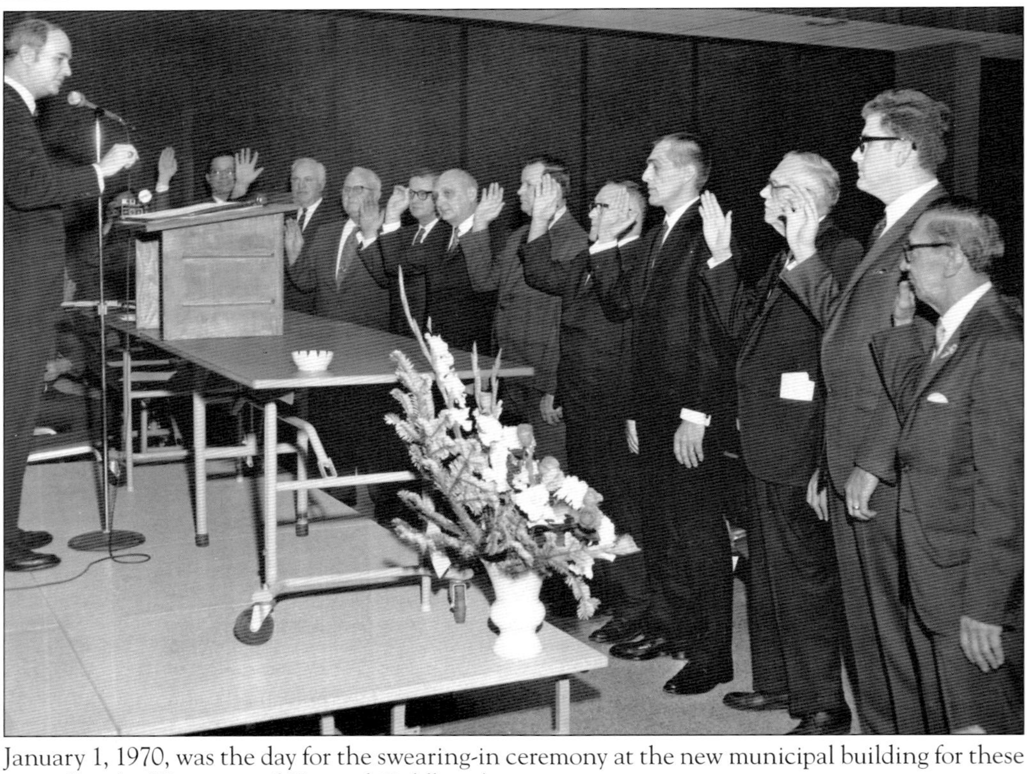

January 1, 1970, was the day for the swearing-in ceremony at the new municipal building for these city officials. (Courtesy of Howard Goldberg.)

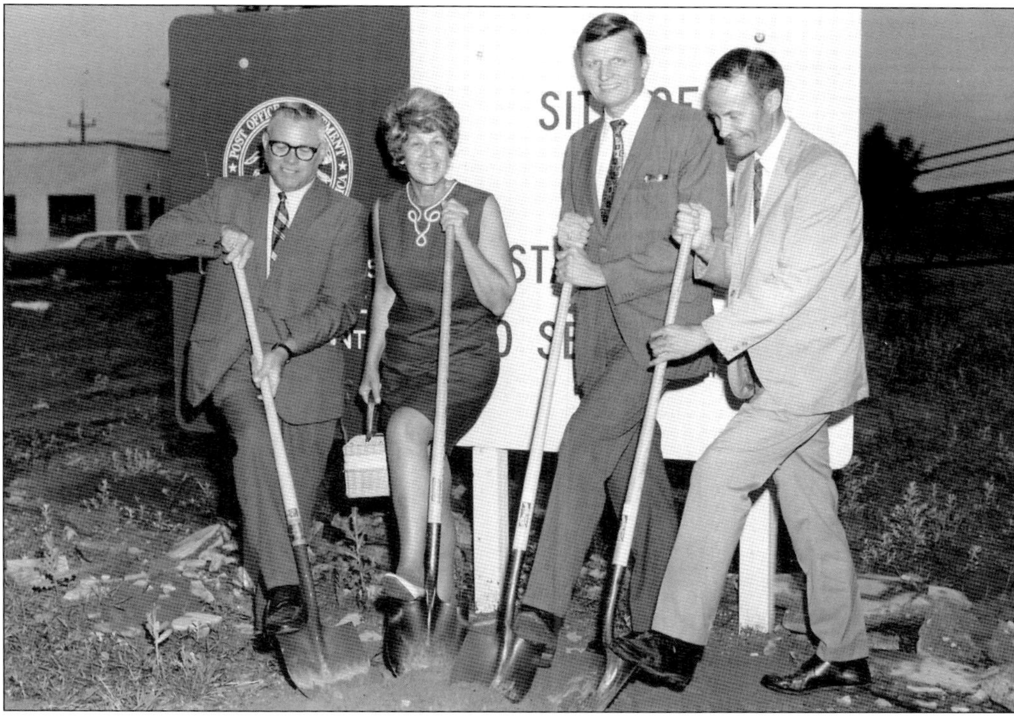

Pictured at the ground-breaking for the new post office are members of the St. Bernard Development Department. They are, from left to right, Rudy DeRiso, Eleanor Berling, Richard Dickman, and Russell Spurlock. (Courtesy of Howard Goldberg.)

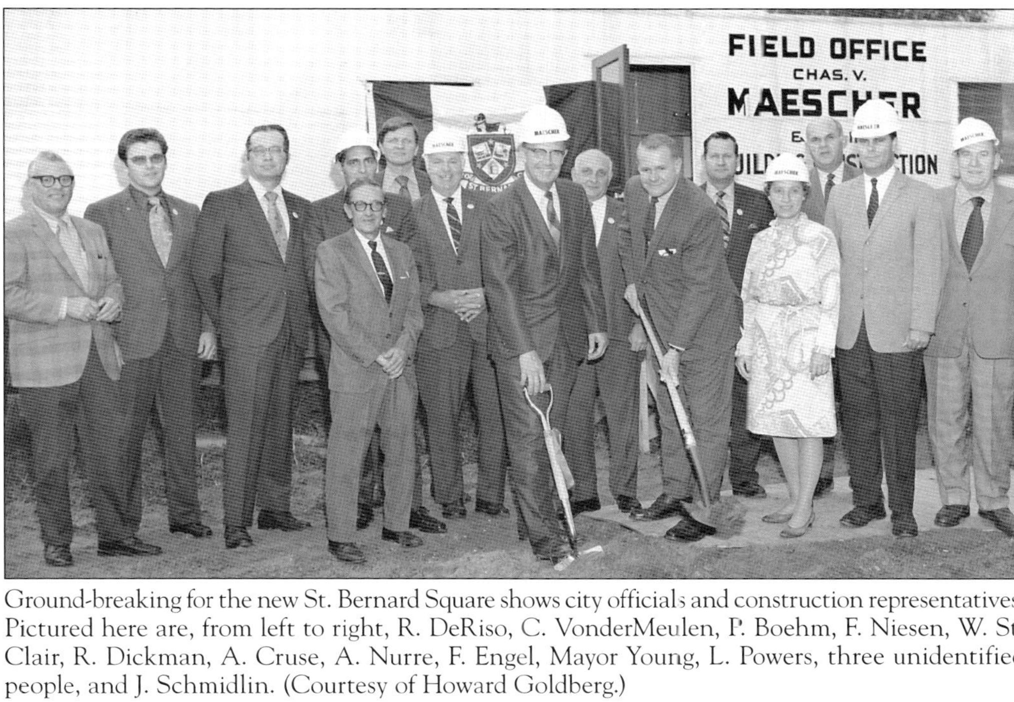

Ground-breaking for the new St. Bernard Square shows city officials and construction representatives. Pictured here are, from left to right, R. DeRiso, C. VonderMeulen, P. Boehm, F. Niesen, W. St. Clair, R. Dickman, A. Cruse, A. Nurre, F. Engel, Mayor Young, L. Powers, three unidentified people, and J. Schmidlin. (Courtesy of Howard Goldberg.)

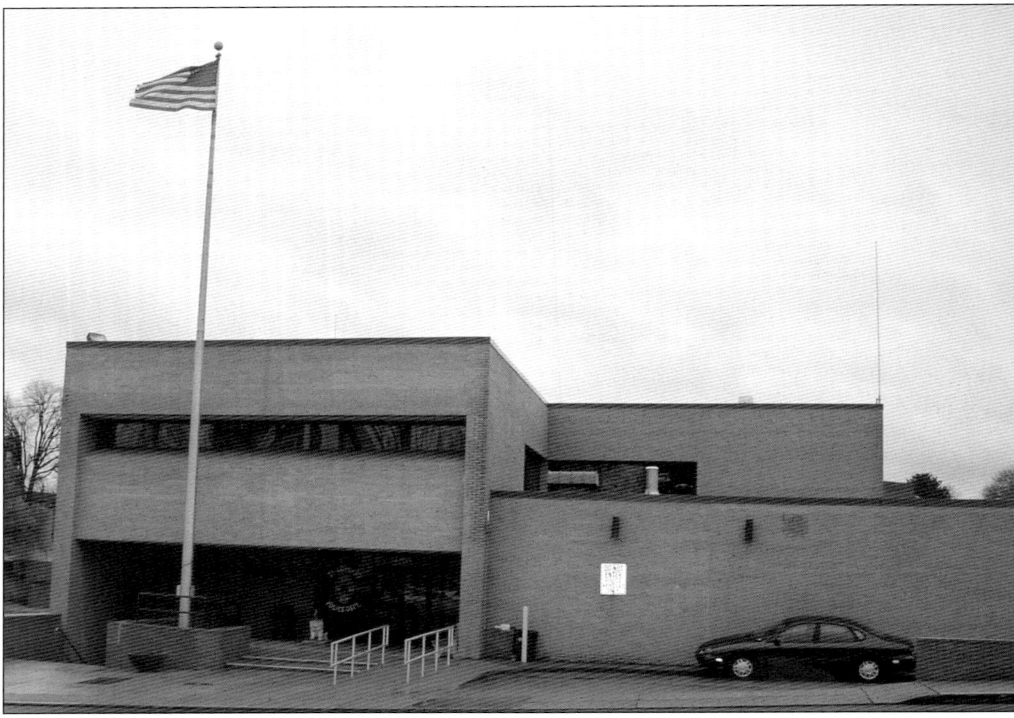

This is today's police department on Vine Street across from the old town hall, where a public parking lot is located today. In contrast to the police offices in the old town hall and later municipal building, computers and up-to-date methods are in place to protect residents and visitors alike. (Courtesy of Barb Jennings.)

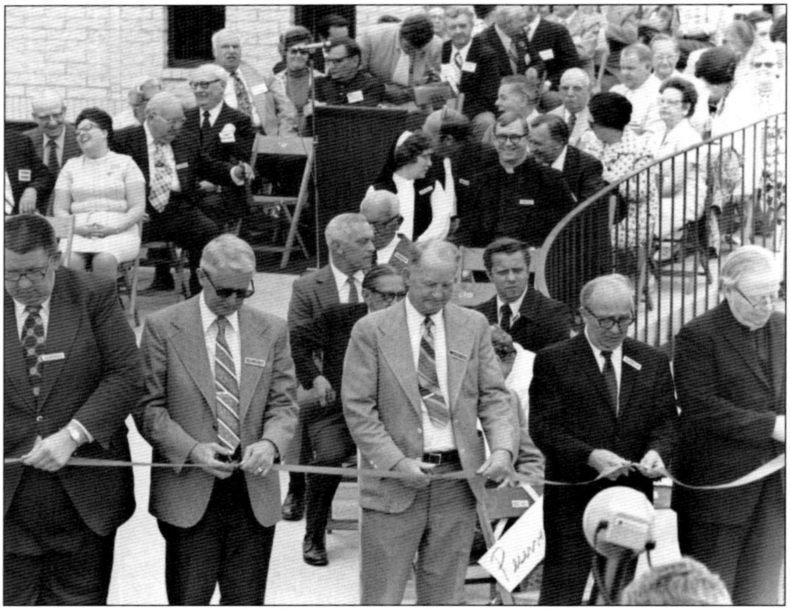

Dedication of the new city hall brought out a crowd of dignitaries. Here, representatives from all local churches assist in cutting the ribbon to the new facility. (Courtesy of Howard Goldberg.)

Barbara Siegel, the first female mayor, served for 12 years from 1992 to 2003. Eight village mayors served from 1878 to 1912. City mayors included Peter Young from 1912 to 1913, Henry J. Nailor from 1913 to 1917, B.H. Wess from 1918 to 1921, Charles Schwegman from 1922 to 1925, George Boehm from 1926 to 1933, John L. Gessendorf from 1934 to 1935, Joseph A. Schottelkotte from 1936 to 1945, Joseph Ellert from 1946 to 1947, George Meyer from 1948 to 1949, Joseph Koetters from 1950 to 1953, Frank Pohlkamp from 1954 to 1961, Joseph W. Haverland from 1962 to 1967, Charles M. Young from 1968 to 1975, Jack J. Hausfeld from 1976 to 1983, Charles L. VonderMeulen from 1984 to 1987, Walter J. St. Clair from 1988 to 1991, Barbara C. Siegel from 1992 to 2003, John H. Estep from 2004 to 2007, and Bill Burkhardt from 2008 to the present.

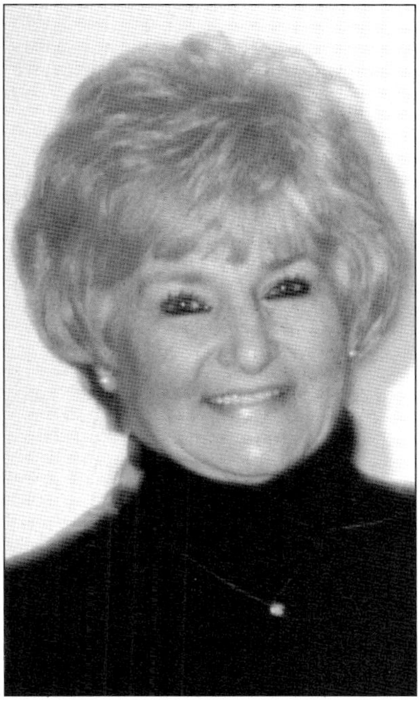

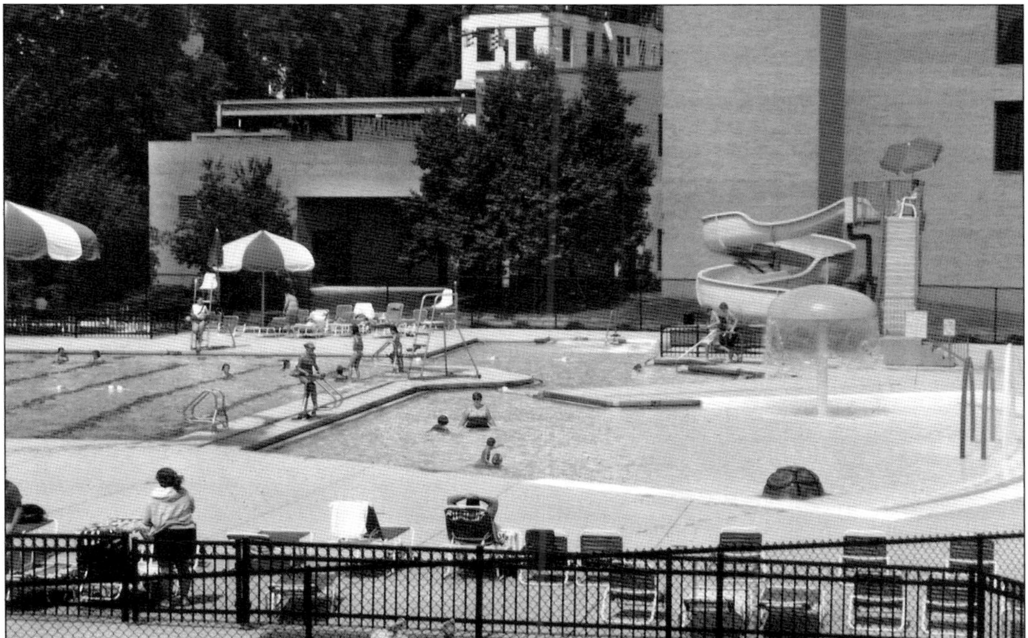

A public swimming pool has been part of a major program of recreation provided in St. Bernard for all ages for more than 50 years. When a major maintenance problem developed under the old pool, this one was the replacement during Mayor Barbara Siegel's term in office. Service Director Ray Schrand, with funds appropriated by city council, modernized the facility as shown here. The St. Bernard Stingrays swim team holds swim meets here, and residents enjoy the benefits during the summer. (Courtesy of Jan Boylan.)

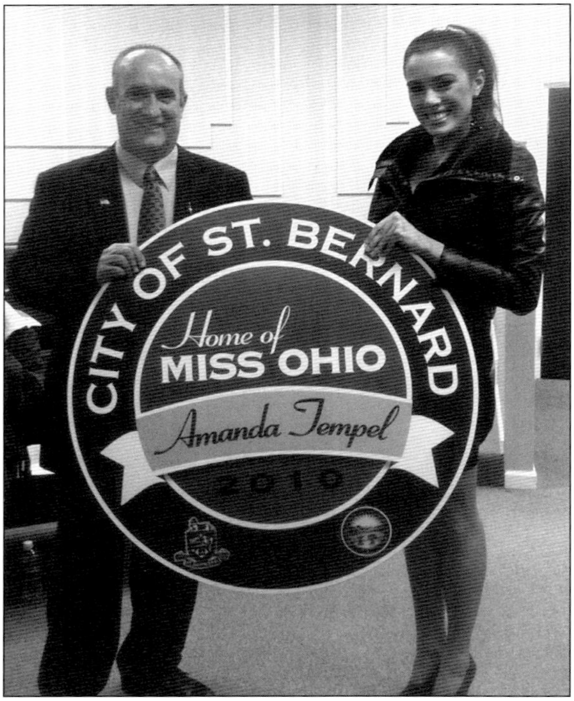

Mayor Bill Burkhardt congratulates Amanda Tempel, Miss Ohio 2010. Amanda is the daughter of police officer Bill Tempel and Stevie Tempel of the service department and is a lifelong resident of St. Bernard. (Courtesy of the St. Bernard Police Department.)

2011 City Officials

Administration

Mayor Bill Burkhardt and Clerk Elaine Sipe
Service Director Phil Stegman, Foreman Mike Wiedmann, and Clerk Heidi Culbertson
Tax Commissioner Edward Geiser, Deputy Commissioner Leighanne Helmes, and Clerk Elaine G. Schmitt Boeh
Planning Director Paul E. Myers and Inspector Walter C. Moeller
Law Director Kate Bedinghaus
Safety Director Rodney Chatman
Police Chief Stephen Moeller, Clerk Sandra Rapien, and Fire Chief Steve Scherpenberg

Council

President of Council Curtis Walden and Clerk Sue Kathman
Ward 1 Councilman Kevin Meier, Ward 2 Councilwoman Peggy Brickweg, Ward 3 Councilman Donald Tobergte, and Ward 4 Councilman John Estep
At Large Councilman Steve Asbach, At Large Councilwoman Cindi Bedinghaus, and At Large Councilwoman Pat Hausfeld

Health Services Commission Board

Medical Director Jonathan Singer, MD
Health Nurse Laura Schmitt, RN, Sanitarian Robert Evans, Plumbing Commissioner Ron Kneidl, Clerk Mary Carberry, and Recreation Director Bob Strotman.

Ten

What Is the Future for St. Bernard?

No longer the "forest primeval," newcomers have left their mark. By 1912, St. Bernard included Ludlow Grove, and the vision was for a bright future. Approaching the 100th anniversary since that incorporation, residents have seen the result of hard work, including the investment of ideas and money to grow from small beginnings to becoming part of global markets. More than 100 years has shown development and urban renewal. Revitalization of St. Bernard is planned to improve the entrance at Mitchell Avenue and Vine Street up to Roger Bacon High School as a welcome to residents and visitors. From Bertus Street north, the homes are good examples of original heritage architecture that appear to anchor the historic character of the community. Architectural and streetscape improvements are under consideration to set the stage for the future. A city centre along Vine Street from Washington Avenue to Interstate 75 can provide a dining, government, and shopping hub for the city. With a nucleus of city hall, the post office, and Fifth Third Bank, efforts will be made to spark an area not fully utilized. An opportunity for office buildings and green space could add value. The potential for concerts and other events will be considered with special attention to make walking and biking paths at or near the city centre.

The research and industrial area already has a strong private business base that can be expanded to meet greater markets. Many key businesses have a long history of forecasting and flexing to meet the increasing demands of their clients. It is anticipated that not only will this continue into the future, but that even greater innovation is in store.

Opportunities to improve existing homes and create new ones will be promoted. The city will work with homeowners to encourage maintenance of the historic character of each neighborhood. A goal is that new housing will fit into the existing areas to add value for older homes with character, and the newer structures will adhere to the solid building qualities for which St. Bernard has become known.

Volunteers of America senior housing at Ross and Greenlee Avenues may free up houses for young professionals or as starter homes for those wishing to remain close to the universities, hospitals, and industries. Consideration of areas for condominiums and townhouses will also be given. Past vision and leadership has constructed the community that exists today, and the current vision will build for the future.

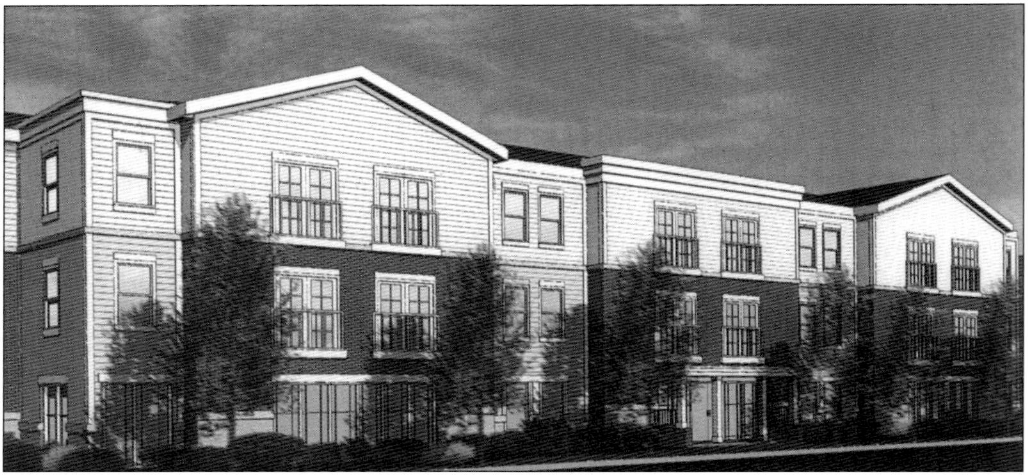

Ground-breaking for a new apartment complex is in the planning process for senior housing at Greenlee and Ross Avenues. (Courtesy of Paul Myers.)

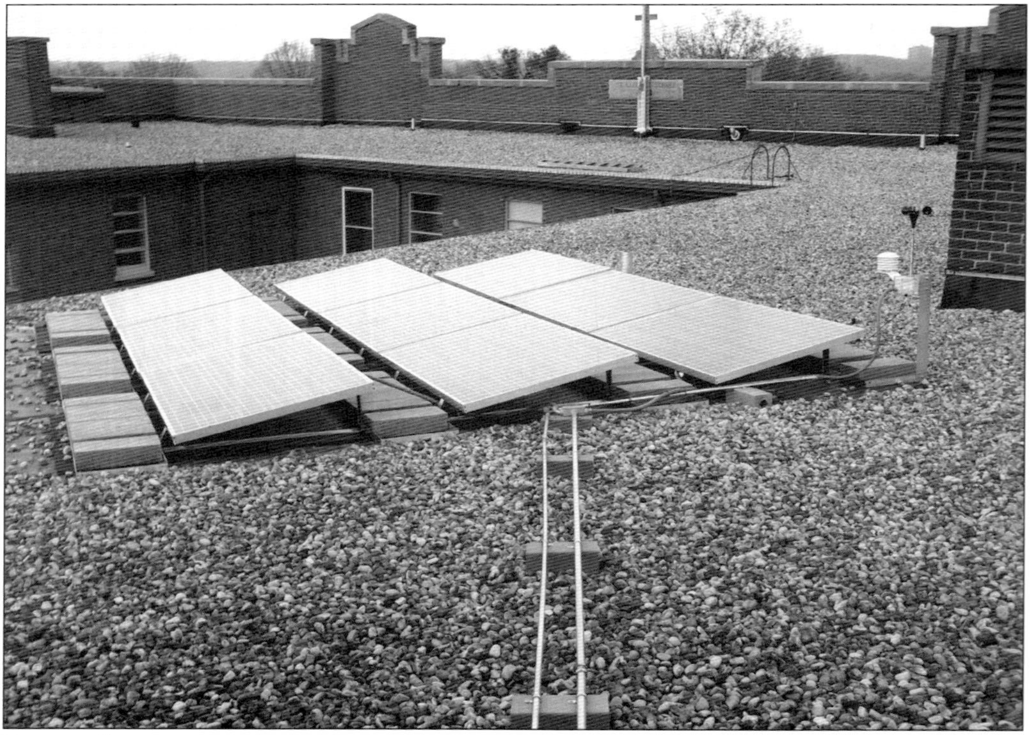

Energy efficiency and concern for high costs may promote cost-saving sources such as these solar panels now located at St. Clement School. (Courtesy of Paula Blessing.)

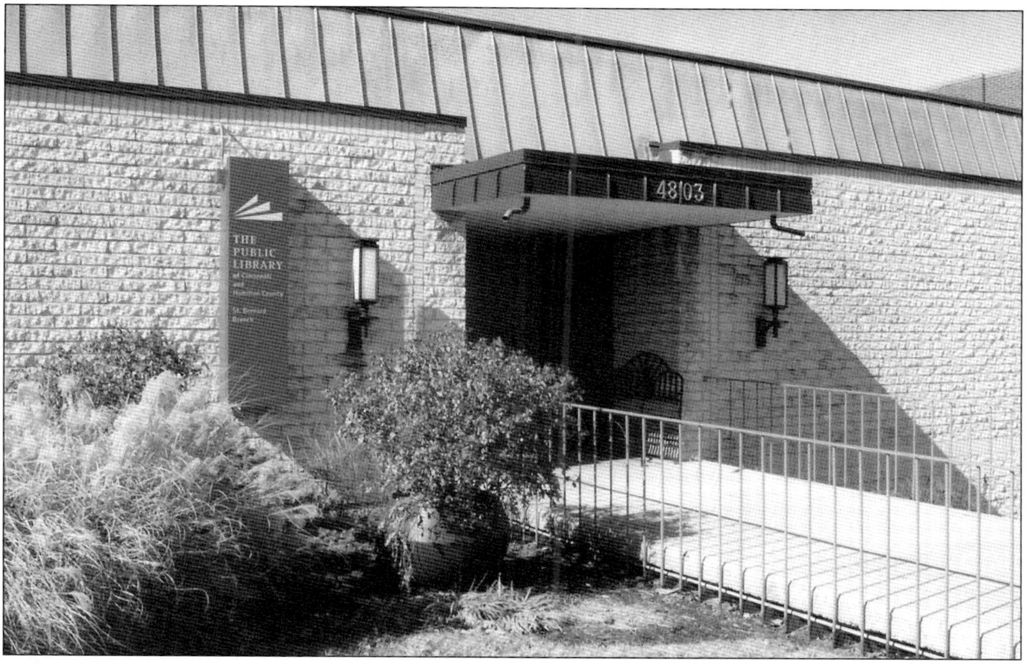

Perhaps the new library will replace the overcrowded branch of the Hamilton County Public Library. It is initially planned for the corner of Vine Street and McClelland Avenue. With universities, hospitals, schools, and businesses creating a need, it is hoped that this new facility will become a reality. (Courtesy of Jan Boylan.)

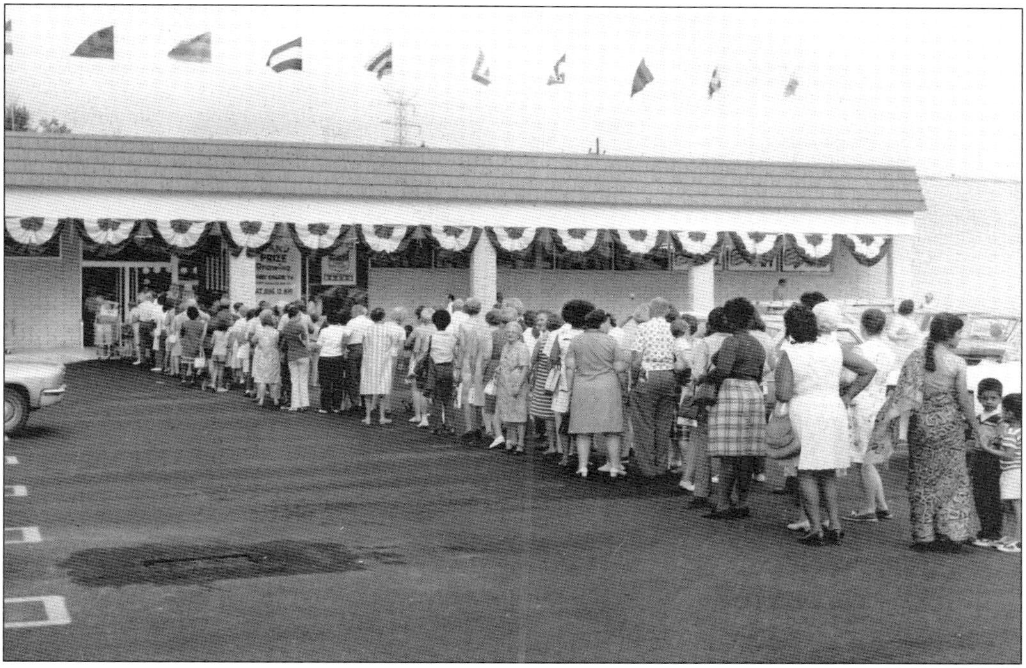

St. Bernard Square was constructed in the 1970s and was a dream for the future. Seen here is the rush of customers at the grand opening of the local shopping center. (Courtesy of Howard Goldberg.)

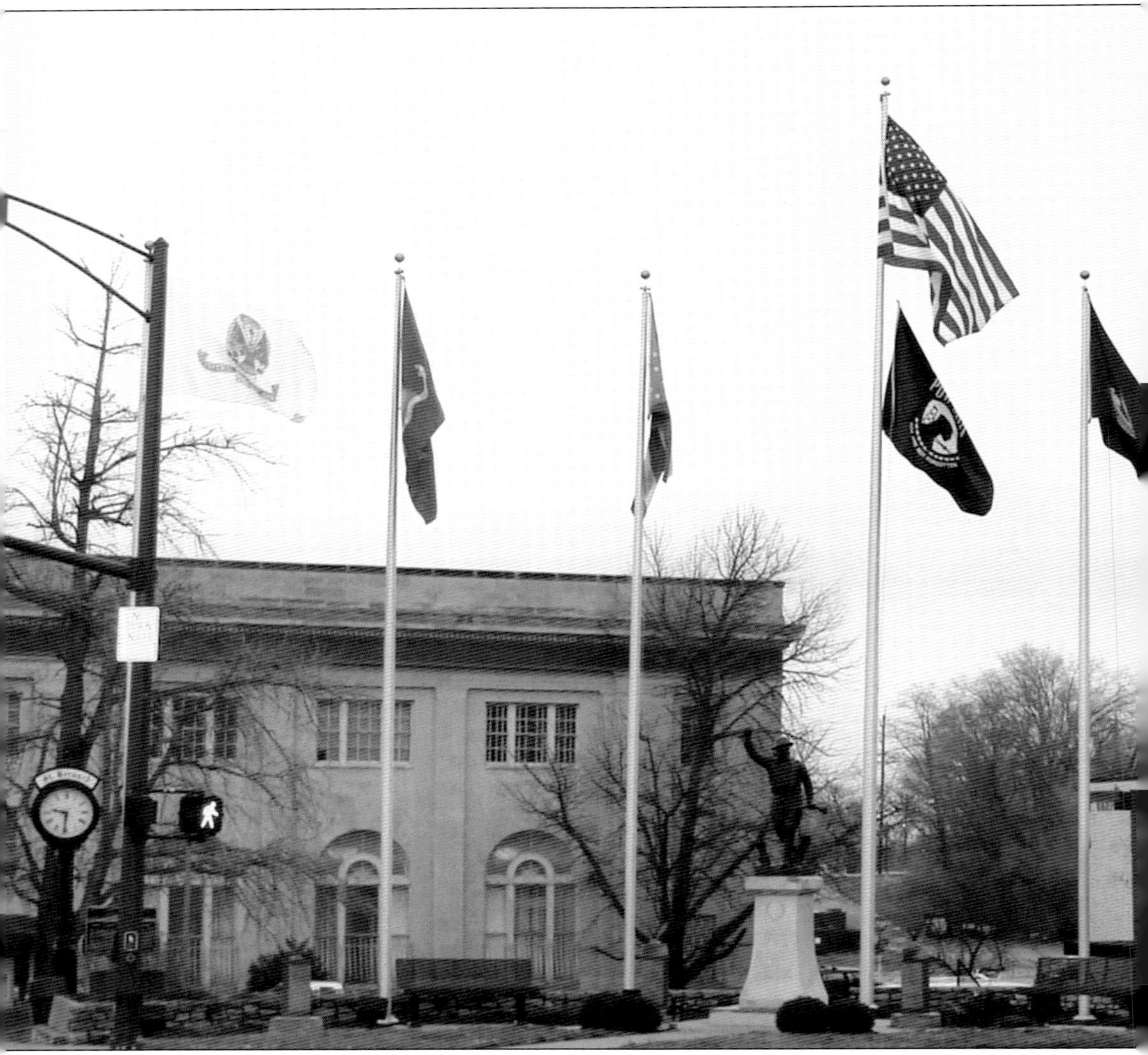

We the people elect those who govern, and it will be the responsibility of us both to assure that the community thrives and grows into the next 100 years. Each person, doing his or her part,

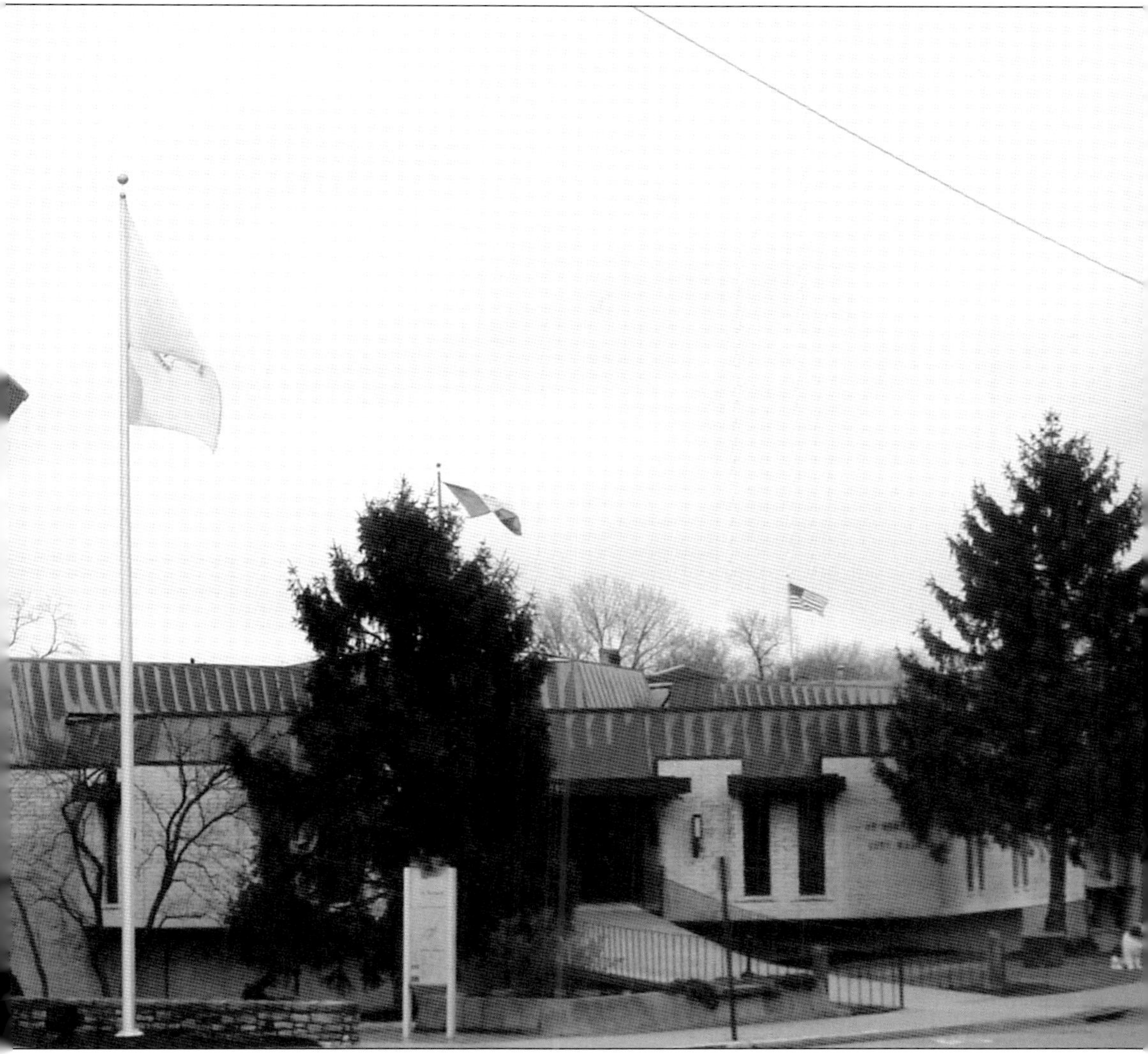

can continue the greatness that has been St. Bernard for all the past years and into the future. (Courtesy of Michael Niesen.)

Discover Thousands of Local History Books Featuring Millions of Vintage Images

Arcadia Publishing, the leading local history publisher in the United States, is committed to making history accessible and meaningful through publishing books that celebrate and preserve the heritage of America's people and places.

Find more books like this at
www.arcadiapublishing.com

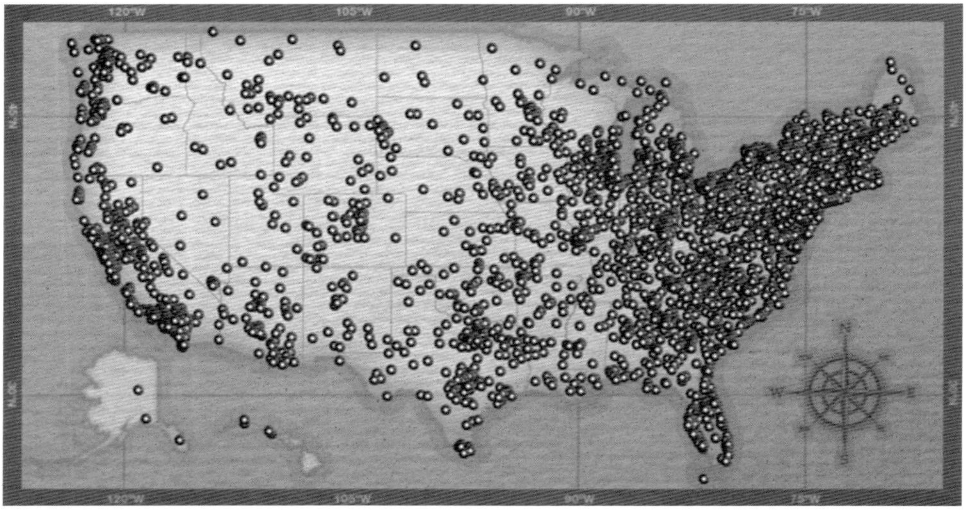

Search for your hometown history, your old stomping grounds, and even your favorite sports team.

Consistent with our mission to preserve history on a local level, this book was printed in South Carolina on American-made paper and manufactured entirely in the United States. Products carrying the accredited Forest Stewardship Council (FSC) label are printed on 100 percent FSC-certified paper.

MADE IN THE USA